Praise for *The Intangibles of Leadership*

"In distilling the essence of leadership, Richard successfully argues that there is a spectrum of qualities that contribute to great leadership. A must-read for all aspiring and existing leaders, whatever your field."

—*Neville Roberts, Chief Information Officer, Best Buy*

". . . Richard Davis has really nailed down in a practical yet very thoughtful way what really distinguishes great leaders, how to identify them, and, even more importantly, how to develop more of them. This book really brings a tangible dimension to the intangibles of leadership."

—*Stephane Charbonnier, Global Head of Talent Management,*
Towers Watson

"This is the most thoughtful book on leadership I have read. Instead of handing out the usual one-size-fits-all approach, Davis realizes that different situations require different kinds of leaders. Insightful, practical, and readable, it is the best book on leadership available."

—*Ford Harding, President, Harding & Company, and author of*
Creating Rainmakers

"*The Intangibles of Leadership* not only details key leadership qualities that Dr. Richard Davis has observed throughout his career, it also provides coaching advice to further develop your leadership essentials through strategies and action plans. I highly recommend this book for any leader who is searching for a leadership compass to guide behaviors and adopt the practices of extraordinary leaders."

—*Judd T. Nystrom, Senior Vice President, Finance, Advance Auto Parts*

"In assessing models of leadership Richard Davis has identified ten intangible qualities, some of which are commonly overlooked or mistaken for other attributes, but which all are central to understanding why certain leaders are able to stand apart and above the rest. His nuanced approach to a familiar subject is both timely and welcome."

—*JP Donlon, Editor-in-Chief,* Chief Executive Magazine

"Unique, insightful, and practical . . . a refreshing take on the true essence of Leadership in a contemporary time."

—*Anne Duncan, VP Human Resources, JTI-Macdonald Corp.*

"This book maps the traits that make good leaders, great. It reinforced for me the behavior needed to make a difference in any organization. Hat's off to Richard for his clarity of insight."

—*Rick Rommel, Senior Vice President, Best Buy*

"If you are in the business of developing leaders and looking to build powerful development plans, you will want to keep this book right next to your laptop. Each chapter provides learning experiences that can be crafted into powerful plans to grow leaders in areas critical for success. Richard Davis offers a career of experience in what really works in developing others—take advantage of it!"

—*Andy Billings, Vice President, Profitable Creativity, Electronic Arts*

The
INTANGIBLES
of
LEADERSHIP

The
INTANGIBLES
of
LEADERSHIP

The 10 Qualities of Superior
Executive Performance

RICHARD A. DAVIS, PH.D.

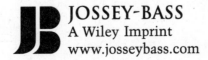

JOSSEY-BASS
A Wiley Imprint
www.josseybass.com

Library and Archives Canada Cataloguing in Publication Data

Davis, Richard A., 1971-
    The intangibles of leadership : the ten qualities of superior executive performance / Richard Davis.

Includes bibliographical references and index.
ISBN 978-0-470-67915-9

    1. Leadership. 2. Success in business. I. Title.

HD57.7.D397 2010   658.4'092   C2010-901551-7

Production Credits
Cover Design: Soapbox Design
Interior Design: Pat Loi
Typesetter: Thomson Digital
Printer: Friesens Printing Ltd.

Editorial Credits
Editor: Don Loney
Project Coordinator: Pamela Vokey

John Wiley & Sons Canada, Ltd.
6045 Freemont Blvd.
Mississauga, Ontario
L5R 4J3

Printed in Canada

1 2 3 4 5 FP 14 13 12 11 10

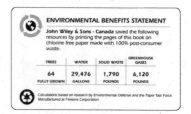

ENVIRONMENTAL BENEFITS STATEMENT

John Wiley & Sons - Canada saved the following resources by printing the pages of this book on chlorine free paper made with 100% post-consumer waste.

TREES	WATER	SOLID WASTE	GREENHOUSE GASES
64	29,476	1,790	6,120
FULLY GROWN	GALLONS	POUNDS	POUNDS

Calculations based on research by Environmental Defense and the Paper Task Force. Manufactured at Friesens Corporation

Dedication
To Eva, Brandon, Aaron, and Lauren—
who have taught me the Intangibles of Everything Else.

Contents

Acknowledgments

A funny thing happened on the way to writing this book: I realized that I really like being an author. Not for the reasons one might imagine, though. For me, it is the process. From concept to writing, editing to publishing, this has been an incredibly rich experience. The original idea for *The Intangibles of Leadership* can be traced back to research I conducted years ago with Gordon Flett, who inspired me to think more deeply about personality and its impact on behavior. When I started to work more extensively with senior leaders, my concept of personality matured, and several brilliant colleagues helped shape how I think about the psychology of leadership.

My sincere thanks go to every RHR management psychologist and consultant with whom I've worked—I have learned so much from them and owe each and every one of them a tremendous amount of gratitude. I would like to call out to a few of those who have spent time reviewing all or parts of this book and adding their wisdom. First and foremost, a special thanks to Tom Saporito for believing in me and in the book. I hope it represents us well. Thank you to Debra Hughes, Rebecca Schalm, Steven Gilbert, Anuradha Chawla, Joanna Starek, Hank Tufts, Julie Wolf, and Toye Honeyman for your comments and input. Thanks also to Lisa Wilkinson and Debi Parker for keeping me in line. In addition, my thanks to Guy Beaudin, who contributed a great deal to these pages. Guy, it could not have happened without you. I am eternally thankful for your mentorship and insight.

Several executives took time out of their busy schedules to discuss their own leadership journeys. Thank you to Richard Peddie, David Denison, Kathryn Hyland, David Orton, Anton Rabie, Todd Soller, Tim Spencer, Michel Poirier, John Rowe, Mary Jo Haddad, and Stephen Foster. Your stories serve as wonderful instruction and inspiration for aspiring leaders everywhere.

As I mentioned, I found the writing process quite a bit of fun. However, fun doesn't necessarily mean good, and making this book coherent required some heavy lifting. A chance encounter with an old friend and master word-smith, IJ Schecter, was a major catalyst to the book finding its way to print. IJ, thank you for all your efforts and for helping to find the story in these words. Likewise, a major shout-out to Don Loney at Wiley, who believed in me and this book from the very beginning. Don exemplifies many of the characteristics contained in this book, and I can only hope that it represents the start of a long partnership.

Apart from the writing, I have learned a great deal about publishing and marketing over the last year. I would like to thank the following people for their guidance in these areas: Jeff Durocher, Ken Ball, Rob Pierce, Patricia Pearson, Ford Harding, Meghan Lantier, and Paige Holden at BlissPR, and Lucas Wilk, Pam Vokey, and Deborah Guichelaar at Wiley. I also thank my friends Elliott, Jordy, Jeff, Kevin, Jason, and Jordan for putting up with me talking about this book when we had much more pressing things to attend to.

Most important, I would like to thank my family. How enjoyable it has been to bounce ideas around with my parents, Allan and Elaine Davis. It would take multiple volumes to describe what I have learned from them about life and leadership. In particular, they modeled how to be a mensch, and I will forever be grateful. Special thanks to Kevin and Nancy for their input and enthusiasm for the book, and Joe, Gail, Steve, Sue, Howie, and Dara for all of their interest and good wishes. I thank my children Brandon, Aaron, and Lauren for their wisdom, patience, and encouragement. Although I don't believe in luck, I am undoubtedly the luckiest man on earth. Kids, always remember these words: *semper ubi sub ubi.* Finally, I thank my wife Eva for her unwavering support and remarkable insight. Intangibles are certainly important, but it is her tangible beauty, both inside and out, that inspires me always.

Foreword

We are going to change the character and
philosophy of business through people.

—Dr. Fred Replogle, Founding Partner, RHR International

In one way or another, every leadership book tries to answer a basic question: Why do certain leaders succeed and others fail? Many books present models of leadership meant to be applied in any given management scenario, as if leadership were a standard uniform that can be slipped on at any time.

As Richard points out in this book, leadership isn't so straightforward. What works in one organization may not work in another. Exceptional leadership at the executive level isn't a pre-fab package that can be bought off the shelf. There is a dynamic relationship between the business demands of an environment and the personal characteristics necessary to lead in that environment.

It is these characteristics that are considered in detail in *The Intangibles of Leadership*. When thinking about selecting individuals for senior leadership roles, it is a mistake to allow ourselves to rely on typical competency models, which are helpful, but ultimately insufficient. Instead, we must ask ourselves, "What are the subtle traits that will make someone successful here? What are the types of behaviors that will lead to success in this role, within this culture, under these circumstances?" Many of the answers to these questions reside within the psychology of the individual and serve as the essence of RHR International.

Founded in 1945, RHR began when Chicago-based psychologist Perry Rohrer was asked by executives at an engineering firm to help them select high-quality candidates for managerial roles. During that time in post-war America, psychometric testing was somewhat in vogue, and it was not unheard-of for corporations to use psychologists in their hiring processes.

What Rohrer revolutionized, however, was the use of clinical insights in such decisions. Beyond using tests, he assessed people through in-depth psychological interviews. He soon joined forces with fellow psychologists Fran Hibler, Fred Replogle, Elliott Janney, and Charles Flory, and they created a consulting company called RH&R (named for Rohrer, Hibler, and Replogle).

Ever since, we have remained true to our founders' original conviction that the principles of psychology are not only pertinent in helping leaders succeed, but essential in enabling them to become better managers of themselves, their teams, and their organizations. Psychologists understand how people develop and progress over time. We believe it is imperative to adapt this understanding to organizational dynamics and the reasons why some leaders flourish and others falter. Today, RHR International services clients around the world in five key areas: (1) selection, assessment and integration of new leaders, (2) CEO succession, (3) accelerated executive effectiveness, (4) team development, and (5) management due diligence for mergers and acquisitions.

Our work is focused on the senior-most leaders of organizations, because it is at the top levels of leadership that the traits discussed in this book have the most impact on the success and sustainability of a company.

I am thrilled that someone has been able to capture the essence of our thinking in an informative and entertaining way. Richard has worked with senior leaders at some of the world's most successful corporations, and here, with characteristic depth of thought, personal insight, and practical counsel, he presents a book that will help individuals of every stripe move forward in their own leadership journey. I hope you enjoy *The Intangibles of Leadership* and take time to draw on the valuable lessons it offers.

Tom Saporito
Chairman and Chief Executive Officer
RHR International LLP

Introduction

Most people aren't familiar with what a management psychologist does. Among other things, we help senior leaders make smart decisions about people. For example, before a company hires a senior executive, we are brought in to assess the top candidates and give a recommendation as to their fit with the company's leadership needs. Given the company's business strategy and operating culture, there are certain behavioral qualities that will make some people successful and others not. We help define and then assess these qualities. And once the successful candidate is chosen, we use that assessment information to help the person hit the ground running.

So, how do I assess people? I gather data from multiple sources, including psychometric testing and, sometimes, 360-degree feedback, but at the heart of my assessment is an in-depth biographically based interview that typically unfolds over three hours. My ultimate goal is to understand how the person ticks and what that means in terms of his or her ability to do the job at hand. Beyond understanding someone's résumé, the goal is to understand that individual at a much deeper level.

In the three hours I have with them, something special happens. At some point early in the discussion, they realize this is going to be a very different conversation than they are typically used to having. We sometimes talk about their upbringing, their families, their experiences in school and in life, their early successes and failures, and the reasons behind certain life decisions they've made. We talk about their careers and their outlook on work, their views on leadership, and their thoughts about the future.

And, at some point, a kind of magic takes hold. As the conversation expands and deepens, these people recognize how events in their life have fit together. The ultimate purpose of our conversation aside, they nearly always come out of it, I like to believe, with newfound insights into themselves.

Afterwards, they often say things like, "I haven't thought about that story in years" or "I've told you things I never tell anyone." For me, of course, this is a great privilege. Doing what I do affords me a unique window into many extraordinary people. It is fascinating, exhilarating, and wonderfully humbling work.

During my first few years of assessing executives, I began to notice patterns. Certain characteristics showed up in those who were successful at getting the top jobs. Some of it was in their pedigree. Some of it was in their expertise. But most of it seemed to exist in the subtle distinctions they displayed. As a behavioral scientist, one of the first things I think about is the research. What did the research say about extraordinary leadership?

What I found was that there were some models of leadership that had been held out as reliable over time. They asserted that a handful of specific personality traits and attributes reliably predicted success in leadership. Still, these models left me wanting more. What did they really tell me?

Existing leadership models offer a basic set of competencies that all leaders should have, but they miss some critical points. First, I found, they said nothing about whether the candidate in front of me would be successful in a *particular* role at a *particular* organization.

Second, they were generally too junior in their description. The competencies that showed up in these models identified basic price-of-admission qualities that many people exhibit. But at the top rung of the ladder, leadership is highly nuanced. The dynamics at the top levels are complex, and what works in one organization may prove completely ineffective in another.

So, I set out to uncover patterns regarding the attributes that truly distinguish those who succeed at the top levels. I pored over research in psychology, philosophy, and literature and met with countless senior executives. I reviewed my assessment reports dating back nearly a decade and asked the opinions of colleagues at the top of their profession.

What I found was that extraordinary leaders possess certain interstitial characteristics—traits that fall between the lines of existing leadership models. Adjust your lens finely enough, and you will see, at the upper end of the leadership spectrum, certain subtle characteristics that emerge as fundamental to executive success. These characteristics are the "Intangibles of Leadership."

This is not a self-help book. Nor is it a manual of what to do and what not to do. I am not so audacious as to impose my perception of how you "should" think, feel, or act in a leadership setting or anywhere else. It also isn't meant to be an exhaustive list of leadership intangibles. Just as each human mind is unique, so is the context of each organization and the behaviors that are best suited to lead it. Leadership is complex, representing a continuous dance between contextual needs and leadership characteristics, and there is much still to be discovered.

This book is a practical atlas of the characteristics that most define extraordinary leaders and their underlying psychological mechanisms. It is a glimpse into the elite executive's mind and heart. It is a reflection of my own experiences and insights as a management psychologist. It is a story of how some people reach the heights of leadership. It is also, therefore, intended to help guide your own thinking and behaviors so that you might adopt some of the practices of these great leaders. It is a mirror to be held up in front of you to help you think about how you approach leadership, hopefully to help you gain insights into yourself that can enable you to grow and develop. This is my great wish for this book and for you.

1

Wisdom

Knowledge is a process of piling up facts;
wisdom lies in their simplification.

—Martin Fischer

The Wisdom of Giving: Part One

Frances had been born in a small town in Kentucky, Harrodsburg, to Bavarian immigrants, Leon and Rosetta. At the time of her birth, she had one sibling; not long afterwards, she had six. Frances learned early about the value of lending a hand.

The family soon moved to Cincinnati. While her father strove to earn money as a tailor, Frances and her siblings attended public school, where she was exposed to children who both looked quite a bit like she did and not at all like she did. Some of them celebrated the same holidays as her family; some celebrated different ones. They had delightfully varied ways of speaking, thinking, and behaving. It was a wonderful miscellany of humankind.

One of these students stood out from the others—Abraham Jacobs—her brother Benjamin's friend. When the two boys headed west to seek their fortune, Frances was crestfallen, but understanding. One couldn't sit around waiting for life to happen. In the area that would later become the frontier town of Denver, Abraham started a general store and operated a stagecoach that went to Santa Fe.

But he had felt the same stirrings as Frances. In 1863, after four years away, Abraham returned to Cincinnati and, in February, they were married. When Abraham and Frances moved to Central City, Colorado, a thriving mining town thirty miles west of Denver, she was amazed. Droves of people seemed to arrive daily, all descending on the west with the same unbridled hope. Nothing but opportunity seemed to lie before them.

At the same time, however, Frances saw the other side of that unchecked optimism—people whose dreams had not worked out, whose lives were not full of aspiration, and who fought a daily battle against desperation and despair. Troubled by what she saw, Frances began volunteering for social work. The ability to help the sick and needy, even slightly, gave her a feeling of worth. She had seen her own parents do so much with so little. Surely she could give of her time.

In 1872, Frances helped found the Hebrew Ladies' Relief Society, and presided over it. The group provided help to those facing the problems of poverty, sickness, malnutrition, and unsanitary living conditions. It was something—but it wasn't enough. The problems of humanity, Frances knew, were not confined to only one community. They affected everyone.

Often, we think of wisdom as something inborn, an attribute some people possess and others do not. We envision a sage sitting in the lotus posture atop a mountain, Confucius-like proverbs floating off his tongue one after the other, as though they had been implanted in his head at birth.

Some of us think of wisdom in a passive sense, something that occurs as a direct and automatic by-product of our experiencing life, so a young person is not able to achieve wisdom and someone old cannot be lacking in it.

Both of these conceptions of wisdom miss the mark. First, none of us is born wiser than someone else—even Confucius was naive in his youth. Second, wisdom isn't passively obtained; it is the result of conscious reflection, evaluation, and decision. Perhaps you're familiar with the colloquial definition of stupidity: doing the same thing as before and expecting a different result. Wisdom might broadly be considered as the opposite: acting in a different way based on a conscious examination of previous experience.

In other words, experience on its own does not equal wisdom. Experience is a necessary prerequisite to wisdom, but to assume that wisdom occurs as a natural consequence of experience is false—and, for someone who wishes to be a leader, dangerously limiting. I have seen many experienced leaders who think that their lengthy résumé predetermines their ability to be successful, that they have all the answers because they have been around the block a few times. However, as leadership coach Marshall Goldsmith aptly puts it in the title of his recent book, *What Got You Here Won't Get You There*, previous experience is not a proxy for capability.

This kind of confused thinking happens often in the boardroom. CEOs are hired because they have been CEOs before, many times regardless of what industry or company they come from. Take the case of Starwood Hotels & Resorts, owners of the Sheraton, Westin, Le Meridien, and W hotel brands. In 2004, then chairman Barry Sternlicht tapped Steven Heyer to be CEO of the global hotel company. Heyer came directly from Coca-Cola, where he was president and COO at the time of his departure. Before coming to Starwood, Sternlicht publicly lauded Heyer as "a marketer who has championed some of the world's most valuable and global brands." Who could blame him? It was Coca-Cola, after all. As it turns out, the culture is very different at Coca-Cola than it is at Starwood, and the leadership style did not translate. What worked there did not work at Starwood.[1] Heyer, who in college was known as "The Tank," had a direct, hard-nosed approach to leadership. Experienced as he was, things didn't work out at Starwood and Heyer left.

A similar fallacy occurs with age. People assume that gray hair is a determinant of success. In the years following the dot-com boom, there was a flight to more experienced CEOs. A case in point is Yahoo!. In 2001, Yahoo! founder Jerry Yang brought in the fifty-eight-year-old former co-head of Warner Brothers, Terry Semel, gray hair and all, to take over the leadership of the online giant. At the time, it was hailed as a great move—an example of a smart decision by young entrepreneurs to let a more experienced CEO take over. The Yahoo! stock price surged, and for a short time great optimism prevailed.

Unfortunately, all of Semel's rich experience did not bring material success to Yahoo!. When Semel finally left in 2007, the company was in a significantly worse financial position than it had been in when he got there. During the years that Semel was at the helm, its rival Google grew its shareholder value twenty-one times that of Yahoo!. Semel reportedly had the opportunity to buy Google for about $3 billion in 2002, but declined. He also could have bought YouTube or MySpace when the opportunities came up.

Not such a great record for a guy whose total compensation over the last five years of his tenure at Yahoo! was reportedly $550 million.

Gray hair is a badge of honor; indeed, it is almost destined to show up on an executive bio. But leaders aren't wise as a result of their experiences. They are wise because of their ability to utilize those experiences. The wise person reflects on their experience—the result is insight into past behaviors and outcomes. In turn, they achieve wisdom and—in the case of great leadership—apply it. This occurs independent of age.

Picture the kind of contraption you might see in a cartoon or Dr. Seuss book where something is shoved in at one end, and then, after the machine chugs, throbs, and whirrs for a while, something comes out of the other end a more refined version of the original. The contraption is our brain. What goes in is our experience. What comes out is wisdom.

WHAT IS IT?

Two disciplines, philosophy and psychology, have attempted to pin down a definition of wisdom for centuries. Our earliest philosophers tackled this dilemma with gusto. In fact, the very definition of the word philosophy dates back to the ancient Greek combination of *philo* (love) and *sophia* (wisdom). Hence, the word philosophy literally translates as "love of wisdom." Plato described three types of wisdom:

1. *sophia*: found in those who are contemplative and who seek life's truths;
2. *phronesis*: found in the kind of experienced, practical wisdom judges, lawyers, and statesmen tend to demonstrate; and
3. *episteme*: found in those who seek to understand the world through the lens of science.

Aristotle added the notion of *theoretikes* or theoretical knowledge of the truth. In his book, *The Psychology of Aristotle*, Daniel Robinson writes that, according to Aristotle, "A wise individual knows more than the material, efficient, or formal causes behind events. This individual also knows the final cause, or that for the sake of which the other kinds of causes apply." Socrates said that wisdom "consists of realizing one's own ignorance, by knowing what one does not know."

Following the tradition of the ancient Greeks, much has been written about the philosophy of wisdom. Early Christian views described the importance of a life lived in pursuit of divine and absolute truth. A complementary way of describing wisdom is the pursuit of the knowledge necessary to lead a good life. Most religions espouse the virtue of seeking truth in some way. In the Old Testament, wisdom is characterized by a sense of justice and lawfulness, personified in the wise King Solomon. In Eastern philosophy, wisdom is famously embodied in two figures, Confucius and Buddha. Confucius said that wisdom can be achieved via three methods: reflection, imitation, and experience. He also said that the love of learning is akin to wisdom. Buddha said that wise people are blessed with good bodily conduct, verbal conduct, and mental conduct. "A wise person," he taught, "does actions that are unpleasant to do but give good results and doesn't do actions that are pleasant to do but give bad results." If only Wall Street executives had paid more attention to Buddha in recent years.

In psychology, the attempt to define wisdom in a satisfactory way has led to two prevailing theories. Dr. Robert Sternberg, dean of arts and sciences at Tufts University, developed the first of these as a result of his own experience with intelligence quotient (IQ) tests. As a child, he performed terribly on these tests, scoring so poorly on one of them that he was sent back to fifth grade from sixth, until his score improved. In grade seven, Sternberg chose intelligence as his science project topic and he devised his first IQ test, selecting a more robust set of indicators than those contained in the traditional tests he was used to seeing.

The Sternberg Test of Mental Abilities (STOMA) not only became a scientifically valid, reliable test, but the same test devised in Sternberg's grade seven science class is still used today. Dr. Sternberg went on to study at Yale and Stanford and, ultimately, he became one of the foremost psychological minds of the last century.

Sternberg's main assertion is that typical IQ tests measure a limited set of intelligence-related factors and there are qualities indicating intelligence that reach beyond those tests. He was interested, in particular, in creativity and practical intelligence—what we might think of as street smarts. In one series of studies, he asked subjects to think of "wise" people and write down as many words as possible to describe them. He then took these words, wrote each of them on separate cards, and asked another set of people to sort the cards into "as many or as few piles as they wished on the basis of which behaviors are likely to be found together in a person."

After having conducted this exercise with several of his subjects, Sternberg devised three dimensions of wisdom:

1. Reasoning well and taking in advice from others;
2. Being perceptive and having good judgment; and
3. Using experience to understand and interpret information and then offering solutions accordingly.

He summarized his findings this way:

The wise individual is perceived to have much the same analytical reasoning ability that is found in the intelligent individual. But the wise person has a certain sagacity not necessarily found in the intelligent person: He or she listens to others, knows how to weigh advice, and can deal with a variety of different kinds of people. In seeking as much information as possible for decision making, the wise individual reads between the lines as well as makes use of the obviously available information. The wise individual is especially able to make clear, sensible, and fair judgments and in doing so, takes a long-term as well as a short-term view of the consequences of the judgments made. The wise individual is perceived to profit from the experience of others, and to learn from others' mistakes, as well as from his or her own. This individual is not afraid to change his or her mind as experience dictates, and the solutions that are offered to complex problems tend to be the right ones.[2]

The second major psychological theory of wisdom comes from a group of scientists at the Max Planck Institute for Human Development in Berlin, Germany. Paul Baltes, Ursula Staudinger, and their colleagues defined wisdom pragmatically, suggesting that it occurs when an individual has deep insight into, and judgment regarding, the ways of life and can offer advice accordingly.[3] They concluded that wisdom is the combination of intellect, personality, context, and expertise—the Berlin Wisdom Paradigm, as it is popularly known.

In this study, the researchers asked their students to nominate people they know as being wise. They then asked those "wise" people and others of similar ages to think out loud about difficult life dilemmas. For example, "Sometimes when people think about their lives, they realize that they have not achieved what they had once planned to achieve. What should they do and consider in such a situation?" Baltes and Staudinger evaluated the responses based on five criteria:

1. deep knowledge of facts;
2. experience;
3. understanding events in their context;
4. knowing right from wrong; and
5. managing uncertainty.

The results weren't surprising: People who are thought of as wise make better decisions and perform better on the dilemmas than those who aren't.

So wisdom, it would seem, begins with basic intellect, but it also involves the ability to synthesize information and be analytical while remaining tied to reality. Of course, there's also the importance of performing conscious reflection on past experiences, in addition to an awareness of the key learnings that have emerged from those experiences. Wisdom also includes the ability to use that information to inform future decisions—and the willingness to apply these learnings across a variety of contexts and situations. Wisdom is like a marriage: You have to work at it. And when you do, the effort can lead to tremendous results.

Wisdom for the Ages

When you hear the highlights of John Rowe's career—a senior chief executive in the electric utility industry, co-chair of the National Commission on Energy Policy, named the best electric utilities CEO in America two years running, chairman of the Nuclear Energy Institute, former chair of the Chicago History Museum, honorary doctorates from seven different universities—you're bound to be impressed.

My colleague Hank Tufts, a twenty-eight-year RHR veteran, has known and worked with John for twenty-five years. Hank describes John as a gifted individual who is not only smart in the traditional sense, but wise with deep perspectives. When the three of us met in John's office overlooking Chicago's downtown, I was immediately struck by the museum-like collection of what appeared to be Egyptian artifacts. I was clearly in the presence of a history buff. As we sat and discussed John's philosophy of leadership, I learned that, beyond his sheer love of learning and curiosity about the past, John looks to history for lessons about the future. His particular brand of wisdom reaches far back, enabling him to see forward.

Let me explain. While John's business card says Chairman and CEO of Exelon Corporation—the biggest electrical utility in the United States, operating the largest fleet of nuclear power plants in the nation—it might as well say "Chief Historian." While he is well known as a visionary with a rare talent for seeing the future, John looks to the past for his inspiration. A voracious reader and historical scholar, he has endowed several university history chairs, primarily focused on Byzantine and Greek history.

As a result, he is often able to see the future in a clearer way than others, allowing him to create positive change. He studies the characters that have walked across the human stage at various times and in different places as well as the events that have shaped the course of world history. He spoke to us about Churchill and Ghandi, Lincoln and Washington, devoting as much attention to their shortcomings as he did to their strengths.

It's not just about how much John knows about the past; it's also about how he uses that knowledge to integrate data. Affectionately known as the dean of the utility industry, John possesses what I call "informed instincts." He is able to see the trends and the larger picture. He was a strong and early advocate for cap and trade, clean air and clean energy—for example, recognizing the social responsibility of sustainability. This is characteristic of the wisdom he displays. When faced with disparate data points, he sees how they fit together. It is because of his ability to understand the landscape from a deep and wide perspective that he is able to make astute, at times "out of the box," decisions and judgments.

Despite his immense intellect, John does not operate as though he has all the answers. Perhaps the best demonstration of his wisdom is his appreciation for the knowledge and insights others can bring to the table. As a leader, he enables those around him to leverage their own minds, artfully surrounding himself with an eclectic group of people rather than only those similar to him.

"Wisdom comes from being wrong," he remarked. "From being open to people and available to advice and differences of opinion." John's only requirement is that people demand excellence of themselves, in whatever form that might take. He appreciates sharp intellect, but also gives superior instincts their due. He deeply respects academic talent, but is equally respectful of the perspectives, the humility, and the "smarts" honed by tested experience and even *failure. As you might imagine, it's important to do your homework if you report to John, but he's happy to hear your ideas, contemplate your advice, and use your input—as long as there is thought behind it.*

Hank had initially described John to me as having a "magnificent mind in the broadest sense." It's easy to see why.

HOW DO YOU KNOW IT WHEN YOU SEE IT?

Think back to the last time you needed advice about something important. Perhaps you were at a major crossroads in your career and wanted guidance on which path to choose. Maybe you were trying different ways to inspire your team to action, none of which were proving successful. Maybe it was something personal—a marital issue, a physical problem, or a poor decision with potentially large ramifications.

Who did you turn to? Your spouse, perhaps? Maybe it was your mom or dad; your rabbi, priest, or imam; your corporate mentor; your doctor, lawyer, or accountant; your psychologist; Jim Morrison's ghost; or perhaps, that guy at Starbucks who seems like he'd have good insight into people.

Whoever it was, you probably sought their counsel because you think of them as someone who possesses a certain amount of insight and discernment. Though wisdom is an elusive attribute, we seem to instinctively associate it with certain traits or mannerisms. Put another way, different individuals in your life probably serve various unconscious needs for you. There's a certain colleague you go to whenever you want to bounce business ideas off of someone. For relationship guidance, there's one particular friend you always call. When it comes to money or practical matters, you speed-dial someone else. And when you feel the need for general life advice, you find there's another person altogether who seems best suited to the task.

Why that particular person? Are they the smartest person you know? Not necessarily. The oldest? Maybe, maybe not. Is it a certain look, a way of speaking? The fact that they own a copy of the *Tao Te Ching*? Unlikely. More likely, they demonstrate a number of the following behaviors.

They are advice-worthy

To be wise, you must have experience. You may be young or old, but you must have experienced a wide variety of life events that have changed you in some way. As Robert Sternberg knew, wisdom is not merely raw intellectual horsepower—it is the combination of that component plus experience and personal characteristics. Those of you who are parents know this to be true. You know the experience of developing wisdom. When you became a parent, you became wiser (though not necessarily smarter).

In my experience, we typically think of our parents as wise. Indeed, I think of both my parents as being among the wisest people I know. If I think of all of the values that I have and the lessons I've learned over my life, my parents were either at the heart of them or uniquely qualified to help me reflect on them. One evening not long ago, when my father and I were having a glass of scotch and pondering the problems of the world, we discussed his perspective on wisdom. "We trust the wise person more than the smart person," my dad said thoughtfully. True enough—trust is critical. As soon as trust is broken, we lose our faith in the wisdom of an individual. This was the case for President Clinton. As a Rhodes Scholar and brilliant academic, Clinton is clearly a very smart man. However, he had lapses in personal judgment and lied to the country. As a result, the psychological contract he had with the American people was broken. People lost faith in his words and ignored the wisdom contained in them.

They encourage others to think about where they've been in the context of where they are

What does a leader's demonstration of wisdom convey to members of her team? That she has read a lot of books? No. That she's always ready with a good quotation? No. That she's erratic and inconsistent? No. It conveys to her team members that they, too, should be self-reflecting as a matter of course. They should always have their antennae up for signals that will alert them to the potential hazards of past behaviors. What was an appropriate response yesterday isn't necessarily appropriate today. They ought to look at their past selves in order to continue to mold the best future selves they can.

Effective leaders communicate the changes they undergo while gaining wisdom to those in their charge, not for the purpose of demanding that everyone else adopt the same stance as them, but to show that they are committed to continuous improvement and self-evolution. If all the members of a team, from top to bottom, are using the lessons of yesterday to be smarter, better, and more strategic today, the team can only move forward. Top leaders know this and work to encourage it.

They exercise good judgment

Wise leaders are rational and have excellent judgment. They have the ability to see through the clutter and get to the heart of an issue. They are able to step back and objectively analyze the situation. This has sometimes been called "helicopter thinking."

In a recent 360-degree assessment we conducted of the new CFO of a major consumer products company, the feedback was not only impressive, but illuminating as well. Everyone described this woman as wise. When we asked them why, no one spoke about her intellectual might or her extensive business résumé. Almost everyone, in fact, gave one version or another of the same opinion: She was able to bring the emotional tenor down, establish focus, and see what was truly important. Because she always brought clarity to discussions and ignored extraneous issues, she made people feel like they were going to get through whatever issue they were facing, even when they had been feeling overwhelmed before. This leader's wisdom manifested in her ability to keep people focused on what was truly relevant and, therefore, make good judgments about it.

They don't speak in banalities

You don't usually sense that wise leaders are *trying* to be wise. Their wisdom often seems effortless and organically formed. But don't be fooled. They think carefully about what they say and how to say it. That's why they are so often able to communicate their ideas, thoughts, or message in a way that is profound and memorable.

This is a crucial quality for any leader to develop, since they are called on frequently to settle disputes, offer opinions, provide guidance, and give direction. To be seen as a wise leader, you must be able to capture the gist of a dilemma and articulate it in a clear manner that sticks. And if you're *really* good, at the same time, you make people take a step back and think. Consider some of the most enduring examples of great leaders who achieved this quality remarkably well:

- John F. Kennedy (quoting Oliver Wendell Holmes): "Ask not what your country can do for you but what you can do for your country."
- Dr. Martin Luther King, Jr.: "I have a dream . . . that my four little children will one day live in a nation where they will not be judged by the color of their skin but by the content of their character."

- Winston Churchill: "Let us therefore brace ourselves to our duties, and so bear ourselves, that if the British Empire and its Commonwealth last for a thousand years, men will still say, 'This was their finest hour'."

Each of these individuals delivered words that continue to resonate today, because those words powerfully and persuasively expressed very specific ideas in a way that made listeners reflect on their own experiences.

They don't rush their words

Have you ever noticed how members of the clergy speak? Slowly and deliberately, usually in a soft voice. This manner of speaking reflects thoughtfulness and perspective. To demonstrate wisdom you must exercise the ability to step back, and in a rational, even-handed way, evaluate a situation and then communicate your views in a way that has impact.

In a set of interesting studies conducted at the University of Texas, researchers looked at how people's vocabularies tend to change as they age. In the first study, the investigators reviewed transcripts of interviews with people who were instructed to discuss traumatic or emotional events. What they found was that older people used more positive-emotion words and fewer negative-emotion words than their younger counterparts. They also found that as people get older, they develop a tendency to use fewer self-focused words (such as I, me, and my) than they had used when they were younger. Older people also employed the past tense less frequently and used the present or future tense more often than younger participants. Finally, the researchers also reported that older people used more "thoughtful" words, (such as think, realize, and reason) than younger people.

Building on these results, the same researchers conducted a follow-up study looking at the language used in the works of famous authors over time. They electronically reviewed the collected works of, for example, George Eliot, Edna St. Vincent Millay, William Wordsworth, and William Butler Yeats, searching for changes in the way each author wrote as he or she grew older. Just as in the earlier study, it was found that these authors, over time and as their careers progressed, used fewer self-focused words, more future-tense words, and more thoughtful words.

What do these findings tell us? That if you want to be seen as wise by those around you, you should use words that focus not on you, but on the people you're addressing. Also, talk more about the present or future than the past. Be reflective and thoughtful. And hey—slow down.

They think independently

Wisdom has nothing to do with rolling over and accepting conventional wisdom. When one points to leaders now considered to be among the wisest people in history, one finds that their stories almost always include moments when the person flouted intellectual convention in order to stay true to their ideas. Few leaders are strangers to this experience. It is a frequent necessity to go against popular thought and stay true to your convictions, and you must be willing to do it. While you need to be open to new information and willing to change your perspective for good reason, you must also be willing to show people that you will hold firm when you believe in something.

The wise leader is wise, in large part, because he considers each situation separately and tries to provide an objective view that will benefit the whole organization. He will often take a devil's-advocate perspective to try to propel new angles or insights to the surface. He will hold his own ideas up to the mirror to be considered. He will get other smart people together in a room to hash out the issues and, hopefully, arrive at a solution that best serves the group.

They are selfless

The wisest leaders bring deep knowledge, but no personal agenda, to the advice they give others. What they say, they believe, and their counsel is always genuinely tailored to the recipient rather than applied indiscriminately or cut and pasted from a previous conversation. When a wise leader is approached with a problem, she lets go of personal biases and abandons any thought of personal gain. She offers the gift of experience only.

Leaders who demonstrate wisdom also do so by encouraging others to develop their own ability to reflect on experience and derive important, and applicable, lessons. It will only do so much for you if I tell you what I think you should do, even if you heed my advice out of respect. Without you actually thinking about the decision yourself, what good will it do you?

Wisdom Checklist

What do I look for when assessing wisdom in a current leader or leadership candidate? Here's a checklist:

☐ **Smarts.** *The person has a high intellect and strong cognitive capacity. One needs to have basic intellectual horsepower in order to be seen as wise.*

☐ **General life experience.** *The person has been through difficult situations. She has seen things that others haven't. She has traveled. She has acquired some street smarts or has otherwise endured crises or complex circumstances.*

☐ **Perspective.** *The person can step back and see the way an individual problem fits into the bigger picture.*

☐ **Root-cause analysis.** *The person is able to cut through the clutter and pinpoint central components of an issue or other matter.*

☐ **Procedural knowledge.** *The person has a diverse knowledge base. He knows how to do a wide variety of things.*

☐ **General knowledge.** *The person knows a lot about a wide variety of things. She is conversant with history, politics, economics, and a number of other areas. She reads the newspaper. She knows what's going on in the world.*

☐ **Teaching capability.** *The person knows how to communicate in such a way that others are able to learn from him.*

☐ **Global sensibility.** *The person does not live in a bubble. She is aware of and understands the most pressing issues affecting the world at large. She is not insular in her thinking.*

☐ **Makes you think.** *The person is interested in hearing others' opinions. He asks clever, penetrating questions and listens closely to the answers.*

☐ **Selflessness.** *The person holds others' interests above her own and gives advice as a means of helping people improve themselves or perform better at their jobs or careers.*

☐ **Awareness of limits.** *The person is aware of what he doesn't know and has no problem admitting to these knowledge gaps.*

☐ **Critical thinking.** *The person is able to weigh assumptions, evaluate arguments, and draw conclusions.*

(continued)

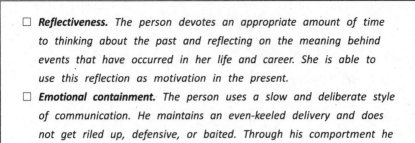

☐ **Reflectiveness.** *The person devotes an appropriate amount of time to thinking about the past and reflecting on the meaning behind events that have occurred in her life and career. She is able to use this reflection as motivation in the present.*

☐ **Emotional containment.** *The person uses a slow and deliberate style of communication. He maintains an even-keeled delivery and does not get riled up, defensive, or baited. Through his comportment he projects calmness and intelligence.*

HOW DO YOU GET IT?

Let's repeat it again: Wisdom doesn't just fall into your lap after you've been on the planet a certain number of days. I daresay we can all give plenty of examples of people we know who have been around a heck of a long time and don't seem to have learned much about anything at all.

Developmental experts have often said that we don't reach our full emotional and mental maturity until age sixty. That's a long time to wait for wisdom. Here are some things you can do to accelerate the process.

Strategy 1: Develop a Teachable Point of View

In a 1999 *Harvard Business Review* article, leadership expert Noel Tichy introduced the idea of a teachable point of view (TPOV). In order to provide advice to others, you need to be clear about your own point of view, and you need to be able to communicate it in a manner that impacts others. A TPOV, in its original form, is a lengthy summary of "what a person knows and believes about what it takes to succeed in his or her own business as well as in business generally."[4]

The leaders of one company I know in particular, a large retailer, use the TPOV to share institutional wisdom regularly. The leaders are continually challenged to identify, and have in their back pocket, not only a perspective on a business issue, but also a way to teach it to others. According to Tichy, in order to develop a TPOV, you need to think about four components: ideas, values, emotional energy, and edge. I will try to simplify this, distinguishing between questions regarding yourself and questions regarding your organization. Go ahead and answer them.

Questions About You

1. What personal experiences in your life were particularly relevant to your current success? How did they affect you?
2. Who were your early influences? What did you learn from these people and how did that stick with you over the course of your life?
3. How would you describe your values? What kinds of people are you friends with or drawn to personally? Who would *not* be a friend of yours? What characteristics do they have that makes you say that?
4. What ideas do you have about the future of your industry and your organization in particular? What will make your organization successful?
5. What tough issues are you dealing with? What are the key decisions you face right now?
6. What holds you back or gets in the way of success?
7. What motivates or energizes you? How do you keep yourself motivated? What do you do to motivate others?

Questions About Your Organization

1. How does your organization currently create value for its customers? What more could it do?
2. What are your organization's values? How does that translate into business practice?
3. If you could reshape your company's existing culture in any way, what would you do?
4. Where does your organization need to improve? What major hurdles do you face as a company?
5. What are the consequences of not doing anything differently?

Your TPOV

Reflect on what you've written for your answers so far. Now, from your perspective, answer the following:

a. What does it take to be successful (as an individual, a leader, and an organization)?
b. What is the best way to motivate and lead others?
c. What needs to change in your organization? What does the company need to do in order to make this a better, more successful place?

d. How will you get there? What do you, and the people around you, need to do, stop doing, or do differently to achieve this goal?

Now that you have the answers, develop a leadership story around them that you can teach others. The results will be powerful.

Strategy 2: Seek Out New Ideas

As a senior leader, you have to devote almost all of your hours to being effective in your role. Still, if you don't know what's going on around you—in your city, country, and the world—you're going to seem less wise and more narrow-minded. Starting today, do the following:

☐ **Read the newspaper every day.** There is no substitute for understanding what is going on in the world. You must be in the know. This is a very basic activity that does indeed take time out of your morning schedule, but it pays major dividends.

☐ **Subscribe to the *Harvard Business Review* (*HBR*), *The Economist*, and any similar publications that interest you.** You need to be acquainted with what is going on in areas beyond your particular scope of work. This is particularly helpful for people who struggle with how to "get more strategic." The *HBR* is a phenomenal periodical that gives a robust view of all aspects of organizations. *The Economist* will inform you about the global economy and geopolitical events. Increase your awareness of such matters by picking up a copy.

☐ **Read a book—any book.** All wise leaders I know are also voracious readers. Why? Because reading exposes them to new ideas and perspectives. It helps them to integrate their thoughts. In many cases, wise leaders read history books, business books, or fiction. I'm not suggesting you need to read every boring business book that hits the shelves. Read something fun, something beyond your typical fare, even if that means following Oprah's Book Club. It will make you a wiser leader—I promise.

☐ **Challenge yourself to learn something new.** Once a year at a minimum, take a course in a subject you know little about or take up a hobby that makes your brain explore new territory. Take a trip somewhere you've never been. The key is not to remain stagnant. Do not accept the status quo. Be a constant learner and you will grow wise.

☐ **Go to a play, movie, concert, or performance.** Once a month or more, get the heck away from business and immerse yourself instead in the arts. Art makes you think, reflect, and react, all crucial steps in being able to build wisdom. It doesn't matter what style or mode of art you most appreciate. I am not much of a ballet person and I have yet to go to the opera, but I do enjoy a U2 concert, I love traditional jazz, and I can get lost in a good art gallery.

☐ **Listen to wise people.** Bring in those with wisdom to share to speak at your organization. This could mean a lunch-and-learn or a full-blown speaking engagement at your company's planning meeting. Sponsor community learning events such as a speakers' series. And if you can't get them to come to you, then you go to them—attend conferences and conventions where they'll be speaking or offer to go to their homes or offices for an hour of face time. A single conversation with someone who possesses true wisdom may be the most valuable one you'll ever have.

Strategy 3: Find a Mentor or Advisor You Trust

In order to provide wisdom to others, you must receive wisdom from someone else. Having a trustworthy mentor or advisor helps you in two ways. First, by listening to the insights someone else has gleaned from their own journey, you will be prompted to engage in your own self-reflection, with consequent insights into yourself. Second, by observing how others impart their wisdom, you will learn how to more effectively do so yourself. Here are some specific ways to seek out and maximize the relationship with a mentor or advisor.

- Ask a trusted peer whom she gets advice from. Who is the wisest person she knows?
- Hunt wisdom. Seek out those who are wise and spend as much time with them as possible.
- Once you've found a trusted advisor, don't let go. These people are rare commodities in the world. Go to them for advice and listen to it. If they challenge you, they are doing it for a reason. The key is to engage in meaningful dialogue about yourself and the world.

Strategy 4: Create Diversity of Thought on Your Teams

The most successful teams have built different *types* of wisdom into them— individuals with varied expertise, different backgrounds, contrasting career paths, and diverse personalities. Teams composed of a bunch of people who think, act, and talk in the same way don't usually go far. The goal for your teams should be to bring together people who are smart, but who represent different kinds of smart—especially if they think differently than you do yourself. If you feel your team is beginning to stagnate or can't unlock the secret to moving forward, have a look around the room. Is it because everyone is too similar? Here are some tips to help shake things up a bit:

☐ **Invite challenges from those who report to you.** Take a hard look at your team and reflect on whether they are willing and able to challenge your thinking and decisions. Is your team susceptible to groupthink? If so, break out of it. Publicly reward or praise people when they present alternative points of view.

☐ **Have different people lead discussions.** Just as members of a family tend to take on established roles over time that, ultimately, are extremely difficult to change, members of business teams can get into ruts because of the roles they fall into—the quiet one, the jokester, the guy who always disagrees, Miss Serious, the one who wants to be the boss, and so on. By forcing people into different roles on a regular basis, you keep things fresh and bring new ideas and perspectives to the surface constantly.

☐ **Bring in people from other offices, other teams, even other companies.** It's easy for those inside an organization to quickly lose objectivity about how the rest of the world sees them. No matter how much internal wisdom you are able to develop, that wisdom is still confined to, and has developed within, your own four walls. Adding someone who can bring wisdom in from outside can be invaluable to the way you devise your organizational strategy.

Strategy 5: Designate Time for Self-reflection

Reserve time in your calendar at least once a week to step back and reflect on the bigger issues. Period. You don't have to formally meditate or sit alone in a room staring at a candle (though if you like that sort of thing, knock yourself out). Just try to avoid getting bogged down in the mire of everyday management activities. Think big and be honest with yourself about the things that come to you. Psychologist Richard Kilburg, an expert on executive wisdom, has his clients reflect about their decisions and actions.[5] Here are some questions you can use to stimulate your own reflective thinking:

• What decisions or actions did I make this week?
• What was the dumbest decision I made? What was the wisest decision I made this week? What was the wisest action I took this week?

- What did I miss this week? Did I fall victim to any blind spots?
- What are the implications for my decisions in the larger context of what I am trying to do here?
- What I have I learned this week? What can I teach others based on what I have learned?
- Who needs help around me? Who might benefit from my advice?

Your own reflection time isn't the only important thinking that should be done; your team, as a group, should be engaging in reflection too. One method you can use to do this is called an "after action review" (AAR). The AAR process was developed in the U.S. military as a way of debriefing and learning from its missions. Military psychologists realized that much wisdom was being lost by not taking the time to really achieve an understanding of both the organization's successes and its failures. So they devised a set of four questions that, if answered rigorously, would reveal the wisdom gained from any given event. As I said, it's only four questions, but together these questions have the power to unlock a world of valuable information. If you aren't already conducting some sort of postmortem on a regular basis, start getting your teams to sit down following the conclusion of an initiative to answer these questions:

1. What results did we expect to achieve?
2. What did we achieve?
3. Why did we achieve what we did?
4. What would we do differently next time?

By asking these questions following a major event, you will learn from the event in an infinitely more robust way. The trick is to be thorough and not allow anyone off the hook. Don't let anyone on the team get away with surface answers or throwaway comments. Go a level deeper and probe for the answers beneath the answers. As happens anytime you open yourself up to the possibility of learning and reflection, you'll be surprised what you can learn.

WHY IT MATTERS

Let me tell you a story about a CEO my company recently advised. This individual had been a star in his organization—a storied Australian holding company that owned a diverse portfolio of public companies. He was brought to North America to oversee a large supermarket company that had been around for nearly a century and was in urgent need of someone to blow off the cob-webs, pump some fresh thinking into the operation, and, hopefully, take it to the next level.

This new CEO had, in his previous position, made a large investment that ended up delivering a huge return. Without devoting too much time to studying the current business climate or the particular circumstances under which the company was operating, he decided to swing for the fences again to see whether he could catch lightning in a bottle not once, but twice. Increasing the risk profile had worked before; why wouldn't it work again?

The new CEO's investments almost ended up sinking the company. In retrospect, it was obvious that they were ill-advised and reckless investments, but at the time, they'd seemed to make sense.

Well, to the CEO, at least, they made sense. But they had not, in fact, made sense because they'd been based only on previous experience with no consideration of the present context. When leaders simply transplant think-ing from one context to the next, they are courting trouble. Knowledge gleaned from previous experiences serves as the foundation to wisdom, but it does not become wisdom until one consciously applies it to new circum-stances. In the case above, the new CEO's failure to undertake the second part of the equation led to a host of other problems. His integrity suffered because he had to hide things from the board after the investments went south. His judgment and efficacy were called into question since he'd hired thousands of people and expanded into new geographies on the basis of his bad bets. Worst of all, by acting boldly instead of intelligently, he lost the faith of his team.

By contrast, those who consciously reflect on the past and apply it to the present are consistently able to transfer their knowledge and experience to current circumstances, and they thrive in their leadership roles as a result. The process of actively nurturing wisdom leads to an expanded per-spective, enables you to be more nimble in a great variety of situations and to more effectively navigate your teams through different waters. It allows you to frame discussions and ideas in meaningful ways so that they make sense to others.

Great leaders don't just think about what happened—they think about why it happened, why they reacted or behaved the way they did, which of those reactions or behaviors led to successful outcomes, and which ought to be dif-ferent next time. Those who do not take the time for such reflection land on the flip side of wisdom. They might as well not have had any experience in the first place, because they aren't doing anything useful with it. Don't aim to be a smart leader. Aim to be a wise one.

The Wisdom of Giving: Part Two

The dust was everywhere and so were the sick. For every fleck of fool's gold dredged up out of the water, there were lungs blackening and people yielding to its effects.

Frances realized she must step up her efforts. The Hebrew Ladies' Relief Society was not adequate for the problems that needed to be faced. It would require the generosity of many, the communal kindness of an entire town.

So in 1874, Frances broadened the scope of her work, approaching people outside of the Jewish community to help found the non-sectarian Denver Ladies' Relief Society. At the same time, she organized Denver's first free kindergarten to help the children of poor families. "God never made a pauper in the world," she said during one of her many public campaigns to promote charity from all corners. "Children come into the world, and conditions and surroundings make them either princes or paupers."

She didn't stop there. Though Colorado's dry air and sunshine were supposed to be a cure for tuberculosis, hundreds of sufferers still appeared day after day. Frances regularly visited impoverished homes to bring food, coal, clothing, and soap. Unlike others, she was not afraid to touch people whose bodies were emaciated. She did not flinch at the sight of blood. She often would stop to give aid to those who were lying in the street felled by hemorrhages.

As her work progressed, Frances realized not only that she couldn't do it all herself, but that she shouldn't do it all herself. She had marshaled resources to help Jewish ladies and then to help all ladies that were in need throughout the city. What more might she accomplish by assembling the right people?

She wasn't the type to wait around to find out. In 1887, she lobbied the city's congregational minister and the Catholic archdiocese to create the Charity Organization Society. The idea, she said, was that this association would act as a central repository for fundraising and other efforts; proceeds would be portioned out across a federation of charities.

Frances continued to be troubled by the number of tuberculosis victims who made their way to Denver in search of a cure, only to find that no facilities existed to give them treatment or even shelter. "Most of the community ignores those who roam the city coughing or hemorrhaging," Frances wrote. Due to the lack of facilities, those afflicted were often transported to the local jail.

Frances sought a new ally—the lately appointed rabbi of Denver's Temple Emanuel, William S. Friedman. The rabbi, sympathetic to Frances' arguments, endorsed her ideas to build a tuberculosis hospital and spread the word loudly from his own pulpit. In April 1890, Denver's Jewish Hospital Association was incorporated and, in October, a cornerstone was laid.

Unfortunately, Frances would not live to see the hospital built. Early in 1892, she herself became ill, but instead of following her physician's advice to stay home and recuperate, Frances clung to her calling, stubbornly continuing to provide assistance for the medically indigent. Soon she developed pneumonia. By spring, Frances was dead at the age of forty-nine.

Her funeral was attended by thousands of people who felt it was their obligation to mourn the woman who had become known as the "mother of charities." The memorial service, open to all faiths, was presided over by Rabbi Friedman and three leading Christian clergymen. Through her tireless efforts, Frances Wisebart Jacobs had forged an enduring legacy and created a powerful model of collective generosity that is still followed today. Which is why the United Way, the organization that the Charity Organization Society would later become, today proudly recognizes her as its founder.

THE BOTTOM LINE

Experience is the basic ingredient in wisdom—but reflection and perspective are what allow it to rise to the surface.

2

Will

Chance favors the prepared mind.

—Louis Pasteur

The Peaceful Fight: Part One

The child was born in a coastal town in fall of 1869. His father, Karamchand, was the diwan, the prime minister, of a small princely state in the Kathiawar Agency of British India. His mother, Putlibai, was Karamchand's fourth wife. The first three, it was said, had died in childbirth. His grandfather was called Uttamchand or, more fondly, Utta.

The combination of his mother's piety and the Jain traditions of the region instilled in the youngster strict values: compassion for sentient beings, vegetarianism, fasting for self-purification, and mutual tolerance between individuals of different creeds. He was haunted by the stories of Shravana and Maharaja Harishchandra, Indian classics both, which imprinted on him the importance of truth and love as supreme virtues.

In May 1883, at the age of thirteen, he was married to a girl one year his senior, Kasturbai Makhanji, whose first name was shortened to Kasturba or, affectionately, Ba. Two years later, the couple's first child was born, but survived only a few days, joining Karamchand, who had died earlier that year.

The young couple had four more children, all sons. At his middle school in Porbandar and high school in Rajkot, the husband remained an average student, passing the college matriculation exam with difficulty. He attended Samaldas College at Bhavnagar, secretly unhappy while following his family's wish for him to become a barrister. But a good son is a good son. In September 1888, just before his nineteenth birthday, he traveled to London and began studying law at University College, all the while maintaining the Jainist vow he had made to his mother to observe the Hindu precepts of abstinence from meat, alcohol, and promiscuity.

When he was called to the bar less than three years later and departed London for his home in India, the news that greeted him there was devastating. His family had chosen not to tell him that his mother had died during his time in London lest they disturb his studies. In subsequent months, things did not become any smoother for him. His attempts at establishing a law practice in Bombay failed. Later, after applying and being turned down for a part-time job as a high school teacher, he ended up returning to Rajkot to make a modest living drafting petitions for litigants, a business he was forced to close after running afoul of a British officer. Next, he accepted a year-long contract from an Indian firm to a post in the Colony of Natal, South Africa, then part of the British Empire.

It was during his time in South Africa that the young man began to encounter the flagrant discrimination toward Indians that would rouse in him the first tremors of social activism. He was thrown off a train at Pietermaritzburg after refusing to move from first class to a third-class coach despite holding a valid first-class ticket. Farther on, relegated to travel by stagecoach, he was beaten by a driver for refusing to travel on the foot board in order to make room for a European passenger. The journey spared him few hardships. He was routinely barred from hotels, ordered to remove his turban, and dealt random punishments. These events proved to be a turning point in his life.

Starting to question his people's status within the British Empire and his own place in society, the young barrister decided to extend his stay in South Africa to assist Indians in opposing a bill that would deny them the right to vote. Though unable to halt the bill's passage, he drew attention to the Indian community's cause. He helped found the Natal Indian Congress in 1894, an organization through which he would mold the Indian community of South Africa into a unified political force.

In January 1897, when he landed in Durban, a mob of white settlers attacked him instantly. He escaped only through the efforts of the wife of the police superintendent. When asked if he wished to press charges, he declined. It was one of his principles, he said, not to seek redress for a personal wrong in a court of law.

In 1906, the Transvaal government circulated a new act compelling registration of the colony's Indian population. In September of that year, a mass protest meeting was held in Johannesburg to oppose the act. There the barrister, now in his thirties, called on his fellow Indians to defy the new law. But the way in which he asked them to do so would change the course of history.

The story of Bill Gates' rise to success and prosperity is well chronicled. He grew up as an extremely sharp child who did very well in high school. Although somewhat awkward socially, he excelled academically. He went to Harvard and considered a career in law. Besides academics, he found himself immersed in a subculture within Harvard of hobbyists, game players, and card sharks. (He was, apparently, a regular and fiercely competitive poker player.)

One day in January 1975, a hobbyist friend of his, Paul Allen, happened to pass by the magazine stand in Harvard Square and picked up a copy of *Popular Mechanics*. Allen took it over to Gates and excitedly showed him an advertisement for the Altair 8800, a mail-order microcomputer kit, introduced for the first time in that issue. Gates and Allen saw potential in the Altair. They felt such a microcomputer would eventually become a popular at-home device. They immediately went to work writing the first programming software for the Altair, an adaptation of a program that was already on the market called BASIC. Gates and Allen quickly sold their program to the company that built the Altair, MITS, likely beating other programmers to the punch by only a month or so.

As a result of having been so quick out of the gate, the pair were able to form a small company and watch it grow modestly. A few years later, in 1980, Gates' mother, Mary, happened to be on the board of the United Way of America alongside fellow board member, John Opel, the chairman of IBM. A proud mom, Mary discussed her son's business, then called Micro-Soft, with Opel who, in turn, mentioned it to other IBM executives. At the time, IBM was looking for an operating system for its new line of personal computers.

Not long after, Bill Gates received a call from IBM and the two companies struck a deal. Through a shrewd business decision by Gates to retain copyright of the software code, the deal between Micro-Soft and IBM launched the fledgling company into the stratosphere.

Such a series of events may lead historians to believe that Gates was a man of great luck and innovation. The fact is, he had neither. Gates is, instead, one of the greatest examples of leadership will. He willed his success through sheer determination, risk taking, and seeing every opportunity possible. His genius lies in both his tremendous curiosity and his eye for a good thing. Gates didn't create BASIC, nor did he create the Altair. Instead, he saw the opportunity in both and devised a way for them to work together. He was able to do the same for Windows when he saw the Apple Macintosh operating system in the 1980s, and again for Internet Explorer when he saw Netscape in the '90s. Let me be clear: There is undeniable genius in what Gates did— survey the market, identify ideas that have an inkling of opportunity, work his tail off, take risks, and make canny business deals. However, his history is also full of products and services that did not work out, but we don't talk about them. When you think of Microsoft, you may not recall Encarta, Bob, Clippie, Windows Me, or the Zune. You remember the giant successes. Gates willed his success by planting enough seeds for a few of them to grow and become those successes.

WHAT IS IT?

Often when I assess senior executives, one theme consistently makes its way into the dialogue—luck. Successful people tend to describe themselves as having a history of being lucky. They describe frequent episodes of good fortune that, ultimately, changed the course of their careers or unexpectedly kick-started their leadership trajectory. To my mind, these people are actually displaying a healthy bit of modesty, because what they're describing isn't luck—it's will.

The appearance of Louis Pasteur's quote at the beginning of this chapter is deliberate. Numerous conversations I've had with highly successful leaders have reinforced to me what Pasteur meant: one must be prepared for luck to occur. Opportunities abound; one just needs to be ready to seize them when they arise.

How do you position yourself for good fortune? Stanford University's Albert Bandura, the father of social cognitive theory, once described his take on this at a landmark presidential address of the Western Psychological Association. He challenged the previous notion that our lives are predetermined in the first few years of our lives, as professed by Freudian psychoanalytic theory. Bandura instead contended that our lives are determined largely by a set of coincidental events, some of which take us off course. "Chance encounters," he said, "have the power to inaugurate enduring change."

Bandura described the psychology connecting chance encounters and life paths. He said there are two factors that should be considered when attempting to understand how luck happens: personal determinants and social determinants. The interaction between what an individual specifically does or has and what the social landscape looks like is what makes up luck.

For Bandura, personal determinants included entry skills, emotional ties, and values and personal standards. To explain these, let me describe a client of mine, whom I'll call Bob, who has been very lucky in life. Bob grew up in a very small town in a family without much money that had never boasted a high school graduate, let alone a college one. Bob was the fourth of seven kids. He was not a particularly strong student nor did he receive much praise from his parents when he did bring home good grades, with so many other children in the family. Bob's logical path seemed preordained—grow up, stay out of trouble, get a job at a nearby factory, and lead a blue-collar life.

In his junior year of high school, however, something fateful occurred. Bob's English teacher died from a freak accident and the district hired a new teacher from a nearby city. This teacher, who had also been a wrestling coach, assembled a wrestling team at Bob's high school. Bob, a big, brawny kid, was an obvious candidate for recruitment. He had tried other sports, typical ones like football and baseball, but had demonstrated a shortfall of talent and interest.

Sure enough, Bob had a natural aptitude for wrestling. He became a star athlete and the teacher became a close mentor to Bob, filling the gap left by his lack of support at home. Bob sought guidance from his teacher and coach on many important decisions. By his senior year, Bob had drawn the attention of scouts from across the country. He was offered a scholarship to a large Midwest college and, on his mentor's advice, enrolled. Once there, Bob continued wrestling with great success, but he also realized that, for the first time, he was enjoying school. Apart from doing well in his math courses, Bob realized he had a penchant for business. He also joined a fraternity and made a number of close friends. The icing on the cake would arrive in the form of a girl Bob noticed one day in his accounting course. It didn't take long before Bob found himself love struck. Luckily, the feeling was mutual.

The woman's father happened to be a senior executive in the consumer products world. Impressed by Bob's seriousness and poise, he offered Bob a job following graduation, during a period when many of Bob's peers struggled to find lucrative or gratifying work.

Fast forward a couple of decades. Bob is the CFO of a huge public company, he has a large family and, by all accounts, an enviable life. He still looks back on those early events and shakes his head at how lucky he was. What would have happened if his English teacher hadn't died? What would have happened if he had ignored the petition of the wrestling coach for him to come out for the team? What if he had accepted a scholarship to a different college and never met his future wife?

According to Bandura, Bob had several personal determinants that, in each of these instances, *enabled* his luck. First, he had entry skills. He had to be able to fit into the social milieu of the wrestling team, the finance class in college, and, later on, the general business arena. Second, he had emotional ties; the bond with his wrestling coach, who, in the absence of parental guidance, ultimately served as his mentor and life-long counselor. As Bandura stated, "Once established, binding relationships serve as a vehicle for personal changes that can have long-range effects." Finally, despite not being able to provide him proper encouragement and guidance, his parents did instill in him solid values and personal standards. It was no coincidence that Bob met his future wife in a finance class at a Midwest college or that her father also came from a blue-collar background, but had moved on to the business world. They both shared a common set of values. Birds of a feather *do* flock together.

Bandura also described the social determinants of chance events. In terms of Bob's journey, the social settings he encountered provided psychological reinforcement. His coach was the first one to show an interest and faith in Bob's talents. From his wrestling team he derived a sense of belonging and acceptance. In his finance class, he felt smart and admired. According to Bandura, in order for Bob to capitalize on the events in his life, he needed to gain some reward from each of them. Moreover, Bob felt a symbolic attachment to things such as being on a high school athletic team, college life, fraternity brotherhood, having a steady girlfriend, and going into business. The symbolic nature of chance events profoundly affected the course of Bob's life.

Throughout history, several prominent figures have noted another important link—belief in one's "luck" is directly linked to one's motivation to succeed. "Genius," Thomas Edison famously said, "is 1 percent inspiration and 99 percent perspiration." Benjamin Franklin asserted that, "Diligence is the mother of good luck."

Psychologists have recently studied the correlation among drive, luck, and success.[1] In a collaborative study done at UCLA and Columbia University, researchers found that people's personal beliefs about luck were directly related to their need for achievement. The study divided luck into two types—stable and fleeting. Believers in stable luck would say that good things happen consistently to some people and not to others—for example, "I consistently have good luck" or "I consider myself to be a lucky person." Others believed in luck, but only as a short-lived phenomenon—for instance, "Something bad always happens after something good happens" or "Luck goes up and down."

After asking subjects luck-related questions, the researchers then tested them on their drive to succeed. Stable luck beliefs were significantly predictive of the drive to succeed, while fleeting luck beliefs were not. This finding stands to reason. If you believe luck is within your control and that you are, in general, a lucky person, you will be more motivated to work hard. But if you're convinced that even good fortune is, at best, transitory, how hard are you really going to pursue it?

THE MOTIVES, VALUES, AND PREFERENCES INVENTORY

What then drives people? If having a strong will is a combination of seizing chance opportunities and having sufficient drive to capitalize on them, what motivates some people to work harder than others? This question has been at the heart of a substantial body of research in psychology. At its most basic level, the research shows that although people are obviously motivated by different things, there are in fact a finite number of motivators that in some combination drive us all. One prevalent taxonomy of motivation has resulted from the work of Robert Hogan, a professor at the University of Tulsa for nearly two decades, who is now the owner of a company providing psychological tests for selecting and developing people in a wide range of organizations. One of Hogan's tests is called the "Motives, Values and Preferences Inventory" (MVPI). It describes ten key factors that serve to motivate us:

1. **Aesthetics** (creativity and artistic self-expression)
2. **Affiliation** (social interaction/being around others)

3. **Altruism** (helping others and improving society)
4. **Commerce** (money and business)
5. **Hedonism** (fun and adventure)
6. **Power** (achievement, competition, and influence over others)
7. **Recognition** (publicity, fame, and credit)
8. **Science** (figuring things out, problem solving, and new technology)
9. **Security** (low-risk environments, predictability, and stability)
10. **Tradition** (history, old-fashioned virtues, and convention)

The ninth dimension of Hogan's model is particularly relevant to will. People who are not motivated by security have a higher likelihood of willing events to occur. Why? One critical component of will is the ability to take advantage of opportunities. To do so, one must be willing to take risks. This may come in a variety of forms: financial risk (putting "skin in the game"); social risk (challenging a superior); creative risk (coming up with a radical new idea and going for it); or intellectual risk (believing in a project so much that you are willing to put yourself, and your job, on the line).

Most effective leaders engage in what is called "reasonable risk." After a thorough examination of the opportunities and threats, they assume the portion of the decision that is unknown at the time, and then pull the trigger. This is a vital leadership muscle to be able to exercise. Without it, one is automatically constrained in what one might achieve.

Finally, what happens if you position yourself for luck, are driven to succeed, willingly seize opportunities, and take reasonable risks to attain your goals, but still come up against significant hurdles?

This scenario is where we arrive back at the core of will, a characteristic that Angela Duckworth of the University of Pennsylvania calls *grit*.[2] According to Duckworth, "the gritty individual not only finishes tasks at hand but pursues a given aim over years." Duckworth and her colleagues created a way to measure one's level of grit, called, appropriately enough, the "Grit Scale." The Grit Scale describes this trait in terms of two factors: first, the extent to which one stays consistent in one's interests, and second, the extent to which one perseveres.

Yes, will is a composite of several attributes. It is the ability to position yourself for "luck." It is the burning drive to succeed. It is the enduring motivation to support that drive. And it is the willingness to come up against a brick wall and keep banging your head against it until you are finally able to crack it.

Will Power

If you've spent even one day leading any group, you know the importance of seeing the forest for the trees. Leaders who become overly tempted by "low-hanging fruit" often do so at the expense of valuable long-term opportunities. To resist short-term gain in deference to the big picture, you must summon not the externally oriented trait that makes others follow—will—but an internally oriented force, will power, which can have long-range implications.

Developmental psychologists have long researched the effects of early childhood will power on later success, perhaps most famously in what is now known as the Stanford Marshmallow Study.[3] In this study, a researcher offered hungry four-year-old children a marshmallow with the caveat that if they could hold off eating the marshmallow while the researcher ran some errands, they would then get two marshmallows. The researcher would leave the room and a video camera recorded how long the child was able to delay gratification and control the impulse to eat the marshmallow. About a third of the children grabbed the marshmallow as soon as the researcher left the room. Another third were able to hold out a bit longer. The final third were able to wait 15 to 20 minutes for the researcher to return, at which point they were rewarded with the second marshmallow.

After many years, the children from the study were tracked down and their life histories recorded. A stark difference was reported between those who had been able to resist temptation years before and those who had not. Children who had eaten the marshmallow right away were more troubled, stubborn, and indecisive, as well as less trusting and self-confident. They had a pattern of succumbing to temptations and impulses when the going got tough. As a result, they also had a higher rate of divorce, lower job satisfaction and income, worse health, and more life hassles.

Those who had been able to delay gratification as children had very different life outcomes. They were more optimistic, self-motivated, and persistent when faced with obstacles. They had more successful marriages, higher incomes, and greater career satisfaction. They had better health and more fulfilling lives. It may seem shocking that a child's ability to resist a single extra marshmallow so powerfully corresponds to what that child's life may look like later on—but this is, in fact, just a testament to the remarkable power of will.

HOW DO YOU KNOW IT WHEN YOU SEE IT?

There are people you know who seem to always be able to get things done. They are probably happy more often than not. People are naturally drawn to them because they get results. Good things just seem to happen to them.

These people weren't handed their good fortune on a silver platter. They have found a source of will within themselves and figured out ways to maximize it. They not only try to directly produce good outcomes, they also create an environment that enables positive outcomes to occur. Their will, over time, becomes something like a magnetic force—pulling or pushing as needed. Sometimes, they have to be forceful. That's because they are determined. At other times, they use their well-developed interpersonal skills to get others onside.

These people have learned to influence the environment they find themselves in, including the people within that environment, the circumstances that created it, and the events likely to come around the bend. People often think of will as mental strength or the power to change someone else's mind. I prefer to think of it as potency of influence. Those who have will are consistently able to assess situations, figure out how those situations need to be shaped to achieve success, and then leverage both their own strengths and those of others in the interests of execution. Such people typically display the behaviors discussed below.

They don't wait for things to happen

Successful executives I've encountered over the years enable things to happen, rather than wait for them to happen. They are frequently described as go-getters, burning with ambition, having engines that never stop, Energizer Bunnies®, never satisfied, not happy to rest on their laurels, always looking for a new way to improve, or constantly innovating. These are the kind of leaders people love to be around, because they tend to remove any worry about organizational complacency. No sooner has one successful initiative been launched than this type of leader is already strategizing around the next one. Her will is unremitting. Somewhere along the way she has been taught, or has learned, that a rolling stone gathers no moss or that a watched pot never boils or that the work isn't going to do itself. It's easy to spot the people who have internalized such lessons versus those who have not. The ones who have are committed to making things happen and they maintain the same expectation of everyone who works with them.

They go the extra mile

Elements of certain leadership intangibles are easy to spot, even before the people who possess them achieve leadership positions. The person you always see working late or showing up early is not necessarily the person with strong influence. To really determine their will, one must observe *how* they work and what that work prompts in others. "Face time" is relatively easy to achieve if you merely plan it right. But those who truly exert will do so by giving an extra 10 percent as a matter of course, not as a means of scoring points with their stakeholders or gaining favor with the team. The person who keeps going until they cross the tape does so because he can't fathom the thought of not doing so. That's will.

They give it everything they have

It is, as I've said several times now, not easy to apply and sustain effective leadership at the best of times. It takes hard work and perseverance. It requires one's full reserves of energy. Leaders with strong will somehow find those reserves, even when their tanks are empty, buoying spirits and inspiring the team. In meetings, in negotiations, or on videoconferences, extraordinary leaders are fully *there*, pouring all of themselves into the mission before them. They can't imagine any other way and it is largely because of this stubborn refusal to do anything halfway that their organizations so often succeed.

They find ways around obstacles

Those people who haven't figured out how to leverage their will are like sticks that drift up against rocks in a stream—they might remain stuck there indefinitely, helpless to find a way out of the predicament or resigned to giving up because the forces working against them just seem too strong. The best leaders, on the other hand, are not like the sticks in the stream, but rather the water—when it comes up against a rock it immediately finds a way around it. Few leaders have seamless paths toward the goals they want to achieve. There are budgets to contend with, competing agendas, manufacturing delays, and client issues. The extraordinary leader finds a way to identify these obstacles and then pulls the team around them.

In the experience of just about any leader I've ever spoken with, opportunities for shortcuts do arise frequently, but few are ever valid. All of us have had moments where we almost fell for, or perhaps did fall for, opportunities that we knew instinctively were too good to be true or that didn't look quite right on the surface. Some need or motivation allowed us to convince ourselves that the prospect in front of us was legitimate, and we learned our lesson the hard way.

Exceptional leaders seldom get fooled. Whatever suggestibility they may possess is overruled by their will. As a result, they stay on the straight and narrow, focused on the objective and the proper course to reach it.

They produce—and own—outcomes

As I said previously, the first way you can recognize leaders with strong will is their proclivity for action. They don't wait for things to happen; they make things happen instead. The corollary to that tendency is two-pronged: first, individuals generate a track record of results over time; and second, they have ownership of those results.

I don't mean that extraordinary leaders succeed all the time. Their profiles are hardly unblemished. The important thing is this: They point to both their successes and failures with equal pride, because in each case they see value and meaning in having made the attempt. These leaders have lots of stories to tell and often those stories form a fascinating map of both advances and regression. A leader who has will takes chances and, therefore, suffers setbacks on the road to eventual triumph. This person's record of past performance does not follow a straight path. It typically follows a circuitous route that includes ups and downs—but ends up at a higher height than the trajectory of those who took the more well-traveled path.

HOW DO YOU GET IT?

You probably think you can't get luckier in life—but you can. You have the power to will events to happen, whether you realize it or not. However, this won't happen on its own. I will give you a secret now, and bear with me while I explain, before you slam this book closed and call me nuts. Will, as I describe it, is in many ways like "The Force" in *Star Wars*. Yes, I said it. Luke Skywalker is able to move objects in space and make people think and act the way he wants them to. While I am not suggesting that you will be able to close your eyes and make things around your office rise into the air, you do actually have the ability to make events turn out in your favor and have good things come your way, much more than you may realize. So, young Jedi trainee, let's learn how you can begin to shape your own destiny.

Prepare for wins to occur

To create will, you must do the necessary homework and make the right preparations for success. The old adage burned into us from the first time we play Little League is true: Practice *does* make perfect. Do you have an upcoming presentation to make that could influence a big decision? How much preparation do you do? Beyond creating the PowerPoint slides, what do you do in advance? Do you practice in front of a mirror or with the assistance of a video camera or voice recorder? Do you anticipate the questions that will be asked and come up with effective responses? Do you speak with people in advance of the meeting to ensure you have sponsorship in the room? If you're not doing these things, you are not *willing* success your way. Extraordinary leaders do far more up-front preparation than you may realize, making it seem effortless. Learn from these leaders and prepare yourself.

Act. Now.

Will requires action. Too many leaders think about what they might do and how they might do it, instead of just doing it. I know leaders who, when faced with a difficult business situation, create the most impressive PowerPoint decks, chock-full of ideas and strategies. However, they spend so much time thinking about the problem that they rarely do anything about it.

Believe me, I am a strong proponent of decision by analysis. I don't think good strategy comes out of thin air. Big decisions require the best thinking your team can muster. However, in my experience, too many organizations, as a function of the leaders who drive them, suffer from paralysis by analysis— too much PowerPoint and not enough rolling up of sleeves. So, using the analogy I started earlier, you must plant as many seeds as possible, but have some kind of rationale for the places where you plant them. Don't plant them on concrete or in the desert. Find the fertile areas.

Don't believe in accidents

Most of us know people we consider perennially lucky. Good fortune is their constant companion; bad things seem rarely to befall them. They have horse-shoes up their rear ends, the luck of the Irish, the Midas touch.

Take a step back and think carefully about these people. Are they truly lucky or do they work hard to create conditions in their lives that, on balance, lead to positive outcomes? The answer is, in the vast majority of cases, the latter. It's a good bet, in fact, that those people you think of as lucky have in fact created their own luck, even though they may not recognize the fact, or readily acknowledge it. They probably roll their eyes when people mention superstition. They scoff at talk of serendipity or divine intervention. Ask them if they consider themselves lucky and they'll probably say something such as, "You make your own luck."

The best leaders do exactly that. They don't sit around waiting for luck to favor them with a visit. They strive to put the building blocks in place for success, whatever degree of effort it might require. Words like complacency and resignation are outside of their working vocabularies. They are willing to try, fail, try again, and then to repeat the pattern as many times as is necessary.

This is most often perceived by others as will, but the individuals themselves might not describe it that way. They would more likely say it is a deep, uncompromising desire to succeed. When I ask most great leaders how they have achieved their success, while out of humility few will say they willed it, not one of them will say, "It just happened."

This chapter began with a wonderful quote from Louis Pasteur: "Chance favors the prepared mind." Samuel Goldwyn was thinking along the same lines when he said, "The harder I work, the luckier I get." In order for you to will events to occur, you must work hard—hard enough so that opportunities will arise. That means looking at problems from as many angles as possible and then coming up with creative strategies to plant seeds in places you had never thought of. You don't think it's possible to be lucky by working hard? Consider it a challenge.

An Uncompromising Vision

Growing up in a blue-collar household in Windsor, just across the border from Detroit, Richard Peddie was obsessed by sports, especially basketball. Unfortunately, he had neither the physical stature nor the natural talent to go far as an athlete. What he did seem to possess was a strong dose of entrepreneurial flair and the kind of instinctive charisma that drew others to him.

While studying business at the University of Windsor, Richard remained spellbound by basketball. To satisfy his craving, he would attend varsity games and cheer on the Lancers. It was during one of these games that he made himself a promise: Someday I will run a professional basketball team. *He recorded the vow in a journal, put it away, and proceeded with his studies.*

After graduation, Richard progressed through a series of increasingly senior positions with large, influential companies: Colgate Palmolive, where he began his career in sales and marketing; General Foods, where he rose to become president of its popular Hostess division; Pillsbury, where he spent several successful years spearheading its Canadian operations; then on to SkyDome (now Rogers Centre), where as CEO he oversaw one of the largest arenas in Canada.

After a few years with SkyDome, Richard found himself recalling his old dream. There was talk of bringing the NBA to Toronto, and Richard put together a bid to start the team. However, to his dismay, Richard's team lost the bid on this attempt and the deal fell through. Richard then moved on to his next gig at Labbatt Communications, which ultimately became NetStar, a division of a major television and sports media company. Not long after, lightning struck again. As "luck" would have it, when a group of his acquaintances began thinking about preparing their own Toronto NBA bid, they came to Richard for advice. He wrote up a brief prospectus and offered recommendations for a successful bid. "They asked me what I would do if I was going to run the thing," he recently told me. "What the strategy would be, how I would market it, what kinds of land mines I would be thinking about, and so on. I wrote up a prospectus with my recommendations around strategy and gave it to them. They called me back later saying how they liked what I had to say and asking me if I knew anyone who could actually execute the strategy. Yeah, I said—me!"

Today, Richard Peddie is CEO of Maple Leaf Sports and Entertainment (MLSE), which owns the Toronto Maple Leafs, the Toronto Raptors, and Toronto FC (Toronto's professional soccer team). The Maple Leafs are the most valuable team in professional hockey; Toronto FC, which Richard had a large hand in bringing to the city, is the second most valuable in professional soccer; and the Raptors are among the most valuable in professional basketball. Beyond these assets, MLSE owns a variety of specialty cable sports networks and an abundance of highly valued real estate. Richard, the blue-collar kid from Windsor, is the proud leader of this empire and the force behind many of its most lucrative deals. Since taking the helm of the company, he has tripled its value to over $1.5 billion.

When I spoke to Richard about his path to success, I expected a lot of talk about luck, good fortune, and being in the right place at the right time. Instead, I listened in fascination to a story about making specific, strategic moves in order to attain a distant, but clear, objective. The decision to enroll in business at the University of Windsor was far from capricious. The choice to accept the role at Colgate Palmolive, a consumer products company, after graduation, seemed to me not to be peripherally related to owning a sports team—until I heard Richard talk about how it helped him learn marketing strategy and the art of the deal. His subsequent roles at Hostess and Pillsbury appeared wholly disconnected from owning a professional basketball team, until he explained how a significant portion of a sports arena's revenue is driven by its food concessions and how frequently leaders in the two industries interact. Equally important was the leadership education Richard received during his time at the two food companies. While there, he was taught the importance of vision and values, aspects of leadership he still espouses vigorously.

By the time we started talking about Richard's opportunity to take on the leadership mantle at SkyDome, I started to get it: This was not, at long last, an entrance into the business of sports—it was the logical next step in a series of strategic moves. It wasn't as easy a decision as one might think. Although it carried a CEO title, the SkyDome role was actually a smaller one than Richard had held at Pillsbury, where he'd been a rising star in a huge public company. But he followed his intuition, and that intuition led, ultimately, to being asked for his advice on bringing basketball to Toronto.

Richard Peddie's path toward fulfilling his dream was not one of luck. It was one of powerful intent, strategic decision making, and a broad vision with a clear ultimate goal. His story seemed to me at first quite serendipitous, full of twists and turns that ultimately found him in the exact place he'd always desired. But the more we talked, the more I realized that, by putting into place all the right pieces of the puzzle over time, Richard Peddie had willed his goal to fruition, decades after he first defined it.

Stand firm

At its simplest, will means showing a spine. If you are seen to be constantly vacillating, those around you will be apprehensive about following your lead. But if you make decisions based on an unswerving, publicly communicated, easily understandable set of values and principles, following you will be easy. You will be seen as having the strength—the will—to step into the fray, tackle issues, and follow through with firmness and conviction. You will encounter resistance and obstacles in any endeavor you take on, and in order to will the outcome you want, you must stand your ground on issues you feel strongly about, and you must push through resistance by working harder and smarter than those standing in your way.

Exercise self-discipline

Remember the Stanford Marshmallow Study? Would you be able to hold off until the researcher comes back or would you dive into the marshmallow with abandon? Don't feel bad if you suspect you'd be one of those who couldn't hold off—you're not alone. At the same time, recognize that self-discipline is a necessary muscle to build if you want to generate will.

You must be able to control your impulses and delay gratification. This gets harder as the scope of your influence increases; however, it's all the more important. Every decision counts—think long-term and don't get distracted by temptation. Keep your eyes on the prize.

One way to do this is to put a system in place for yourself. This may sound simple, but the best solutions often are. Avoid distraction by devising a process that will keep you focused. Build discipline by forcing yourself to be accountable; this is the entire basis behind weight-loss programs such as Jenny Craig and Weight Watchers. To avoid getting distracted or falling into short-term traps, members go to weekly weigh-ins and record their caloric intake daily. I generally advise my clients to use one of three systems:

1. IT systems (for example, using Microsoft Outlook to schedule a weekly time for you to think about, and work on, a major project);
2. Human systems (for example, hiring a good executive assistant to keep you on top of a project); or
3. Organizational systems (for example, a monthly progress meeting with your team).

Every strong executive I interact with shows, in one way or another, the discipline necessary to achieve great things. Some have been marathon runners, training mile after mile in the early mornings despite cold weather and a family asleep at home. Others have endured demeaning grunt work early in their careers—at the expense of their egos and personal lives. What are you willing to sacrifice in order to reach your long-term leadership goals?

Don't quit

Too many people give up before they reach success—often, *just* before. Studies have shown that the hardest part of reaching any goal comes just before you actually reach it. If you have ever tried to quit smoking, you know this to be the case. At the beginning, the cravings only get worse, not better. Then, at some point, they peak and begin to subside. Unfortunately, most people who are trying to quit give in just before the peak. They think it is impossible to reach their goal because the effort only seems to be getting harder and harder. What they don't realize is that it is just when their struggle seems most difficult that they are on the verge of attaining their goal.

This is also the case in the workplace. Will requires you to have "stick-to-itiveness." You can't quit. You need to be tenacious. When obstacles keep getting in your way and it seems that you'll never meet your objectives, remember this: You are probably just a hair's breadth away.

WHY IT MATTERS

Leaders in every space have a virtually constant need to catalyze, galvanize, and rally people around them in pursuit of a common goal. Some leaders do this subtly, exercising their influence in so delicate a fashion that those around them happily follow without questioning why. Others use more insistent methods, forcefully staking out their territory at the front of the pack and spelling out the reasons why their vision makes more sense than anyone else's. Both of these methods, and every one in between, require will. It's a competitive world out there. Lots of people have great ideas, deep business knowledge, and broad skill sets. But when it comes to exceptional leadership, it's the ability to make things happen that proves the biggest differentiator.

The Peaceful Fight: Part Two

Satyagraha *was what the barrister called his method of defiance— devotion to the truth. He was asking his people to defy the new law, but also to suffer the punishments for doing so. Non-violent protest, he asserted, was the most effective way to exert the collective will of so many.*

So great was the Indian people's respect and esteem for this man, they adopted the plan willingly, leading to a seven-year struggle in which thousands of them were jailed, flogged, or shot for striking, refusing to register, burning their registration cards, or engaging in other forms of non-violent resistance. Though the South African government was successful in repressing the protesters, its methods spurred a public outcry. Finally, South African General Jan Christiaan Smuts was compelled to negotiate a compromise with the barrister, whose belief in satyagraha only became stronger.

Challenges to satyagraha would arise frequently in the years to come. In 1906, after the British introduced a new poll tax, Zulus in South Africa killed two British officers, and in response, the British declared war against the Zulus. The barrister actively encouraged the British to recruit Indians, arguing to his people that they should support the war effort in order to ultimately legitimize their claims to citizenship. The British refused to commission Indians as army officers, but accepted the barrister's offer to let a detachment of them volunteer as a stretcher-bearer corps to treat wounded British soldiers. It was delicate progress, the barrister knew.

At the outbreak of World War I, he found volunteers for the Ambulance Corps. In 1915 he returned to India and in 1918 he agreed to actively recruit Indians for the front lines—though in a letter to the viceroy's private secretary he stated that he personally would "not kill or injure anybody, friend or foe." And in the waning days of the war, he exposed the deplorable conditions in which British landlords had left Indian villages, leading to the cleanup of these villages, the development of schools and hospitals, and the official condemnation of social evils.

Using non-cooperation, non-violence, and peaceful resistance as his weapons, he continued to lead the struggle for justice and independence, becoming famous throughout the vast nation of India. People began to address him as "Bapu" or "Father" and "Mahatma" or "Great Soul." In 1921, the barrister was invested with executive authority on behalf of the Indian National Congress, and he expanded his non-violence platform to include the policy of swadeshi, boycott of foreign goods—especially British goods. He advocated that all Indians wear homespun cloth instead of British-made textiles, exhorting Indian men and women, rich or poor, to spend time each day spinning the cloth in support of independence. In addition, he urged the people to boycott British educational institutions and law courts, to resign from government employment, and to forsake British titles and honors.

Non-cooperation began to earn favor across Indian society, but just as the movement reached its apex, it was blotted abruptly as a result of a violent clash in the town of Chauri Chaura in February 1922. Fearing a turn towards violence, the barrister called off the campaign of mass civil disobedience. He was arrested, tried for sedition, and sentenced to six years' imprisonment.

Without the barrister's unifying personality, the Indian National Congress began to splinter, and cooperation among Hindus and Muslims, strong at the height of the non-violence movement, began to disintegrate. The barrister attempted to bridge these differences through many means, including a three-week fast in the autumn of 1924, but with limited success.

Still, he pushed on. In 1928, he called on the British to grant India dominion status or face a new campaign of non-cooperation, with complete independence for the country as its goal. Two years later, he launched a new satyagraha against the British tax on salt, emphasizing his resolve by marching 241 miles from Ahmedabad, his home, to the coastal village of Dandi to make salt himself. Thousands of other Indians joined in, marching the entire distance alongside him. Britain responded by imprisoning tens of thousands.

Eventually, the British agreed once again to negotiate with the Mahatma. They consented to free all political prisoners in return for the suspension of the civil disobedience movement. But when a new British campaign to subdue the nationalist movement arose, the barrister again rallied his people in a mass non-violent protest and, again, he was arrested. This time, the government tried to negate his influence by isolating him from his followers. But they failed. And when World War II broke out, the Mahatma declared that India could not be party to a war ostensibly being fought for democratic freedom, while that freedom was denied to India itself.

In later years, the barrister's focus shifted to vehement opposition to the movement to partition India to create Pakistan. Splitting India into two countries, he argued, would only encourage conflict. But eventually, India's Congress leadership accepted the partition plan as the only way to prevent a Hindu-Muslim civil war. Devastated, the barrister gave his assent.

Despite the division, he talked with Muslim and Hindu community leaders endlessly, with the aim of peaceful resolution. But passions continued to rise, and in response, the Mahatma launched a "fast unto death," asking that violence on both sides be ended once and for all. Not long after, Hindu, Muslim, and Sikh community leaders assured him they would renounce violence and call for peace. The barrister then broke his fast, taking a few sips of orange juice.

A few days later, in the early evening hours of January 30, 1948, the Mahatma met with India's deputy prime minister and an associate, and then proceeded to his prayers. Near the garden where the prayer meeting was to be held, a Hindu fundamentalist lay in wait. Moments later, Gandhi's life was over.

"Friends and comrades," said Prime Minister Jawaharlal Nehru, "the light has gone out of our lives, and there is darkness everywhere, and I do not quite know what to tell you or how to say it. Our beloved leader, Bapu as we called him, the father of the nation, is no more." But then he added: "Perhaps I am wrong to say that."

For Nehru had, in that moment, realized the profound truth that Mohandas Gandhi was only physically gone. Through the love he had preached, the truth he had urged, and the philosophy of peace through which he had summoned the will of an entire nation, he would live on.

THE BOTTOM LINE

Be accountable for your own luck. Will success to occur.

3

Executive Maturity

When dealing with people, remember you are not dealing with creatures of logic, but creatures of emotion.

—Dale Carnegie

Order on the Court: Part One

He was dazzled by the Franklin Wonder Five. Swept up in Hoosier Hysteria along with the rest of the state. Most of the Wonder Five had followed their high school coach, Griz Wagner, to Franklin College, and now they were simply dominant, steamrolling over opponents big and small—Notre Dame, Illinois, Purdue, Wisconsin, any and all comers.

The way they moved the ball around, sharing it so unselfishly. The way they hustled, each man inspiring the other. How they passed and moved, how they worked as a single, fluid unit, how they kept their game faces no matter what the circumstances—watching the Franklin Wonder Five was poetry in motion. It wasn't surprising that they cruised to the state championship three years in a row. What was surprising was that any other team had come close.

There were, in fact, eight players in the Wonder Five. You had Burl Friddle and Ralph Hicks. You had Paul White and Sima Comer. There was Snake Eyes Gant, Harold Borden, and Pete Keeling.

And there was Fuzzy Vandivier, John's favorite. Though John was only ten, he couldn't imagine anyone had ever seen a player better than Fuzzy. Fuzzy was as cool as he was talented, always intense, but never rattled. One of the rules in the Seven Point Creed that John's father had given him was, "Make each day your masterpiece." Fuzzy must have felt that about each basketball game.

John and his family moved to Martinsville, and Fuzzy and the Franklin Wonder Five were consigned to a cherished part of his memory. Now fourteen and coming into his own as an athlete, John began to make his own mark on the court, leading his high school team to the state finals three years in a row, and, in 1927, winning the whole thing. At Purdue, under the guidance of Piggy Lambert, he continued to build his basketball résumé, following three All-State selections with three nods as an All-American, the first person ever to accomplish the feat. In 1932, the Boilermakers were named National Champions—by a panel, rather than the NCAA tournament, which would only start in 1939—and John came to be referred to as "The Indiana Rubber Man" for the suicidal dives he would make to get the ball back at any cost.

The professional ranks followed. John had earned a place in the basketball stratosphere. He was among the elite—one of the very best to play a game millions loved. All the while, he happily sacrificed himself for the game, for the Indianapolis Kautskys, and then the Whiting Ciesar All-Americans. John remembered the lessons he had learned from watching the Wonder Five and Fuzzy Vandivier. He tried to be unselfish in his play. He hustled all the time, hoping others would follow his example. And he tried never to lose his game face. If Fuzzy couldn't be rattled, neither could he.

It helped enormously, this silent lesson that Fuzzy had taught. Keeping a rein on his emotions helped John stay in control of himself on the court, poised, able to calmly see a moment ahead, instead of reacting to what had happened a moment before. It helped him to sink 134 consecutive free throws over forty-six games.

He taught the same approach to the high school players he had started to coach: Keep it together. Remember that it's not about you, it's about the team. Don't let one bad play get you down; focus on the play coming up instead. And they listened, mostly. And it worked, always.

When John came home from the war, his high school coach, Glenn Curtis, who had been coaching at Indiana State, accepted an *offer to coach the Detroit Falcons, a pro squad. The Indiana State job was left vacant and John was asked to step in to fill Glenn's shoes.*

John continued to build on his mantra of equanimity, insisting to his players that they must behave the same whether winning by ten or losing by twenty. He demanded intensity, but punished emotionality, enforcing composure both in his players and himself. He gave no rah-rah speeches or contrived pep talks. His players were prohibited from exulting after scoring on an opponent or brooding after being scored on themselves. He told them that if they let their emotions take over, they would be outplayed, and if they were outplayed, they would be outscored. He maintained the same posture in a preseason game as he did in a national championship. And following either one, he made sure to conduct himself in such a manner that one could rarely tell whether his team had won or lost.

The formula worked wonders. John's team won the Indiana Collegiate Conference title in 1947 and received an invitation to the national tournament in Kansas City. But John refused, citing the tournament's policy banning African American players. Thanks, he responded, but no thanks. I and my players, Clarence Walker included, would rather not participate.

The following year, the tournament reversed its policy, and this time John's team played, reaching the finals but losing to Louisville. It would be the only championship ever lost by a team he coached.

Some of television's greatest dramas are played out in shows where one expects it the least. I happen to occasionally enjoy watching hold 'em poker. I know, not exactly cerebral stuff, but it can, in fact, sometimes make for incredibly intriguing TV. Literal fortunes are won or lost by the turn of a card. Joe Cada, the 2009 World Series of Poker champion, took home $8.5 million for that tournament.

Beyond the staggering numbers, what I find most interesting is how people react under tremendous pressure. What makes poker on television work is that we, the audience, can see what no one else at the table can see—all of the players' "hole cards" (the cards hidden in each person's hand). As the viewer, you get a real-time glimpse into what it looks like when someone is lying. They may have nothing in their hand and they're pretending to have aces. Or they have a powerhouse hand and are faking nonchalance.

Emotions communicate a great deal. People make inferences about content depending on the emotion in which the message is framed. Like the poker player, it is critical for the executive to be in control of his emotions. Emotional outbursts that are unplanned or unintended can have deep and detrimental effects. However, carefully planned expressions of emotion can be a powerful communication tool. Aristotle said, "Anyone can become angry—that is easy. But to be angry with the right person, to the right degree, at the right time, for the right purpose, and in the right way—that is not easy." Handled judiciously, emotional expression can be a powerful tool in the effective leader's repertoire.

WHAT IS IT?

At a basic level, executive maturity is about regulating our emotions. Emotions affect the way we see the world, the way we make decisions, and the way we are perceived by others. When we're feeling down or depressed, we really do see the world through gray-colored glasses. Everything seems blander than it would on a day when we're happier or more pumped or looking forward to the possibility of romance. On those days, colors are more vibrant, food has more flavor, and smells seem more fragrant.

Moods can also distort our perceptions of our surroundings, sometimes in odd and wonderful ways. In a recent study, scientists at the College of William and Mary found that emotional arousal influences our perception of height. That is, if you are standing on top of a building, the happier you are, the more you'll distort how high—literally—you feel. The same effect can also be produced by showing people in different states of emotional arousal a picture of someone *else* on top of a building. Those who are ramped-up emotionally will believe the person in the picture is higher up than they really are.

In the workplace, emotions affect us in many ways. In fact, much has been written in the past decade about the importance of emotional intelligence. Daniel Goleman and others have built an entire industry around that concept. Emotional intelligence is indeed an important attribute—how you understand emotions in yourself and others can contribute to your overall well-being and your success in the workplace. I have no doubt about that.

However, at the executive level, I believe that it is not just how well you can read and understand the emotions in others, but how effectively you can control your own emotions that differentiates the extraordinary leader.

The author of the Foreword to this book, Dr. Tom Saporito, CEO of RHR International, once told me a story about emotional regulation that affected him in a visceral way. I think it applies here:

Many years ago, I was providing consulting services to McCormick, a global provider of spices, seasonings, and flavors. In one instance, there was a division that was in tremendous turmoil. I was working with a group president named Clayton Shelhoss. Clayton called me at one point and said that he was going to have to fire one of the division heads. I had worked with the group and knew how emotionally charged the situation would be. Clayton asked me how to communicate the decision in a way that would be best received by the team, and I gave him some advice.

Instead of just listening, he said, "Okay—come with me." And he brought me with him to the meeting. I will never forget the walk from his office to the divisional building. He exuded absolute calm. I could feel the intensity throughout my system as we walked into this charged situation, yet he showed none of the same emotion. He was composed and in control. In the meeting itself, he used his calm composure to infuse a sense of stability and resolve. It inspired others and redirected everyone to focus on the task at hand. He took the emotion out of the situation. It was a seminal moment for me, both as a management psychologist and a leader myself. I saw how controlled he was and the impact that had on everyone else.

Read the story again. It isn't a story about not having feelings. It's a story about choosing when to put feelings on display and when to shelve them in deference to the task at hand. The best leaders I have worked with are masters of their emotions. They rein in their emotions when the situation demands it, or let loose with their emotions when it will have maximum impact. There are times when you need to be still and impenetrable; at other times, you need to be able to pound your fist on the table. The key is not whether you are typically a calm or intense person. It is your ability to gain mastery over your emotional tendencies and reactions. You must develop the ability to fit the emotion to the demands of the situation.

This is, of course, no easy feat. Think about the last time you were enraged. How easily were you able to contain yourself? Were you able to maintain calm or did you lash out?

I like to think of executive maturity as a high-functioning emotional filter. Any information you receive has some degree of emotional valence—it triggers in you a certain level of anger, fear, happiness, suspicion, or memories of your first love. Some people always react immediately to the information; others take time to process it and then react appropriately. Those in the first group have a short filter, if any. Those in the second group have a long filter. It is the leader with a long filter who ultimately wields greater influence—first, because she considers her reaction before having it, and second, because others see her thinking first and acting second.

For those with well-developed executive maturity, the choice that results from this moment of consideration isn't necessarily the same each time. The judicious leader doesn't just choose a default approach. Deploying our emotions effectively isn't as simple as that. In a recent two-part study conducted in England, researchers reported a fascinating set of findings. In the first part of the study, they asked a large group of participants to recall a distressing event. Then they asked some of the people to try to suppress their negative feelings. Those who had purposely tried to suppress their emotions reported being in a better mood.

However, in the second part of the experiment, things were flipped. Another group of participants repeated the same procedure, but this time the pressure was increased. They were asked to remember a nine-digit number, thus increasing the complexity of the process while mimicking a real-life scenario of needing to control one's anxiety in the face of stress. The results were quite different this time. Those who were asked to suppress their emotions ended up in a worse mood than those who weren't.

In other words, when the heat is on and your blood pressure is rising, it may do more harm than good to just bottle up what you're feeling. You'll feel worse and, eventually, that negative feeling is going to come out. Emotional regulation involves recognizing your own emotions as they form, matching them to the situation you're in, and channeling them appropriately.

* * *

Here's an easy test to assess your basic level of executive maturity: How well do you control your impulses? Every day we are inundated with choices. We are confronted with decisions that have short- and long-term implications. These can be basic, core implications such as physiological benefits (Should I eat that piece of cake or not?) or financial benefits (Should I cheat on my tax return?). There may also be more complex benefits that address some underlying need

(Should I pursue this career path? Should I fire that person on my team just because she made a single inappropriate comment?).

These choices and their drivers have been the source of study in psychology almost since the beginning of the discipline. Freud believed famously in the "pleasure principle"—simply that we do things that bring us pleasure and avoid things that bring us pain. Furthermore, we have a system of checks and balances when confronted by a choice that may be outside the boundaries of social acceptability. Our superego protects us from doing things we shouldn't. It is our benevolent conscience, the angel residing on our right shoulder.

"Healthy" adults have a strong superego, according to Freud, and are able to fend off impulses issued by their more crude ids. The less mature among us cannot muster up enough superego to do this.

Say what you might about Freud, or call the process by whatever label you'd like, but clearly we do have a system of checks and balances. There is a part of us that wants to follow our impulses and take care of our most basic needs. The devil on one shoulder says, "Do it." The angel on the other shoulder argues mightily, imploring us to delay the gratification and think about the bigger picture. It is the most mature among us that resist the devil most consistently.

In my clients, I witness this struggle all the time. Money and power bring strange opportunities to follow impulses. In some cases, these opportunities are relatively benign, such as pursuing a pet project that is more fun than profitable, or promoting someone who has been more loyal than capable. In other cases, the impulses are much more sinister, such as making an acquisition because of personal financial incentives rather than the actual viability of the deal, playing nasty politics in order to win, or even engaging in scandalous adventures like corporate espionage, succumbing to sexual escapades with staff, or the kind of fraudulent behavior that has practically filled the news over the past few years.

The "healthiest" leaders, Freud would suggest, get what he was saying. They stare down temptation and blot it out by holding paramount their sense of the bigger picture. The most successful CEOs quietly forgo quick wins, easy fixes, temporary boosts, or transient power grabs in favor of long-term success. Their maturity enables them to keep their impulses at bay, so they end up sticking around a lot longer, and they are more successful as a result.

Research shows that older people tend not to get as "hot and bothered" in response to social tension than younger people do. Older people are also prone to using more passive strategies, like ignoring the situation or walking away, than younger people, who favor more active strategies, such as direct confrontation. In one recent study, when older people were asked why they opted for the passive means of dealing with tension, they reported that their aim was to preserve harmony and avoid conflict.

They weren't just retreating, in other words. They had a specific goal. Any aspiring leader should take note of the wisdom of their elders. Most of us do not envision an ultimate goal when we are confronted with an intense situation, particularly a negative one. Instead, we react, trying our best to tip the argument, get the green light, or secure the thumbs-up. Though such wins may feel good, they don't always contribute to a shared objective. A more adaptive strategy is to establish and remember the goal. Most often, preserving harmony will achieve the best outcomes, so defusing the situation is typically the best option. Those of you less experienced in such matters, take note: The goal of the mature leader is never, "I will change this person."

Finally, executive maturity is not just an inwardly focused capability. Extraordinary leaders regulate the emotions of others as well. What good does it do for the captain of a ship to remain poised under pressure if the rest of the crew is coming apart at the seams? Only by pooling their resources in a focused, calm way will they prevail.

We, of course, influence the emotions of others all the time and we use various techniques to do so. Sometimes this is a conscious effort, sometimes not. You can probably think of a time when someone tried to cheer you up when you were feeling lousy. You can probably think of other times when someone, perhaps a college friend with a cruel streak, purposely made it their business to embarrass or anger you. Perhaps you can think of a strong leader who was able to lift your spirits or inspire you in some way. What did that person do, and why was it effective? Thinking back on the situation now, did he buck you up with a general "You can do it," or was it a specific quality of yours he emphasized? While all managers, through what they do and say, impact the emotions of their subordinates, exceptional leaders do it with a purpose.

HOW DO YOU KNOW IT WHEN YOU SEE IT?

Are some people naturally calmer than others? Yes. Historically, this trait was referred to in psychology as neuroticism. It's a term that has been misconstrued and grossly misused. What it actually refers to is emotionality—specifically, the extent to which someone emotionally reacts to events.

People who are low in this trait express a narrow band of emotions and don't visibly react to events. (They're the ones who make great poker players.)

People who are high in this trait tend to wear their hearts on their sleeves. They are passionate and sensitive, and visibly show when they are anxious, excited, or thrilled.

So, is it better to be low or high in neuroticism? While people who are not emotionally reactive tend to occupy more leadership roles than not, the majority of *unemotional* people miss a critical aspect of executive maturity: They cannot summon the emotional response when the situation calls for it.

One executive I work with, the CFO of an automotive company, is completely even-keeled. Nothing fazes him. His face is expressionless and he is as calm as a toad in the sun. Throughout his career, this quality has helped him immensely. He has achieved great success because he possesses aplomb. But in his current role, he is struggling. The nature of his work now requires him to be much more passionate, to inspire his people and rally the troops, to push back and challenge the assumptions of the rest of the leadership team. And this ability to summon passion doesn't seem to be within him. His example is highly relevant. I don't want you to confuse having executive maturity with being emotionless. Executive maturity refers to the appropriate, intentional use of emotions to match the situation.

Great leaders practice deliberate emotional regulation in the context of the broader goals or purposes they face. The results, and the impact on those around them, are often powerful. Our intellect and our emotions are natural adversaries and it is never wise to try to ignore one for the benefit of the other. Both insist on being acknowledged. Extraordinary leaders know this and they have developed a crucial mix of skills in response. As a result, they are able to read situations, adapt their style and behavior accordingly, and, ultimately, make emotions their ally instead of their foe. You can spot these types of leaders in a number of different ways.

They can mix it up

Sometimes, of course, it is okay to let loose. Done strategically, raising the emotional intensity of a situation can yield results. I know a very mild-mannered CEO of a financial services company in the southern U.S. He is an incredibly smart guy who also happens to be quite introverted. He talks very quietly, to the point that I sometimes have difficulty hearing him when we're on the phone. Everyone around him knows him to be kind, considerate, and highly empathetic. He has a very even temperament; I rarely have seen him lose his cool.

I do, however, remember one particular time. I was sitting in on a meeting with a small group, his top team. The discussion was about a long-standing problem that hadn't yet been solved. As usual, the tone of the meeting was analytical and objective, without much emotion. Then, out of nowhere, the CEO raised his voice, literally pounded his fist on the table and loudly admonished the team for their lack of movement on the issue.

The sudden outburst was extraordinarily jarring, making everyone in the room (including me) jump in their seats and straighten their postures. The meeting ended quickly thereafter, and I had some private time with the CEO. I asked him, "What happened? I've never seen that side of you." He told me, "I did it purposely. I know the impact it will have. Sure, it may not be so natural for me, but did you see how everyone reacted? When I need to move the needle on something that just isn't moving, I turn up the heat." Sure enough, by the end of the following day, the team had come up with a plan to solve the problem.

The Leadership Brand

Soon after Michel Poirier became CEO of JTI-Macdonald, a division of tobacco giant JT International, the company was hit with a lawsuit north of a billion dollars. "That was enough to make anyone panic," Michel told me.

But then Michel did something of profound importance: He took a little time. Before showing a public reaction to the rest of the company, he reflected behind closed doors, staying in his office and thinking things through.

It was the type of patience and rationality he had acquired at an early age. The second youngest of eight kids, Michel grew up an observer. In particular, he watched the way the interpersonal dynamics in his family unfolded, the way conflicts arose, and how they would get resolved. One lesson, he says, stood out. "I saw that visible reactions always made things worse."

By the time his father, a janitor, sent him out into the world at the age of eighteen, Michel had already developed a degree of poise that would, ultimately, serve as the hallmark of his leadership style. He started in sales at Alberto-Culver and then moved on to Procter and Gamble, where at only twenty-seven he became a regional manager. When an opening for a bigger role came along, Michel applied for it, but was told he was simply too young. He reacted not emotionally, but analytically—by going out and looking for a better opportunity.

And there were other opportunities. He joined Johnson & Johnson, becoming the vice president of sales. "But the amount of travel involved in that role became very strenuous after my daughter was born," Michel told me, "and at that point in my life I knew it wasn't right for me." It didn't take him long to move on to bigger and better things. "A month later, I was hired as VP of sales for Revlon." Now more firm in his approach and experienced as a leader, Michel thrived. He became known as a smart, analytical, and thoughtful leader who challenged those around him to bring objectivity and strategy to sales. He challenged long-held assumptions and used data to influence change.

After a successful run at Revlon, Michel was hired into JTI-Macdonald as VP of sales and then promoted quickly up the ladder— eventually to the very top.

It was under the glare of that billion-dollar lawsuit that the results of Michel's leadership journey were most effectively demonstrated. After taking that time to compose himself, to ask himself what his employees needed most from him, he armed them with an important gift—information. "You have to take away the emotions. Get people thinking analytically instead." He talked to his staff about the suing party's motivations, JTI's position, what the process was going to look like, and why he felt they were going to come out on top. He helped give them answers to the questions their families were likely to ask. He told them how they'd get through this, what it was going to take, and how long it might last. He brought them from the emotional side to the rational side. "I tried to help them substitute reason for emotion."

His basis for this strategy was, and is, the philosophy that the leader sets the tone for the organization. "The leader portrays the brand," Michel said to me. "He can either reinforce it or kill it. For that reason he has to remain calm under scrutiny. He has to have a high threshold for frustration. And if he is going to show emotion, it must have a purpose."

When Michel does choose to show emotion, it absolutely has a purpose. Most of the time I'd describe him as highly composed and extremely rational. He almost always seems to be in control and solution-focused. He is immaculately put together, professional to the bone. However, that doesn't mean he's stoic—quite the contrary, in fact. He is also amiable, empathic, and fun to be around.

I've even seen him get good and ticked off on occasion. This he does sparingly and in the company of select people. Every emotion he reveals has a tactical reason for being allowed out. "When I feel passionate about something," he says, "I show it, and hopefully it creates a fire in the belly. Emotions are a good thing—as long as you know how to make them work for you."

Michel's attention to the impact he has on others and his understanding of leadership as a frequent exercise in branding have resulted in major successes for his organization. Beyond JTI-Macdonald's strong financial performance, it is clear that his people are thoroughly engaged: Since the billion dollar lawsuit some 11 years ago, the company was named one of the Top 50 Employers in Canada by Hewitt Associates and the Globe and Mail for 10 of those 11 years. Michel now serves as Regional President for all of the Americas at JT International. He knows who he is as a leader. Even more important, he knows what others need from him.

They don't get defensive

Senior executives are under constant attack—from employees, The Street, competitors, and customers. Some leaders opt to fight back. You've seen them: their face gets red and their blood pressure begins to rise. Then, they usually either attack the messenger or deflect the message. This is defensive behavior and it is surprisingly common among leaders. Why is that so? Many are confident, as they need to be to reach a certain level of success (see Chapter 8 on self-efficacy), so much so that any time someone comes close to bruising their egos and knocking their self-confidence, they can't take it. Extraordinary leaders, on the other hand, take in feedback, listen to people's concerns about them, and then process it. They don't always agree with what they are hearing, but they listen thoughtfully. Such non-defensiveness is a rare commodity and characteristic of the mature executive.

They take a moment

Of course, no matter how prepared we might be for a certain situation, surprises will occur. Sometimes these surprises are brought to the surface purposely by others—media, adversaries, or loose-lipped colleagues.

Effective leaders do not react hastily. They think before responding. Sometimes this pause consists of a fraction of a second, but watch the difference between (a) the person who looks urgent in his desire to speak next, who leans forward waiting for a spot to jump in, pouncing as soon as there's an opening or, more often, interrupting before the other has finished, and (b) the person who listens actively and fully to the person speaking, then allows a beat to pass and responds in a relevant, direct, considered way. The first person introduces tension and agitation to the conversation, making it an inadvertent competition to see who can get the most words in. The second person, because she pays attention to her interlocutor and thinks about her words before reacting, is always heard.

They acknowledge emotions but deal with them intellectually

As we'll discuss further, extraordinary leaders open up and reveal themselves, but they do it in a way that is accessible and purposeful. They have a mature perspective. One leader I assessed reflected on how angry he had been as a kid and how that now translates into sometimes going overboard when he is upset with his subordinates. He admits to falling into such traps occasionally, but he understands where it comes from and does his best to mitigate it.

They demonstrate emotional bandwidth

When emotions go awry, people can't function effectively. About 2 percent of the population of North America has a psychological disorder called Borderline Personality Disorder (BPD).[1] It is characterized by pervasive instability of moods, causing major disruptions in one's life. You may recognize people with BPD when they have bouts of anxiety, depression, or anger that just don't seem to fit the circumstances. Their moods can change from moment to moment and these swings tend to be powerful. People with BPD experience emotions in black-and-white terms. There are no mild emotions, only extremes. While it's nearly impossible to diagnose someone from afar, you can probably think of some well-known cases of young Hollywood stars who show signs of such behavior, which also includes substance abuse, promiscuity, acting out in public, and demonstrating acute anger. Sound pleasant? It isn't and it remains a very difficult disorder to treat.

While perhaps not as extreme as what I've just described, I've seen similar exhibitions of BPD in the workplace. Emotionally immature leaders ride the same roller coaster with enough twists and turns, loops and dives, to make anybody sick. They are fine one moment, then burst out in anger the next. Even worse, they express emotions that don't fit the circumstances—getting angry when it doesn't help or anxious when the situation calls for calm. Leaders who manage by crisis are notorious for this behavior, which proves extremely counterproductive.

Similar emotional immaturity arises in executives who are narcissistic. They are self-centered, need admiration, and lack empathy. At times, when they should show sensitivity and understanding toward others, they appear dispassionate and indifferent. Their need for attention and power stems from immature fears of their own adequacy.

Here is one example of inappropriate emotions. A large conglomerate had acquired a small high-tech company I was working with. A town hall meeting was held in which the CEO of the conglomerate came to greet the hundred or so employees of the company they had just bought. What he may or may not have known is that the acquisition was seen as a disaster by most of the employees. They expected that their small office would likely close or be severely downsized, just as the acquirer had done with previous companies it had bought. There was a somber, subtly angry mood in the room prior to the CEO's coming on stage.

I happened to be invited to the meeting at the request of the small company's president, to give her my read on the CEO and to help her come up with a strategy for dealing with him. The room was tense, quiet. All of a sudden, the CEO burst into the room. Wearing a smile from ear to ear, he gleefully approached the podium. He then proceeded to announce the excitement he was feeling about the acquisition, how happy he was, and how the company would surely benefit as a result of the new purchase. Someone handed him a bottle of champagne, which he popped open, symbolically marking the celebration. Then, without taking a single question from the audience, he abruptly left the room. Meeting over. I don't believe I've ever witnessed such a gross misread on the part of a CEO in my career. The audience was aghast—and determined to set things right going forward.

At the other end of the emotional spectrum, the best leaders I work with are able to match the visible emotion to the needs of the situation. They have a relatively wide range of emotions, showing intensity when the pressure is on or showing joy when a win is being celebrated. However, they are keenly aware of how their emotions will be interpreted and utilize them accordingly. Leaders with executive maturity know how to leverage their position through the occasional strategic moment of exaggerated emotion. If they time their "big" reactions well and use them sparingly, such instances can have tremendous impact. Executive maturity does not mean exercising perfect equanimity at all times. It means recognizing that there is a time for fist pounding and a time for steadfast composure. The best leaders play both parts to equal effect.

They stay cool under pressure

I said earlier that managing one's emotions doesn't simply mean staying calm. I also said that the ability to stay calm, especially under pressure, is indeed one of the hallmarks of a leader in control. When the going gets tough, people want someone they believe can navigate their way through a crisis. They are unlikely to put their faith in someone who doesn't seem able to stand the heat. About the latter type of person you will hear comments like, "She lets her emotions get the best of her" or "He folds under pressure." On the other side of the coin is the mature, self-managed leader, who simply doesn't break. Inevitably, this resilience extends to their team; they draw strength from the leader's example. Instead of *telling* them to stay tough, he *shows* them how. He is in control, but not controlling. The difference is critical.

They help others deal with emotion

There are two types of executive maturity: self-oriented and other-oriented. I've talked extensively about the first—management of one's own emotions, reactions, and behaviors. Exceptional leaders, however, demonstrate the second type as well, whereby they manage the collective personality and behavior of those around them.

Those who individually self-manage are perceived as rock-solid leaders who seldom get their feathers ruffled. But those leaders who extend their sense of maturity, so that they see themselves as chief ambassadors for the entire organization, often have much more forceful and widespread influence. Their behavior serves as a symbol for the company and others follow suit. From this kind of broad executive maturity often emerges a strong, clearly branded organization whose members represent it proudly and consistently.

Think for a moment about the conduct Rudy Giuliani demonstrated as the mayor of New York City in the wake of the devastating 9/11 terrorist attacks. Within hours of the attacks, Giuliani seized the reins of leadership and rallied millions of people by exuding composure and clarity at a time when most were hollering for blood. By acting stalwart but not hysterical, he managed not only to exhibit control over his own behavior, but also to recognize the turbulent collective emotion of countless people and transform it into positive action. Because Giuliani made it his first order of business to manage a fever-pitch situation, potential chaos turned into a sense of powerful solidarity and cooperative purpose.

For a telling contrast, consider the behavior of George W. Bush during the same period. The words he offered the millions of citizens in his charge were, by and large, ineffectual, characterized by empty rhetoric and vague posturing. Perhaps his worst offense as president was to provoke emotion ("We'll get him, dead or alive"), rather than defuse it.

They don't hold grudges, obsess over lost opportunities, or pursue vendettas

Extraordinary leaders act in the interests of the organization—always—not themselves. They don't do things in order to get back at those who have wronged them or to "I told you so" the person who said their risky idea didn't stand a chance. Their behaviors are always aligned to the organization's goals. It's a simple approach, but one championed by every outstanding and enduring leader.

HOW DO YOU GET IT?

Executive maturity does accrue over time, though not always. The most emotionally mature executives are often the ones with the most experience leading. However, not all experienced leaders exhibit it. Likewise, executive maturity can be accelerated. Here's how.

Learn to read between the lines

People give subtle hints about how they're really feeling, but these can sometimes be very difficult to interpret. You need to have a taxonomy of emotions, an atlas of expressions. If it helps, recruit an expert to help you understand the cues others give when they're feeling certain ways. Your own executive maturity depends on your ability to recognize not only your own signals, but also those emitted by others. Study these signals. See if you can detect them in the members of your own teams or your family. Count how many times a day you give off cues yourself that you weren't aware of before. If there are people you trust to ask, get feedback from them on whether others pick up on your signals and how they interpret them. And then adjust your behavior accordingly if need be.

The day-to-day responsibilities of a typical leader are so time-consuming that most leaders rarely—or never—sit down and reflect on how they react to certain circumstances or in certain situations. But it's imperative that you do find the time to do this. You cannot develop and deploy strategic behavior for a given situation unless you first come to understand how that kind of situation typically causes you to respond. You need to know your own triggers and hot buttons. Does the pitch of someone's voice strike a chord in you—positive or negative? How do you react? Do you get ticked off every time a direct report challenges you in an open forum? What do you do? Be realistic. Don't fool yourself. Once you know these things, you know whether your usual behavior is effective—and if it isn't, you can start to figure out what might be getting in the way.

Put together your own "personal board of directors"

As we've discussed, although it is occasionally appropriate and often effective for a leader to lose it, in most cases, the esteemed leaders are the ones who remain cool as a cucumber at all times, without betraying their underlying emotions.

But we all like and need to vent. Are there people in your close network who can serve as sounding boards for you? People you can trust with the rare bitch session or diatribe? If there aren't, can you think of anyone who *could* occupy that role? Most senior executives have trusted advisors, intimates with whom they share their feelings and experiences. Finding such a group of people within the organization can sometimes prove impossible for the top dog. If that is the case for you, look elsewhere. Include people who have training and experience in understanding and re-framing emotions, and make sure they are people you can trust to give you honest feedback, no matter how difficult it may be to hear.

Recognize that others have emotions they need to manage

It's an ongoing truth that we rarely see in ourselves the things that we can spot in others. Be cautious not to criticize others for their lack of emotional management, especially if the same trait isn't evident in your own behavior. To make such an accusation, even when presented constructively, is hypocritical.

Instead, take the approach that you can help the people you lead manage their own moods and feelings, accelerating their own impact as leaders. Personal stories and relevant analogies are especially effective teaching tools. Relate the fact that, early in your career, the hardest thing for you to do was listen to someone all the way through without interrupting them. Talk about how becoming an active listener was crucial in enabling your career path. By telling your own stories, you help people understand the feelings behind your behavior and, in turn, you help them appropriately channel theirs.

You need one-on-one time to do this. Take your people out for dinner or invite them over to your home. Let them in, invite them to express themselves. To be clear, I'm not suggesting that you hold "Kumbaya" sessions or ask people to cry on your shoulder. Quite the opposite. I'm advising you to show emotional maturity by recognizing that emotions do affect how people act and that they need to be understood and managed effectively.

Use humor

While your role may be serious, you can't take yourself too seriously. The most effective leaders use humor to defuse tense situations. Some of the best executives I know are really, really funny people. Just make sure the humor you use is appropriate. Insults or offensive material can get you in trouble. I know of at least one CEO of a public company who got sacked because of his foul mouth. I also know a few other leaders who made attempts to be funny, but those attempts landed with a resounding thud, because they simply just aren't that funny. So do yourself a favor: Use humor, but only if you're good at it!

Be fit

Executive maturity depends on your ability to be insightful, reflective, perceptive, and adaptable. These mental behaviors are much easier to perform when your faculties are firing on all cylinders. It's no secret that psychological and physical health feed each other, so if you aren't giving your body and brain the nourishment and exercise they both need, start now. Do yoga. Go for a run every morning. Lift weights at lunch. Yes, your schedule is packed, but this is too important not to incorporate into your routine. The more energy you have and the more efficient your overall physical functioning, the sharper you are mentally—and the better able to manage your emotions and respond effectively to the emotions of others.

Get out of town

You need downtime. Don't be a hero and think the world will stop if you are in the Bahamas for a week. This applies to people at the top of the house and right on down.

Travel enables you to think, to gain perspective, and, if you're going somewhere interesting, to learn a thing or two. Don't put it off until next year, because next year chances are you'll say the same thing. There is never a perfect time to take a vacation. And don't feed me the line that you find it more stressful when you're vacationing—that's only an excuse you've told yourself because you haven't really disconnected from work in a long time.

So get up off that desk chair and book a holiday. Oh, and a "working vacation" is an oxymoron. Ditch your BlackBerry. Leave your laptop at home. Bring your iPod instead or a good book. Get outta town!

WHY IT MATTERS

As a leader, your ability to master your emotions will determine your fate. Skill and knowledge may help you make good decisions, but it's your interpersonal effectiveness that will enable you to lead. An awareness of your emotional patterns and triggers, and the ability to manage those emotions across situations and circumstances, are paramount to fully formed leadership. In sports, it is often said that when competitors are equally skilled, those best able to manage themselves emotionally are the ones who come out on top. I encounter many business leaders who have the same skills, background, and acumen, but there are only a remarkable few who are masters of their emotions and lead with executive maturity.

Order on the Court: Part Two

The call from UCLA came prior to the 1948 season. John's wife, Nell, preferred to stay in the Midwest, and John had been led to believe by the University of Minnesota that he was first in line for the job of coaching the Golden Gophers. However, he knew not to look a gift horse in the mouth. UCLA it was.

Except, he learned a short time later, the Golden Gophers hadn't lost interest at all. Minnesota was simply in the middle of a bad storm. Their officials hadn't been able to call. John had given his word, he said, thanking them. He was a Bruin now.

John immediately began to impart his emerging philosophy to the UCLA players, who had endured that most horrible of athletic experiences, a season of mediocrity, the year before. Failing to prepare, he told them, is preparing to fail. Flexibility is the key to stability. Most important of all, be quick, but don't hurry. Once you lose control of yourself, you're the other team's lawful prey.

His players took these lessons to heart and the results were stunning. From an average team, the Bruins transformed into conference champions. Under John's direction—or, perhaps more accurately, his regulation—they began playing a game characterized by both intensity and self-possession. They moved the ball constantly from one pair of hands to another. They encouraged one another equally, never betraying more emotion to any one teammate than any other. They learned the system, focusing on execution rather than emotion. Whether UCLA won or lost, his players behaved the same. And because of this, they usually won.

Years later, long departed from both the playing and coaching spheres, John would reflect on his harsh antipathy for emotion. "A leader who is ruled by emotions," he would write, "whose temperament is mercurial, produces a team whose trademark is the roller coaster—ups and downs in performance; unpredictability and undependability in effort and concentration; one day good, the next day bad. Good judgment, common sense, and reason all fly out the window when emotions kick down your door.

"A volatile leader is like a bottle of nitroglycerine. The slightest knock and it blows up. Those around nitroglycerine or a temperamental boss spend all their time carefully tiptoeing back and forth rather than doing their jobs. It is not an environment, in my opinion, conducive to a winning organization."

One ought to suppose he should know. After all, John Wooden's UCLA Bruins won ten NCAA championships in twelve years. To say this track record has not been broken is a vast understatement. It has not been touched. Even today, decades after Wooden's greatest accomplishments on the court, the numbers for those teams seem almost unreal. A winning streak of eighty-eight games. Four perfect seasons of thirty wins and zero losses. Among the ten championships, seven were consecutive between 1967 and 1973. No other college coach has won more than four—in total.

Picture Wooden on the sidelines, however, and you discover an interesting thing. No matter how hard you might try, no matter how many of his games you watched, you never see this coach waving his program in the air or mopping his brow or hollering at the official. You don't see him berating his players nor even praising them much. You don't catch little gestures of frustration, sighs of relief, or grins of self-satisfaction. You remember nothing of the sort. Wooden coached for over thirty years, in thousands of games—yet when you picture him, you are only able to come up with one image, one posture, one expression.

That's because he never showed you anything else.

THE BOTTOM LINE

Master your emotional reactions, and use them to influence others.

4

Integrity

Integrity is what we do, what we say,
and what we say we do.

—Don Galer

Doing Some Good: Part One

They came from opposite ends of the world. One, the son of a computer science professor and computer programming instructor in Lansing, Michigan, fell in love with the machines himself at an early age and built an inkjet printer out of Lego® bricks. The other, after emigrating with his family from Russia to avoid increasing anti-Semitism, received a Commodore 64® for his ninth birthday and never looked back.

When they met while doing graduate work at Stanford, the personal chemistry wasn't instant, but their interest in data mining was. Soon they had created a software system called BackRub, dropped out of university, and begun devoting themselves to the large-scale pursuit of a simple, but—they felt—profound task: finding and organizing information better.

In 1998, they decided to bring their idea to life, naming their company after a word referring to the number one followed by 100 zeros. As it turned out, their inkling was right: people did appreciate well-organized information. The company exploded, going from dozens of employees to thousands, and literally bringing an entire industry back from its knees. They became endearing enigmas, saying things like, "We try very hard to look like we're out of control" and "We don't generally talk about our strategy, because it's strategic." They implemented principles like "20 percent time," allowing employees to spend a fifth of their time on personal interests. They built enclosures for their projectors so the sound wouldn't disturb people during their meetings. They invited people to bring their dogs to work. They hired the Grateful Dead's former chef to oversee the cafeteria. And they organized their company priorities not by using complex programs, but in the most straightforward way possible: by writing them down and putting them in order.

But there was a catch to their meteoric rise. When you've surpassed your wildest expectations, what do you do for a follow-up act? Seemingly overnight, they had become a billion-dollar company that had revolutionized behavior across the globe. People used their product three billion times every day. The company name itself had acquired official verb status, earning a place in the Oxford English Dictionary. *They were suddenly on top of the world. There now lay a new question before them. What next?*

In every organization, there are one or two people at the senior level who operate as chief ethics officers. You know them—they're the ones you go to when you need to talk with someone you can trust, the ones who seem to have good judgment, the ones you can rely on to do the right thing. Think for a moment: Who occupies this role in your workplace? Who do you think of when you think of the word integrity? Now picture that person. What is it that made you think of them? What creates the perception of integrity? Is it the way they behave under pressure? Did they keep a confidence in the past? Do they follow through on everything they say? It may be all of these things, but one thing is indisputable: Integrity directly affects your credibility as a leader and it makes or breaks careers.

We all understand the ongoing challenge to integrity that daily life serves up. We collectively consider this characteristic to be one of the highest human virtues, because all of us know how difficult it can be to uphold. We tend to describe those with integrity in vague terms—a "good person"; someone who "makes the right decisions"; an individual who "always has your back"—but with rock-solid sincerity and conviction. Such is the power of an intangible trait: Even if we may not be able to describe it precisely, there's no question we feel its impact.

Let's start this chapter by disclosing something that most people don't talk about when they mention integrity in management courses—you don't need integrity to become a leader. I have known strong leaders who are experts in their domains and some who have done great things, and yet, at the same time, they have terrible scruples. Shocking as it is, many people do achieve leadership roles by playing some pretty dirty games. It's not fair, but it's true.

What I have seen, however, is that all of these unscrupulous leaders eventually get stung by their dishonesty. They don't win in the end. Instead, they crash and burn, usually in a very public and disgraceful way.

Trust is not a one-shot deal. To evaluate someone as having integrity, one must have multiple data points, usually over a long period of time. Integrity cannot be built overnight and it is, for the most part, an all-or-nothing proposition. You can work on understanding it and learning how to create the perception that you are a leader with integrity, but it's not about perception. It's about living an honorable life and doing the right thing—not once, not twice, but all the time. Let me also tell you that you will be a much better leader as a result.

WHAT IS IT?

Over the past decade, a lot of attention has been paid to the notion of integrity. Of course, the reason for this is the frequent evidence of the very deficiency of this quality at the highest echelons of corporate America. Newspapers have been filled with headlines highlighting the moral lapses that seem to have become the rule rather than the exception. New governance regulations have sprung up faster than you can say "Enron." Commissions have been formed, targeted executive education has been created, and new regulations such as the *Sarbanes-Oxley Act* have literally reshaped the business landscape.

Yet for all the talk and all the measures undertaken to prevent unscrupulous activity, it seems integrity has less of a foothold in the boardroom than ever. Why is this? Have we become a less ethical society? Is our collective integrity on a slippery slope?

Let's dig a bit deeper into the meaning of the word.

Integrity is a multi-dimensional construct. It has three main facets: trust, consistency, and a moral compass.

Trust

Let's start with trust. It won't exactly floor you to hear me say we exhibit less trust today for the leaders in our society—political, religious, business—than we seem to have done in previous generations. (Ever watch *Fox News* or one of those "investigative journalism" shows? Cynicism toward leaders is ubiquitous, and taking people down has become a new blood sport.) Is it because our leaders are less trustworthy, or have we just become more cynical? Trust can be thought of in a couple of different ways: first, as a behavioral intention. Professor of organizational behavior at Carnegie Mellon University, Denise Rousseau, and her colleagues describe it like this: "[Trust is] a psychological state comprising the intention to accept vulnerability based upon positive expectations of the intentions and behavior of another."[1] She means that we believe in certain people based on what they have done in the past and consequently we make ourselves susceptible to being deceived and potentially harmed (physically or psychologically) by them. Trust can work for you or against you, in other words. That's why, when you hear someone described as a "trusting person," you aren't always sure it's a compliment.

Others have described trust differently, as an internal action—a more black-and-white decision or judgment. When you're listening to a car salesman tell you about the features of the model you're considering, you're making a deliberate decision to trust what he says or not (probably not—pity the car salesman). It's a binary decision, biasing you distinctly in one direction or the other. You may even decide whether or not to buy the car based solely on your feeling of trust toward this individual. In this way, trust is a conscious choice.

Other experts take a different tack, expressing trust as a personality characteristic, a stable aspect of who you are as a person. If you're one of those people who is instinctively trusting, the researchers in this camp assert you've probably been like that from the get-go, and you probably aren't going to change anytime soon.

A look at the various theories in aggregate yields two critical slivers of the trust pie. First, in order to trust someone, you need to be able to allow some degree of vulnerability. Trusting someone else means exposing yourself to the possibility of loss or pain. You've heard this reflected numerous times in the words of friends dealing with breakups, or actors in formulaic Hollywood romances: "I laid it all on the line." "I put myself out there." "I trusted him."

Second, with trust there is inherent expectation. Trust isn't unilateral; when you give it, you expect a certain type of behavior in return. If someone rewards your trust by satisfying the expectation it implies, it becomes easier to trust again. The opposite scenario can be terribly profound in its effect. Ask anyone who has been "burned" in a political battle how easy it was for them to completely trust the next person.

Trust Me

It is not nearly enough merely to know what trust is. The much more vital consideration is how to inspire it. John Gabarro, professor emeritus at Harvard Business School, studied newly appointed managers over a three-year period, specifically focusing on what made people trust them (in his words, "the bases of trust"). He found three such bases: ability, character, and what he termed integrity.

First, in order to be seen as trustworthy, one must have ability. How often have you privately thought this: "In order for me to trust my boss, I need to believe he has the ability to make me, and the company I work for, successful." Gabarro posited ability as a culmination of skills, knowledge, experience, and the interpersonal skills needed to be successful in an organization. Think of who you seek out as a trusted advisor—someone you confide in with your most private thoughts, ideas, and aspirations. No doubt that person has these abilities.

Gabarro described the second of his bases, character, also as benevolence: being loyal, open, caring, and supportive. This stands to reason, especially in today's global, job-hopping, and economically uncertain environment. You may have thought this about your manager: "It's going to prove difficult for me to trust someone unless I believe she truly cares about me, is in tune with what I want for myself and my career, and has my best interests at heart."

When Gabarro talks about his third basis of trust, integrity, he's referring to fairness, justice, consistency, and promise fulfillment. You may have murmured this under your breath: "If I see you acting unfairly or inconsistently, best of luck earning my trust." Most critically of all, not just in the workplace but in any leadership context, if you want to win the trust of others, the best thing you can do is demonstrate to them that you follow through on your promises.

So, in order to inspire trust and be seen as trustworthy, what do you need to demonstrate to others? The ability to get things done and the benevolence that shows you truly care about and support them. And the sense of justice that tells people your word is gold.

I would add two more important attributes: trust in yourself and your own decisions, and the ability to trust others. People believe in those who rely on their instincts and abilities. It's difficult to fake that. While arrogance or defensiveness will turn people off, truly feeling comfortable in your decisions and believing in yourself will inspire trust.

Consistently, studies have shown that trust is a two-way street. The first step in being able to inspire trust is being able to trust others yourself. The research tells the story. People who have a propensity to place their trust in others take more risks, connect better with those around them, perform better in senior roles, are more often seen as mentors or advisors, and as a result, end up being more successful leaders.

Consistency

The second major component of integrity is consistency. Consistency doesn't mean acting the same way all the time. Think of consistency instead as the bridge between a vow and the corresponding behavior. A huge body of evidence suggests that the best predictors of success in the workplace are conscientiousness, reliability, and commitment to doing what one says one will do. I'd be willing to wager that, if I ask you to name someone in your life who has integrity, the person who enters your mind is someone you feel you can rely on, someone who will step up to the plate when you need them, someone who's always there in a pinch.

It's this aspect of integrity that causes us to shake our heads at the endless procession of politicians who make glowing campaign promises, only to abandon or modify them once they're elected. President Obama, despite his initial positive ratings, is now dealing with this very issue as his initial promises fall under constant scrutiny. He talked a great deal about issues such as education, energy, health care, and foreign policy, and had made specific pledges regarding each of them. Some have been dealt with, including landmark (and controversial) healthcare reform, some not. Public expectations for what any political leader, even the president, can accomplish and how fast they ought to be able to accomplish it are sometimes unrealistic. Nonetheless, public perception of Obama's integrity has waned and, once this happens, it can be difficult to reverse the trend. Time will tell how the president will go about projecting consistency in order to recapture his radiant status in the eyes of the populace.

Going with Your Gut

Several years ago, when I was managing New York Life Worldwide (Bermuda) Ltd., I was looking to hire someone to support the underwriting function. This person would be based in New York and be the interface between brokers submitting applications and supporting client

(continued)

---

information, clinics and medical facilities contracted to conduct medical tests, underwriters based in Toronto, and staff actually maintaining files and issuing policies in Bermuda. I interviewed a number of applicants for the position and chose a woman whose background work and experience appeared to be the best fit for the position.

The parent company's human resources department was helping out with the recruiting process and the paperwork. The applicant indicated that she had received an undergraduate degree from a university I wasn't familiar with. Unbeknownst to me, Human Resources contacted the university to verify the information and discovered that the applicant had attended the university, but had not graduated. The information was relayed back to me, but no action was mandated.

I struggled a bit with the decision. I didn't care at all whether the woman had a degree, as it would not impact the job. Given the job and the nature of the degree, it would, at best, have had some initial selection effect, which would have long since worn off. I decided to pass on the candidate. My concern was that this was a key position, which involved the relay of sensitive information and a trust relationship. If she would willfully lie about something so trivial (in my mind), was it appropriate to trust her on issues of key business significance?

I decided to hire another woman of about the same age with no university degree who had insurance experience, but much less familiarity with medical and financial underwriting. This time, the selection was highly influenced by my gut instinct regarding trustworthiness. Despite my initial reservations regarding her shortage of immediately relevant experience, Sue Ellen turned out to be one of the best hires I ever made—not to mention one of the most trustworthy individuals I've ever worked with.

—Kathryn Hyland, Senior Vice President, Americas Life Risk Management, Swiss Re Life & Health Canada[2]

Moral compass

The final component of integrity, a moral compass, is the one that has been blighted the most by recent events. By moral compass, I mean the set of values that guide your decisions.

People are judged enormously on the decisions they make—the individual, in-the-moment decisions, and the patterns those decisions seem to underscore over time. On what basis do we make these decisions? Most leadership decisions are based on incomplete, ambiguous data. Even when all the information required to make a decision exists, making it isn't necessarily easy.

So we rely on the only other guide we have—our intuition. It is in these kinds of situations, when we are forced to use no other guide than our gut, that integrity tends to be illuminated or obscured.

The thing is, that gut instinct—our hunch, sixth sense, instinctive gravitation toward one choice or another—doesn't arise accidentally. It's been shaped over time by our exposure to lessons from others and our own observations of people we do or do not wish to emulate. Our moral standards are, of course, highly informed by religion. People learn standards in religious schools, places of worship, through social networks, and, of course, from their families. Many, many people in corporate America base their business ethics on the question: "What would God want me to do?" Whether you realize it or not, you may be a product of the religious teachings you received as a child. What I want to make clear here, however, is that I would never assert that religious belief has anything to do with leadership effectiveness, nor would I ever espouse what "good" religious values are. Integrity is not a function of a particular set of values, but rather a function of the presence or absence of values in the first place. Whether you have Judeo-Christian, Muslim, Hindu, Buddhist, or other values, or you follow your own "code of values," it matters not. What *does* matter is whether you *have* a set of morals or not.

To be an *effective* leader, you must have a basic understanding of right from wrong and a personal code of conduct. Often, in my assessments of senior leaders, I ask them to share some of the lessons they learned as kids—the messages they heard around the dinner table, the moral-driven stories or repeated proverbs, the phrases they knew would always come up in response to certain behaviors.

For me, there were four: "Always do your best," "Education is the key to success," "Be a solid citizen," and "Do unto others as you would have them do unto you (the 'golden rule')." These morals were drilled into me in a variety of ways, but none was more recurring than the story of *The Little Engine that Could.* I can still hear my mother's deliberate cadence and the way she would look at me to make sure I was absorbing the mantra that made the story so popular: "I think I can, I think I can. . . ." I couldn't have known then how deep-rooted a value this idea would become in my life.

These learnings accompany us throughout our lives and become the basis for our emerging moral compass. As we progress into the teenage years, we make an intense exploration of these ideas of right and wrong, testing the limits of certain beliefs, and in the course of that exploration, start to solidify our moral convictions.

It is also around this time, with our moral ideas becoming more firmly embedded, that we start to make conscious decisions about who we want as friends. Why is it so common for people to remain close many years later with the core group of friends they made in high school? Because those friendships were not made idly. Though we may not have been aware of it at the time, they were made based on close correlations of values, judgments, and behaviors.

It is for this reason that one of my most favored ways to get a sense of a potential leader's moral compass is to ask about his friends. What things do his friends have in common? What characteristics does he find himself attracted to? How closely aligned are his friends' views on common issues? The answers I receive help begin to paint a clear moral picture of the person I'm assessing. How about the opposite question: What are the traits you consider unattractive? Yes, I'm essentially asking for a list of interpersonal turn ons and turn offs—and they speak volumes. Point the lens at yourself for a moment and ask yourself these same questions. See if you don't suddenly get a very clear idea of your own sense of right and wrong.

One of the most interesting aspects of integrity is its resistance to measurement or prediction. For decades, psychologists have attempted to quantify integrity. The tests they've developed to specifically assess it fall into two categories—overt and covert—neither of which, unfortunately, have been particularly valid in screening out shady candidates. The overt tests ask direct, obvious questions like, "Have you ever taken any supplies home from work?" or "There is nothing wrong with telling a lie as long as no one gets hurt (true or false)?" The covert tests assess personality factors closely linked to poor integrity, for example, "Would your friends describe you as impulsive?" or "Would you consider challenging an authority figure?" These tests don't make direct inquiries into one's overall behavior; they probe one's attitude as it relates to integrity.

Though such tests are used widely throughout North America, especially in evaluating potential hires, their validity is dubious for the very reason you're probably thinking right now—they're ridiculously easy to fake. When you're up for a job and a test asks you whether you've ever lifted supplies from work, well, let's just say you don't have to be a rocket scientist to figure out what the test is trying to get at. They might as well put a Rolex on the table and see if you go home with it.

In other words, reams of research over time generally points to one conclusion: When it comes to integrity, the proof is in the pudding. It seems there's really only one way to accurately assess whether someone has integrity. Watch them in action and evaluate the decisions they make.

Operationalized Integrity

Maybe it was being the fifth child of seven that taught David Denison about integrity in all its various facets: truth, honor, and reliability. "I had to learn how to fend for myself," he told me of his childhood in Montreal. But fending for himself also meant respecting the fact that he was part of a larger collective unit. His father, an academic, had high expectations for David and his siblings. He wanted them to be able to look after themselves. In order to teach them to stand their ground, he would have them participate in debates at the kitchen table. If your turn was called, you had to step up and perform.

But you also had to do it right. David was taught not only to prize intelligence, but also to show respect. Brains counted for little unless accompanied by a strong sense of values. It was this combination—intellect plus values—that propelled David forward from an early age. When I asked him about the career path that took him from teaching to public accounting to internal finance and, finally, to CEO of the Canadian Pension Plan Investment Board, the country's largest pension fund, David said this: "I've never had a master plan. I just had a constant need to push myself. That's what drives me—I need to feel challenged."

Those challenges have been marked by success at every level and that success has been underpinned by two lessons his father taught him: be smart and behave with integrity. The examples are numerous, from small acts to big. As a teacher, David learned that, "the quicker you give feedback to students, the better they'll learn." So he made a commitment to always give tests back a day after they were taken. As the leader of a huge organization today, he espouses strategy and discipline equally. "I'm a principle-based, value-based leader," David told me. "How we conduct our business, the way we choose to act both internally and externally, is critical."

My favorite part of talking to David was this: Even though he occupies a very high-profile role and even though he oversees a portfolio of more than $120 billion, he still talks, acts, and relates to people like the kind of teacher you wish you'd had. Even when he speaks about big issues like information leaks—"We believe in being transparent here," he says—you get the feeling he sees the people in his organization the same way he looked at a classroom of students. First, as equals. Second, as people who depended on him. Third, as a group with the potential to be greater than the sum of their parts.

To ensure that his people operate with the same kind of integrity he expects of himself, David treats the concept as something not just to be thought about, but also, as he puts it, "operationalized." To address the fact "people have different meanings of that word," he conceived an exercise that now serves as an integral part of every employee's onboarding process. A series of case studies is presented describing situations where people are asked to make important values-based decisions. These case studies run across functions and departments, from HR to operations. Employees are required to talk about the issues described and the ways they would go about trying to solve them.

The discussions, in which David actively participates, accomplish something very important to him: They bring integrity to the forefront, making it part of the ethos of the organization. Echoing his father's philosophy, David Denison sends a clear message: It's not just what we do that matters. It's how we do it.

HOW DO YOU KNOW IT WHEN YOU SEE IT?

Integrity is notoriously difficult to accurately assess. As a management psychologist, I have years of experience appraising senior executives for a variety of complex roles and situations. I have many tools at my disposal to assess leaders. Yet, in a single assessment, the one intangible of leadership I can only get a partial picture of is integrity.

Why? Because to predict such behavior accurately, you must know someone over a significant period of time. You must hear from people who know that individual, learn about how she dealt with potential conflicts of interest or how she handled confidential information, and ascertain how reliable she is over time.

I can, of course, evaluate someone's values and the basis upon which she makes decisions. I can get to know her judgments and how she goes about building trust and loyalty. For the rest of the picture, I rely heavily on information gleaned in reference checks and 360-degree feedback. The result is a powerful and robust read on the individual's level of integrity.

Beyond such an assessment, what are the signs of someone with integrity? How will people recognize it in you?

For starters, those who possess integrity tend to behave in a highly consistent manner, guided by strongly entrenched principles and beliefs; those who lack it tend to behave less predictably and their decisions from situation to situation seem to be made according to motivations that aren't always clear. Take a close look at the behavior of some of the leaders you know. Those with integrity will demonstrate almost all of the following behaviors.

They don't lie, they don't cheat, and they keep their promises

The basic tenets of integrity seem absurdly easy at first blush. Don't lie. Don't cheat. Don't steal. Do what you say you're going to do. Don't do what you say you're not going to do.

But putting these ideas into practice is more challenging than people realize. You shouldn't discount how difficult it can be to always live by these rules in a complex business environment. Situations come up all the time that test our commitment and resolve.

You need to follow these principles all the time, in every situation. There are no exceptions. No transgression is too minor; every decision matters. The moment you break a promise, even the moment someone believes you broke a rule, you lack integrity in their eyes.

Leaders who operate on the basis of integrity don't carry the anxiety that they might be "found out" or constantly have to look over their shoulders for fear that their skeletons might be exposed. They tell the truth. They do things on the up-and-up. They engage in fair, ethical business practices. And they deliver on their promises.

Seems simple, doesn't it?

They're mensches

During the Age of Enlightenment, the term *Humanität*, or humanity, was used to refer to the concept of humanism or "a better human being." This concept was translated into the German word *menschlichkeit*, then refined into *mensch* in Yiddish. Eventually the word made its way into the English vernacular, where it is often used today to mean, roughly, a good person. In the German translation, a *mensch* is "a person of integrity and honor." According to Leo Rosten, author of *The Joys of Yiddish*, a *mensch* is "someone to admire and emulate, someone of noble character. The key to being a real *mensch* is nothing less than character, rectitude, dignity, a sense of what is right, responsible, decorous."

That's quite a lot of positives to live up to in a single syllable. Yet the word sets a fair standard for extraordinary leadership. Be a good person and treat people well. Act respectfully and use high ethical standards in conducting your business affairs. Be a *mensch*.

Even though they're nice, they don't finish last

Let's not get the wrong idea about being a *mensch*. It doesn't imply being a doormat. "Nice" doesn't mean "weak." "Good" doesn't mean "soft." "Admirable" doesn't mean "pushover." Adopting the qualities that go into being a *mensch* doesn't preclude success; it facilitates success.

Very often, those climbing the leadership ladder assume that if they act "too nice," they'll inevitably be trampled on by someone more ruthless taking aim at the same spot. Nothing could be further from the truth. Nice guys do not finish last—not in business or any other pursuit. Nice is not the factor that tips the balance. Other related factors may limit your leadership runway, such as being a pushover or not having conviction. However, you can be a good person and have a backbone as well. In fact, some of the most extraordinary leaders I know are, at their core, nice, genuine, and thoughtful people who also stand firm in what they believe, are highly committed to excellence in whatever they do, and tactfully challenge others and the status quo.

They rarely deviate from their principles . . .

Just as exceptional leaders serve as anchors to their teams, they themselves are anchored by a set of personal principles—a code of behavior they refer to anytime they face a decision, no matter how small or large. They walk the talk. A leader who, at her core, values the customer will be more likely to adopt a truly customer-centric strategy and probably take the time to regularly get out in the field and interact with her customers. The leader who passionately espouses the importance of work-life balance is more likely to be seen having dinner at home with his family on weekdays, rather than in the office.

At a recent dinner meeting that included some of the top minds in the organizational behavior field, I asked the guests what integrity meant to them, and the general consensus was, "Knowing what you believe in and acting like it." Acting in a manner consistent with their stated beliefs is one of the most powerful and easiest things a leader can do. Such behavior puts members of the organization at ease. It makes them feel that they know their leader and what she stands for.

"Do as I say, not as I do" doesn't apply to leaders with integrity. They're known to deliver on promises—to follow through on their word. People around them accept verbal contracts and handshake deals because they trust their word. By behaving according to the same set of parameters they ask of those around them and establishing a track record of honest, fair dealing, the best leaders forge a sense of equality and naturally generate followership. People around them don't carry the perception that there is one set of rules for the leader and another set for everyone else.

. . . but they're open to change

The fact that our politics and principles change over time is a well-documented phenomenon. For instance, we tend to get more conservative as we age. Many of us, when we look back at ourselves five, ten, or fifteen years ago, are amused, or even troubled, by the people we were or the things we stood for. Would you now vote for the same people you voted for that long ago?

Sometimes it's a major, life-changing event that causes us to shift gears in our overall philosophy and belief system; sometimes it's nothing more than the passage of time. But we do change and the people around us can easily accept those changes if they know the reasons behind them. For organizational leaders, the importance of communicating the reasons for a directional shift is magnified tremendously. People rely heavily on their understanding of their leaders' values; when those values appear to change, it's unsettling. On the other hand, a more communicative approach to dealing with change helps people around you understand the reasons behind it and enables them to more quickly hop on board.

They put others first

Leaders with integrity are not all about themselves. When they offer advice, you can rely on the fact that they have your interests at heart. When you open up to them, you can trust that they'll hold what you say in confidence. And when they give you their word, you can believe it.

That's because they place a high premium on helping others. Unfortunately, this aspect of integrity is proving a rarity today. We are more inclined to look out for ourselves and take care of our own interests. I believe history will look back on the early part of this century as a "Me Decade," akin to the way the 1980s were characterized. We've temporarily stepped off the path of integrity.

I further believe, however, that this will change. I am hopeful that over the next decade we will see a shift toward putting others first. I believe we will witness a rise in large-scale global philanthropy initiatives, despite the negative shifts in the world's economy. The term "corporate social responsibility" will become synonymous with good leadership and it applies to doing the right thing not only as an organization, but also as an individual.

They lead by example

It isn't just that leaders behave in a manner consistent with their stated beliefs and principles. They also behave in a manner that offers an example for everyone else in the company to follow. People tend to feel safe following their example, because it consists of behaviors that don't waver from one day to the next. They are predictable, meaningful, and relevant. They're consistent with the organization's goals. They reflect its corporate philosophy. They are extensions of its brand. They represent a steadfast, dependable form of leadership—one built on integrity.

HOW DO YOU GET IT?

The "acquisition" of integrity is almost a misnomer. All humans have a built in sense of trust, of consistency, of right and wrong, but some find it easier than others to act on these instincts.

Or they've identified more of a reason to do so. As a leader, you've probably had to do things on your way up that you weren't always proud of. You did what you had to do. You weren't one of those "I'll crush anybody I have to on the way up" type of leaders. It's more that you maintained a hard focus on the path forward, encountering and dealing with plenty of different circumstances along the way. You managed to navigate your way through those waters, and now here you are. Looking back, it's hard to believe you actually did it.

At a certain level of leadership, the eyes start focusing on you. You become the beacon of integrity, the standard-setter of how your people conduct their affairs. Now that you occupy your executive position, it's important that you recognize how symbolic integrity is. You must become willfully aware of your obligation to be a pillar of decency and uprightness for all those around you. Challenges will arise constantly, from all sides. It isn't necessarily easy or natural to repel them. The best way to do so is to embed integrity-driven behaviors into everything you do—behaviors like the ones described below.

Write down your personal code

When I ask people I'm assessing if they have values they believe in, most of them, of course, say yes. But when I then ask them to elaborate in more depth on what they stand for personally, what they believe in, what specific values they live by, many have a difficult time articulating a coherent answer. Most of us think we have a strong idea of our own values, but we don't normally sit down and clarify exactly what these are or are not. We don't write them out or have the need to formally communicate them to anyone else. When push comes to shove—that is, when a nosy organizational psychologist is asking you a bunch of questions about your value system—we often suddenly find we're a lot less clear about what drives us than we thought we were.

Having a personal code enables you to clearly define what you stand for. It's not an easy exercise, but it is an exceptionally valuable one—not only for you, but also for your organization. Values are initiated from the top. You set the tone and the clearer others are about what you stand for, the easier it will be for them to align their own behaviors accordingly. Organizational integrity involves everyone striving for the same goals in the same way. Write down your personal code and don't be shy about posting it, communicating it, and highlighting it again and again. People want to know what you're all about. Tell them, and just maybe, find out yourself.

Don't hedge

People have many contradictory qualities. One of these is that we're instinctively both trusting and skeptical of others. In other words, if you're trustworthy, people will generally figure it out and, if you aren't, they'll probably sense that too. From a leadership stance, hedging is one of the worst behavioral practices, because it runs directly counter to the trust and transparency that are so critical to the integrity you need to project.

Be as forthright as you can. Make a conscious habit of being up front with information and doing it quickly, before rumors or lies can start. More often than you think, people will know when you aren't divulging the whole story and you don't want the kind of waves such suspicion can create. If you're hedging, holding back, or hesitating, the behavior is going to be construed as caginess. Remind yourself that, even when the news is less than rosy, people prefer to know what's going on rather than having to guess as a result of your evasiveness. So, do two things. First, provide information whenever possible, in a clear, direct, and honest way. And second, when you simply can't give out information, tell them why you can't. And then tell them when you will.

Align what you think, say, and do

From a leadership perspective, the consistency between your actions and words is nothing less than fundamental to the way you will be perceived throughout the organization. Few things can agitate people more or make them more cynical about your leadership abilities than seeing you pledge one type of behavior and then swing the other way. If they don't think you walk the talk, there's little you can do to win them over.

Displaying this kind of integrity means staying consistent across the behavioral spectrum. Glowing praise is nice, but not if it's followed by a behind-the-back insult. Warnings and challenges can be effective if they have real consequences, but not if they remain empty scare tactics. People's tolerance for gaps between your words and your behaviors will fade quickly and your credibility as a leader will suffer. As a leader, you must always think hard about what you say, what you promise, and what you believe—because everything you do after will be assessed against those words.

Be a mensch

Be nice! Let other people win occasionally. Be thankful, polite, and respectful to others. Conduct your affairs honorably.

Let me re-emphasize that last point. You are judged by how honorable you are during negotiations and deals. Don't get overzealous or kick someone when he's down. Seek an outcome where everyone can come out saving face.

Let me give you an example of how being a *mensch* leads to positive business outcomes. A major part of my practice is working with private equity (PE) firms in mergers and acquisitions (M&A) transactions. My colleagues and I provide pre-deal due diligence of the target companies' management teams on behalf of the PE firm. In other words, the PE firm is looking to acquire a company, and before they do, we come in and assess the leadership team of the target company to give a read on what the PE firm is buying from a leadership perspective. We then give our recommendations on whether to do the deal, what changes to make, and how to maximize the performance of key executives once they own the target company.

As a result of seeing PE firms in the process of conducting large deals, I get a glimpse into how they conduct their affairs. What I have seen is a stark difference in the way some PE firms do their deals compared with others. One firm I know, Birch Hill Equity Partners, is a model of integrity in the industry. The firm is composed of incredibly smart, thoughtful, and genuine people. They treat people as partners, not as assets, and have earned the respect of their community by being honorable and respectful.

Make no mistake, they will make aggressive acquisitions or pull the trigger on management if they have to, making tidy profits for themselves and their investors, but it is always done in a way that shows integrity. Contrast that with other PE firms I know (I'll hold off on naming them, thank you very much)—those who earn the Gordon Gekko-like reputation as cutthroat takeover sharks that only care about profitability and are willing to stomp on anyone who gets in the way. Which type of firm do you think attracts more prospective sellers? When a CEO is thinking about selling a major stake in the company, whom do you think he would rather partner with? PE firms live and die by their deal flow (their ability to find new acquisition opportunities) and it is those firms who conduct themselves with integrity that are able to source these deals most effectively.

So, be a thoughtful business partner. Engage your employees and stakeholders in a manner that promotes ethical and pro-social behavior. Give some of your time and resources to charity. Operate as a *mensch* and you will reap the rewards.

Make sure you and the company are a good match
Many people are unwittingly leading organizations whose values differ from their own. It's a much more common problem than you may realize. Are you

more aggressive than the people around you? Do you wish that people would be more accountable? Less hierarchical? More employee-focused? These are signs that your values just don't match your environment.

It happens pretty innocuously: You join an organization thinking it has certain values that you believe in, typically espoused by recruiters, board members, or other key executives. Then you arrive, only to find out that the place is very different from what you anticipated and the values seem dissimilar to your own.

You have a couple of options. If the organization's values diverge greatly from your own, making you feel you're compromising, get out. If it is merely an uncomfortable gap between your values and the organization's culture, try to effect change by exerting a positive influence. Put a plan into place that will initiate culture change, align the right resources and people, and execute it.

Before all that, though, the biggest piece of advice I can give on this front is to do your due diligence before you join any company. You may not be getting a sufficiently realistic preview of an organization for a variety of reasons. Maybe you get very excited about new opportunities and are overly optimistic, maybe you get seduced by potential financial windfalls at the expense of seeing people for who they really are, or maybe it's just not a strength of yours to read people and their motivations.

In that case, you need to find alternative strategies. Ask more probing questions up front, enlist the support of your network to find out information about a company's culture, use the Internet and social media to do your own intel, or call up people who have previously left the organization and find out why. Whatever the strategy, doing your homework up front will be a valuable investment and mitigate the risk of landing in an environment with values at odds with your own.

Stay away from gossip and politics

Career suicide anyone? Leaders court disaster when they share information they shouldn't, say things that might reach the wrong set of ears, or offer "opinions" about others that may be taken as flippant. Confidentiality is the means through which people will test your integrity. Don't break their trust by falling prey to gossip, loose lips, or politics. Keep personal information confidential. On work-related matters, only agree to keep quiet on matters that do not affect performance, legal, or ethical breaches. Make sure your position on this is known before someone confides in you. Rebounding from a failed initiative, reversing a negative balance sheet, or overcoming developmental gaps in your skill set—these things are all possible. But once you're caught up in the powerful current of office politics, trying to swim back to shore is often futile. Eventually, you go under.

WHY IT MATTERS

As we've all seen far too many times in recent years, just as the presence of integrity can benefit an organization, the absence of it can cause permanent wreckage. An unfortunate number of cases have demonstrated what can result when otherwise skilled, smart leaders go about their business without a firm ethical arrow pointing the way. Yes, a group of leaders might be, to paraphrase another title, the smartest guys in the room. That doesn't count for much when integrity isn't even a blip on their radar screens.

No leader can maintain consistent performance at the top levels of business without her decisions being anchored by a consistent set of values. The moral compass may wobble slightly, but it must be firm enough that anyone in the leader's charge will know what she stands for and how she will act under a given set of circumstances. This stability and steadfastness affects every relationship the leader has. A leader who displays such qualities is seen as trustworthy, objective, and a confidential sounding board; a leader who does not is seen as undependable, biased, and injudicious.

So powerful is a leader's display of integrity that those with disagreeable but consistent values are still more likely to be followed than those whose stances are vague or prone to constant change. A highly aggressive executive who behaves according to a consistent compass still gets more respect than one whose values appear to slide back and forth. This may not be an appetizing idea, but it's true. We can predict the behavior of someone whose values are clear, so we will follow them into battle. If we do not know what someone believes or what will influence his decisions from one moment to the next, we are less inclined to follow his command. That is why, from an executive leadership perspective, integrity is not a nice-to-have quality, but one that is a need-to-have. Unfortunately, not all leaders demonstrate this quality, making it a rare and precious commodity in the leadership market.

Doing Some Good: Part Two

As they had always done, the duo decided that a simple principle would serve them best. The company would be governed by a clear, straightforward maxim: Don't be evil. *It was the best way, they decided, to continue performing innovative work while also using their stratospheric success to do something meaningful. When they took the company public, they wrote a letter to Wall Street saying they were committed to carrying out their objectives as a company that was "trustworthy and interested in the public good."*

And, although today they are each worth several billion dollars, others tend to find them disarmingly down-to-earth—or, as one interviewer put it, "less interested in the billions of dollars on the horizon than in the day-to-day challenge of running a hugely successful company that provides a valuable service, does good in the world, and is fun to work for." They drive Priuses. They rent modest apartments. At their most formal, they dress business casual. "If we were motivated by money," they say, "we would have sold the company a long time ago and ended up on a beach."

Unlike the leaders of many other companies, their statements are backed up by their actions. They released a free, powerful e-mail service that has hundreds of times greater storage than comparable programs and whose operating principle is: "We will not hold your e-mail hostage." They set up a philanthropic foundation whose express purpose is to leverage the company's information and technology to build products and advocate for policies that address global challenges. They developed a grant program that gives free advertising space to over 150 different global charities and whose results include a Singaporean businessman sponsoring the education of twenty-five Vietnamese girls.

But most important to Larry Page and Sergey Brin, the founders of Google, is the same goal they set for themselves when they first put their heads together as students interested in finding and organizing data: "We have a tremendous ability and responsibility to provide people the right information. Someone wrote that he was having chest pains and wasn't sure of the cause. He did a Google search, decided he was having a heart attack and called the hospital. He survived. We want to make the world a better place."[3]

THE BOTTOM LINE

Do the right thing, be consistent about it, and lead with your values.

Social Judgment

Do I need to be liked? Absolutely not. I like to be liked.
I enjoy being liked. I have to be liked. But it's not like this
compulsive need to be liked. Like my need to be praised.

—Michael Scott, *The Office*

Ice Time: Part One

The idea, it seemed, held nothing but promise, and the ultimate journey, nothing but glory. Yes, the Norwegian Amundsen had beaten him to the pole, but there remained one great object of Antarctic passage—the crossing of the continent from sea to sea via the pole. The "Imperial Trans-Antarctic Expedition," he would call it. It was a fitting name for a grand voyage and a decisive feather in his cap.

He had come a long way since that initial trip as third officer on Scott's "Discovery Expedition." He'd been in his late twenties then, only a pup, really. How embarrassing to think now that he'd been sent home, that his body and mind had both lacked the strength to endure.

How fiercely he'd resolved to make amends and how satisfying redemption had proven. An incredible feeling it had been, reaching farther south than any human ever had—only 112 miles from the pole, curse it, but, as he'd now been quoted many times, "a live donkey was better than a dead lion."

The discovery of the Beardmore Glacier. The first ascent of Mount Erebus. Even the race against starvation they'd faced on the way home, surviving on half-rations—all of it was worthwhile, preparing him for greater conquests and teaching him vital lessons about leading a crew. How fascinating it had been to discover that keeping them happy and focused had as much to do with spirit and camaraderie as with nourishment.

The ceremony when he'd been knighted—the king himself bestowing the status—a sailor becoming a noble. The Gold Medal from the Royal Geographical Society, the hero status accorded him at every turn. That amusing headline in Dublin's Evening Telegraph: *SOUTH POLE ALMOST REACHED BY AN IRISHMAN.*

But that was the past, and his restlessness had never allowed him to dwell too long on the past. He had a new focus. The crossing would be his claim and no one else's. True, he had told Emily he would never again venture south, that his permanent place was now home, but he knew this latest idea was within his grasp. Bruce, the Scot, had already imagined the course—landing in the Weddell Sea, then across to McMurdo Sound, a second ship taking a support party to lay out supplies—only to abandon it. Eighteen hundred miles all told.

Generating interest in the expedition had hardly proved difficult, if the five thousand applications were any evidence—this despite the notice he had posted: "Men wanted for hazardous journey. Small wages. Bitter cold. Long months of complete darkness. Constant danger. Safe return doubtful. Honor and recognition in case of success." Generating funds was another matter, though he seemed up to the task. After £10,000 from the government, £24,000 from the Scottish jute magnate Caird, £10,000 from the industrialist Docker, and a generous helping from the tobacco heiress, he was set. Now it was just a matter of selecting the crew.

Previous voyages had taught him that character and temperament were as important as ability. That's why he asked the physicist if he could sing. That's why he trusted himself to accept some people on sight. That's why all men, the scientists included, were expected to share equally in the chores. If they felt it was below them, the Endurance *had no place for them.*

With the funds in place, the crew chosen, and preparations made, the landmark voyage was at hand. The captain and his crew departed on December 5th, casting off from South Georgia Island in the South Atlantic and moving southward.

It wasn't long before they encountered the ice.

There are book smarts, there are street smarts, and then there are people smarts. The most effective senior leaders I've worked with possess all three.

Book smarts are a function of one's raw intellect and formal education. It is critical for senior leaders to possess such a capability, to be analytical, innovative, and to understand business complexities. To succeed at an executive level, superior mental capacity is required. Beyond sheer intellect, having a good education enables critical thinking and a diverse knowledge base.

Street smarts, on the other hand, are a function of more practical intelligence. They are the result of circumstance, experience, and "learning the hard way." Some CEOs are successful despite limited book smarts. Others succeed with only partial street smarts. However, few, if any, are successful if they don't have people smarts.

The reason for this is that business, of course, is not just a matter of transactions. It is about people. Leadership, by definition, requires that people follow you. To generate followership, one must understand and have insight into people. Being a senior executive in any organization is really about managing relationships, both internal and external. Yet despite the significance of people smarts, I have found that most people overestimate their own aptitude for acquiring this type of intelligence. Part of the reason for this is that no one really teaches us how to gain insight into others; we mostly need to pick it up on our own. Likewise, because our perceptions of others are so subjective, we generally have few ways to really measure our own success at it. In this chapter, I hope to show you how.

In an earlier chapter on executive maturity, I discussed the crucial need for leaders to be able to manage their emotions and corresponding behaviors across a variety of situations. Those leaders become even more successful when they apply this self-management to a thoughtful consideration of the social psychology of the organization. They are keen social spectators and strategic social participants. They exhibit effective, ongoing social judgment.

I say social judgment rather than mere social awareness in order to assert a vital distinction. To achieve a top leadership position and maintain positive status and influence that cuts across the organization, it is not good enough just to recognize the corporate social landscape; you need to be able to influence it. Most executives I know recognize the politics of their environment, but they have minimal strategy for influencing it. Adopting this position is akin to walking into a minefield without any forethought or plan of attack. Study the minefield and you have a good chance of navigating it successfully.

Walk through it blindly and you have no idea which buried shell might represent an irretrievable misstep.

WHAT IS IT?

Social judgment might be thought of as the ability to analyze people and situations, then make good decisions based on the information collected. After all, our impressions of others are the basic building blocks of our social lives. Whether right or wrong, based on long-standing relationships or brief encounters, we instinctively construct mental models of every individual we meet, and those models come to shape our friendships, our choices in romantic partners, our hiring decisions, our political preferences, and our daily interactions.

This is a very basic and critical intangible that nearly all successful people have. When you first meet someone, what do you pay attention to? Is it what they say or how they say it? Is it something in their body language that gives you information about them? Is it their clothes? Is it how they interact with others? Probably it is a mix of all of these.

What you may not realize is that you pay attention to a lot more than this as well, much of it in the blink of an eye. Some people are quite expert at this exercise—their brains process the information accurately and attend to the right cues. Others are less proficient—they tend to pay attention to the wrong things, make errors in how they interpret what they've observed, and, ultimately, make erroneous decisions about the people they've come into contact with.

One mechanism we use to size people up is comparing them to ourselves. Subconsciously, we use a mental scale with ourselves as the index. We then rate people we meet on a variety of dimensions against our own absolute zero. If you perceive someone as better looking than you, you stamp that person with a positive rating. The same applies to intelligence and a host of other dimensions.

What we are effectively doing when we carry out this unconscious exercise is both logging a raw evaluation to that person and assigning them a rating in comparison to ourselves. A significant body of research suggests that the more insight we have into ourselves, the better able we are to assess others. I will talk more about the importance of self-insight in a later chapter. For our purposes here, suffice it to say that in order to really know and understand others, you must know and understand yourself.

Blind spots and biases

Early on in my work assessing candidates for senior executive roles, I found myself regularly ascribing negative judgments to those people who displayed reasonably appropriate levels of confidence. I kept assessing people with a healthy level of poise and assurance as "arrogant" or "cocky." In fact, the over-confidence I was observing was perfectly in line with what a senior executive needs. It took me a few years to realize that I had a blind spot which was coloring my evaluations.

Two things were working against me. First, I am by nature competitive. Perhaps because it was early in my career, those who were smart and success-ful represented threats to my own self-worth, so I unconsciously wanted to knock them down a peg. Second, it had been drilled into me at an early age that pomposity or egotism would not for a moment be tolerated. As a result, my reaction to kids who acted pretentious or stuck-up was severely disapprov-ing. Psychologically, I came to equate the slightest bit of arrogance with gen-eralized badness, and any time I observed even an inkling of it, my unconscious bias emerged. As a result of these two factors, anytime I saw a candidate who exhibited a bit of confidence, I negatively inflated the attribute.

Inevitably, my distaste for arrogance surely bled into other characteristics. My overall evaluation of highly confident people was disproportionately neg-ative. Finally, through the comparison of my insights with colleagues and a good bit of self-reflection, I realized the subconscious trap I was falling into. I also came to understand the importance of having high confidence in the executive suite and how it can be a necessary contributor to success at senior levels. Accordingly, my yardstick was recalibrated.

The cognitive bias I committed is very common. Or, more accurately, its flipside—the halo effect—is common. First described by Edward Thorndike in the 1920s, the halo effect occurs when we observe a positive trait in some-one and it overwhelms our overall perception of them. The halo effect causes us to decide that someone who is happy is also friendly, or that a person who is quiet must also be timid.

We all fall victim to the halo effect from time to time. It can be difficult, if not impossible, to dodge, because we typically don't recognize it. In fact, there is a biological reason this effect works on us so easily. We can't possibly take in all the information available to us when we first meet someone, so we use mental shortcuts. More than half a century ago, psychologist Solomon Asch famously showed the effect that attractiveness has on our perception of people. Not to make us sound too shallow, but, the truth is, we like attractive people more than non-attractive people. We think they're smarter and more capable than they necessarily are.

As a parent and management psychologist, I see the halo effect make its rounds in the schoolyard all the time, where those children who are more verbal, more articulate, or more sociable with adults automatically are ascribed greater intelligence by the moms and dads who encounter them. "That Rachel," they say. "She's such a smart little cookie. Probably win a Nobel Prize when she grows up."

What they mean, of course, is that little Rachel talks up a storm and doesn't turn mute in the presence of grown-ups. The truth is that intelligence is only loosely related to these attributes. The list of shy, quiet geniuses throughout history is long, but psychological traps can be powerful and we are easy marks.

Behavioral benchmarking

Measuring others against ourselves upon first meeting isn't the only comparison we make. Just in case we aren't giving them a hard enough time already, we also weigh them against other people we know. Again, parents offer a great example of this instinct. If you are a mom or dad, then you know it's virtually impossible not to size up other kids against your own. It isn't a productive instinct, but it is a persistent one.

Naturally, we exercise this bias in social relationships too. When you go on a date or meet someone in a social context, what do you do? You think about how they measure up to others you've met under similar circumstances.

Again, to provide ourselves shortcuts, in our minds we create archetypes or blanket embodiments of a certain quality. "Joe? That guy is modesty incarnate." "What do I think of Sally? Absolute, hands-down sweetest person in the world." "Carl? He's a complete schmuck." Each of these judgments gives us a benchmark against which we assess all others on a particular trait. The next person we meet, though they don't know it, has Joe as a yardstick of humility, Sally as the gold standard of sweetness, and Carl as the personification of idiocy. And when we work alongside exceptional leaders, they too come to claim an archetype in our minds. "Judith? She's the kind of boss you feel lucky to work for."

Strong social judgment, then, requires some perspective into your own tendencies and an ability to effectively benchmark people's capabilities. But it also requires the ability to translate simple observations into deeper understanding.

This need practically defines my job as a management psychologist. In every conversation I have and every assessment I conduct, I'm seeking the meaning behind behavior. I pay close attention to the way people talk, respond to questions, and react to the things I say. Often, I see discrepancies between what people say and do. The person who tells me how much she cares for people and how sensitive she is, yet shows no emotional inflection whatsoever, piques my curiosity. The individual who tells me how social he is, yet presents as being utterly introverted, probably is trying to create a certain perception of himself to get the job or promotion. It's my responsibility to try to see through the superficial façade and develop a sound understanding of who the person is at his or her core. My job, in fact, depends on my ability to do this. As a senior leader, your job probably depends on it too.

Process observations

Social judgment isn't just the ability to understand people. It's also the ability to understand situations.

By situations, I mean the way people interact with one another in a certain context or environment. If you want to see this attribute in action, there's no better place to observe it than in a meeting.

When executives interact, they focus mainly on the content of the discussion at hand, hoping to get consensus on decisions or find resolutions. But the most astute among us understand that lots of useful information can also be derived from what occurs outside the pages of the meeting agenda—not what people are saying, but how they are interacting. This ability to read situational dynamics is called process observation and it can provide critical insight for those willing to look for it.

Top leaders are able to make process observations while still keeping a handle on the content of the discussion. They may code how much nervousness exists around a particular issue or how enthusiastic a group or person is about a certain topic. They will notice the discernible quiet that suddenly dominates the room when two particular individuals exchange conflicting views. They observe how constructively someone disagrees, the manner in which a person is able to effectively synthesize differing perspectives, and the number of side conversations that persist while the main topic is being discussed.

The information gleaned from this exercise is often more important than what is gained from the content of the discussions. I'll talk more later in the chapter about how to put it to use.

Understanding people. Understanding situations. Both are critical, yet neither are useful unless translated into behavior that reflects the understanding. Being able to read people and the dynamics between them is a good party trick, but this ability only becomes meaningful when something useful is done with the information. Social judgment, though intangible, manifests observably when keen assessments of people and their tendencies are used to produce effective behaviors.

HOW DO YOU KNOW IT WHEN YOU SEE IT?

The best leaders have an indefinable ability to "connect" with people. Like other key intangibles of leadership, this ability is, in fact, quite definable, and those who possess it exhibit common traits and behaviors. How do extraordinary leaders create chemistry with so many different types of people in such varied positions? How are they seemingly able to read people, anticipate their needs, and influence their behaviors and decisions? It's not accidental. They are exercising social judgment. Look closely and you'll see that they display the following behaviors.

They stay attached

Yes, when you rise to a prominent leadership position, things change. You're looked at differently, thought of differently, approached differently. Even your simplest decisions are influenced by multiple factors and have potentially widespread implications. Your interactions with just about everyone seem to have a different tenor than they did before. Even brief greetings may start to feel less natural, more contrived.

The fact is, once you're at the top, things do become different. You've been separated from the pack in a highly visible, deeply affecting way. The trick is how to manage this.

The shrewdest leaders recognize that, even though they cannot operate socially in quite the same way as everyone else, they still need to be part of the social gears of the organization. They participate; they don't detach. Although they can't be as high-touch as they used to be, they seize opportunities for informal social time with key people. That might mean a lunch with a younger, high-potential leader or joining the senior sales team for their annual barbecue. Often, leaders cherish these types of interactions, since they are so hard to come by.

Effective social judgment begins with outward focus. You can't hide in your office! Those who are focused myopically on their own goals will rise only to a certain level, no matter the type of organization, because eventually, others will either "gang up" against them or they simply won't be able to execute their mandate without the support of their peers. Many a potential leader has fallen short due not to a lack of intellectual horsepower but because of a failure to connect meaningfully with others around them.

They personalize their interactions

The successful leader does not carry out transparent, indiscriminate, one-size-fits-all contact with other individuals. Exercising social judgment does not mean calling everyone "Chief" or "Ace" or saying, "There's the man," nor does it simply mean being "nice" to everyone all the time.

The best leaders overcome this problem by infusing their interactions with true meaning. Jack Welch, famed ex-CEO of General Electric, was a master at this. He reportedly knew the names and roles of over 1,000 people in the organization. He was highly personal in his communications with people throughout the company. He sent handwritten faxes to people when he felt they deserved it (either to congratulate, motivate, or course-correct).

In addition, Welch personally reviewed everyone who reported to him, writing lengthy in-depth evaluations that, at times, ran several pages. People throughout the company felt a sense of pride and personal connection to their leader when they received such personal attention. As a result, everyone knew Welch as "Jack."

Consider the story of a regional managing partner at a leading global consulting firm. He oversaw an office of 200 people, half of whom were consultants, the other half of whom were support staff. The structure of the firm had him dealing frequently with those on the consultant side, both junior and senior, but apart from his own executive assistant, he seldom dealt with the rest of the support staff. The problem was that he physically encountered everyone in the office on a regular basis, leaving him feeling constantly visible, but personally distant, to half the office.

He solved this issue by carrying out a series of meaningful, personal interactions with the support group, both on an individual and group basis. For example, this managing partner was preparing to present the firm's strategic plan for the following year to those in the office. Given the size of its main presentation space, he would have to present to the consulting staff and support staff separately. The consultants, he knew, would be most interested in the numbers. But when it came to tailoring the presentation to the support staff, he found himself struggling. He knew that the previous managing partner, in his valedictory presentations, had told the support staff he'd always connected with them on a "more emotional level," a statement that had been met with private smirks given (a) the embedded insult that he couldn't have connected with them on an intellectual level, and (b) the fact that he'd barely interacted with them at all over the course of his tenure.

Being smarter about these things than his predecessor, the managing partner scheduled a meeting with one of the veteran members of the support staff, and when she entered his office, thanked her for coming, told her about the upcoming presentation, and asked plainly, "For this group, what would a meaningful message be?"

Somewhat surprised, the veteran assistant said simply, "Let them know how valuable they are."

The managing partner gave two very different presentations. The first, to the consultants, was heavy with plans, figures, models, and projections. To the support staff, he tailored his message in a very different way, not only communicating the key parts of the strategic plan, but also talking specifically about the important role they would have in launching and sustaining it, the kinds of client calls they might expect to receive once it kicked off, and, of greatest significance, the critical work each of them had done to help the practice reach its current level of success.

Both the consultants and the support staff felt their presentation had been customized in a meaningful, useful way. It's almost beside the point to note that the strategic plan ended up being wildly successful. More important to this discussion is the fact that the managing partner continued to make smart social choices. He maintained the practice of meeting with individuals at different levels for casual lunches in order to get to know them better and have them know him better in turn. That led to specific, meaningful interactions even when he would pass people in the hallway. "There's the man" became "Gordon, how are your daughter's cello lessons going?" It's nearly impossible to overstate the ongoing ripple effect of such a gesture.

They're genuine and curious

Have a conversation with an extraordinary leader, whether as part of a formal meeting or in a more casual setting, and the feeling you get will be one of sincere intimacy and interest. She won't break eye contact to see what's going on elsewhere. She won't act like an interrogator or try to unduly control the dialogue. She won't interrupt or dismiss your thoughts.

Most elite leaders are naturally interested in the talents, views, and backgrounds of others around them. The difficult thing is often finding the opportunity to get one-on-one time with so many different people. Great leaders find a way to schedule this time and, once there, they are fully present. They turn off their BlackBerry, focus on the conversation at hand, and ask lots of questions.

They communicate on a symbolic level

Those senior leaders who are especially astute at communicating on a symbolic level intentionally create opportunities or orchestrate specific events for the purpose of staying connected. This can be as simple as creating a photo opportunity for the company newsletter or taking a particular individual out to lunch to celebrate a major success. Politicians are particularly adept at creating such opportunities and, despite what we might think of their motivations, one can learn a lot about the effectiveness of this technique by observing them.

Where politicians often come up short in our estimations is on the most critical dimension of symbolic action—sincerity. The message needs to be honest and genuine or the effort will be seen as its natural opposite: contrived and manipulative. Lunches, employee meetings, and conferences—there is no shortage of opportunities to connect with those in the organization. Employees will make inferences about what is important by virtue of the content that the leader brings up in such instances.

Socially adept leaders also strategically shape their physical environment. The physical office space of an executive speaks volumes about the things that are important to him or her. Is the office decorated lavishly or modestly compared to the norms in the company? Is it kept neat or is it drowning in piles of paper? Is the door generally open or closed? Is the office accessible or protected by a group of assistants who act like sentries? None of these elements are insignificant; each can have a deep effect on what people perceive as important to the executive and, in turn, how they are expected to behave.

When a company's top dog maintains an imposing office layout, for example, and never comes out from behind his desk to meet with people, others will infer that he holds himself above others, the result of which is increased social distance. Everyone begins to act cautiously around him, removing him further from the pulse, the lifeblood of the office. It takes only slight alterations in one's physical space to bring about the quick result of making people more comfortable and, therefore, more apt to ask advice, discuss difficult issues, or approach the leader on a number of other fronts.

Another symbolic component of a leader's environment is her executive assistant. What does the assistant's demeanor and style communicate to the entire organization about the kind of relationships the executive wants to have? Does the assistant act like a gatekeeper or a facilitator of contact and accessibility? The sophisticated executive is aware of just how much symbolic impact stems not only from her own actions, but also the actions of everyone associated with her.

Playing the Field

The ability to get the most out of others may be a more significant trait in the sporting arena than it is anywhere else. And when you listen to David Orton connect his leadership success today directly to his athletic endeavors of yesterday, you really believe it.

Growing up in Dunedin, Florida, David lived close to the water and was a naturally active kid. He played a lot of team sports and excelled at pretty much all of them. He was one of the top racing sailors in the country. He was the quarterback.

However, athletic prowess aside, he didn't know what he wanted to do. Neither his father, a salesman, nor his mother, a nurse by training who stayed home to raise David and his two siblings, told him what he should do. Nor did David get much direction from his guidance counselors. By the time David graduated from high school, his room was decorated with plenty of trophies and plaques, but when it came to what he wanted to really do with his life, he had no idea.

But he did have three things going for him: serious ambition, raw intellect, and, like any great football player, a keen ability to see the field and make good judgments. David applied to Wake Forest, mostly on his own, and he got in. There he majored in math while continuing to play the sports he loved. Near the end of his junior year, a classmate of his said she was going to graduate school in electrical engineering. It involved applied math, which David preferred to the theoretical stuff. Talking about the football is one thing; feeling it in your hands is another. David took the cue from his classmate and pursued the same path, earning a spot in the program at Duke University. By recognizing his own strengths on the playing field and being open to the advice of others, David Orton had, almost without realizing it, begun to carve out his path.

Today, David is CEO of Aptina, one of the world's leading imaging solutions companies. Between the program at Duke and now, he has undertaken a fascinating, highly successful, forward-moving journey characterized by astute decisions driven by sound judgment. After graduating from Duke, David landed a coveted job at Bell Labs where he found himself, at an early stage of his career, amongst a bevy of high-profile talent. After a few years, David's wife decided to go back to school to complete her PhD, so the couple moved back to North Carolina. It was 1983, and one of the few companies hiring at the time was GE, specifically for its emergent work on semiconductors. David won a position with the company, unaware that it was a breeding ground for blossoming superstars in a dynamically growing industry. He was successful at GE's Graphicon division, working his way up to the position of director of engineering.

During a trade show in Texas, David met Wei Yen, a well-known industry executive at Silicon Graphics (SGI), the computing and graphics giant. After hearing David give an impactful speech about the direction the industry was going in, Wei approached him and asked if he'd like to work for him. No, said the former football player—I want to beat you guys. David's competitiveness impressed Wei, and the two stayed in touch. Eventually, Wei's persuasion worked and David joined SGI. Moving to Silicon Valley was a huge career accelerator for him. He was now in the middle of the action, playing a key role in an exploding industry.

In 1999, David took the plunge and went to a start-up called ArtX, where he served for the first time as CEO. Not a year later, 3D graphics company ATI acquired his company. Remarkably, David's leadership talents were recognized during the due diligence process and the acquiring company made him President and COO of the merged organization. A few more acquisitions later, and David today finds himself heading up a Silicon Valley company with a very bright future.

In his current incarnation, David is as much a scout as a player. His place on the field firmly established, his role now is to assess others. "I look for people who are on the upslope," he says. "People who want to learn, who can be good player-coaches. I want people willing to roll up their sleeves. Are they driven? Are they self-sufficient?"

David runs his business like a coach running a football team. "I don't need levels of hierarchy," he says. "I believe in a flat organization. I try to get people to think about problems differently, then I operationalize them. I have a model in my head, then I let them shape my thinking about the model."

In other words, David works hard to transmit his own sense of judgment to the members of his team. He doesn't want people blindly following a set playbook; he wants them to help design the plays. This sense of collective engagement, of all for one and one for all, permeates his leadership style. "When we do offsites, I really focus on the interaction among people more than the content of what we're talking about. I design the sessions to focus on interaction." David already knows he has smart people on the team. Like a basketball coach trying to coax group chemistry out of individual talent, he leads from an inclusive perspective, engaging people on a personal level at every opportunity.

You can see it when he talks to people. His conversations aren't interrogations, but he's certainly focused on getting the most out of his players. He asks probing, logical questions to get to know the members of his team, and then, like any great coach, allows them to be individual performers while still holding onto the overall reins. David calls this a "hand-off," as opposed to "hands-off," style. He leverages the experience and perspective of his team, then delegates the work in a way that maximizes results.

And those results speak for themselves. In the six years he was at ATI, the company grew from $1 billion in revenues to $2.4 billion and was subsequently acquired by industry giant AMD. I spoke to some of David's former employees, who told me he was known as a highly passionate and engaging leader. Everyone was important to him and was allowed a voice, regardless of whether they were a senior VP or an analyst. When you had a conversation with him, they said, he really listened.

Like so many great leaders I speak to, David attributes his tremendous success largely to luck and timing. And, as I say so often about these types of leaders, I respectfully disagree. Luck has very little to do with it. To me, David's constant upward trajectory is a function of his competitiveness and drive, his ability to see the playing field, his knack for making intelligent decisions, and his firm belief that an individual is only as good as the team he plays on. "I never tried to stand out more than others," David told me. "I just always felt we should get things done." The more I spoke to him, the more I felt I was talking to both a great leader and a great teammate. The one who understands his teammates and how to utilize their strengths to win. The guy you'd want to lead your business and the guy you'd want on your squad in the championship game. Same guy.

They have peripheral vision

It's much easier to read people and situations when you are a bystander, observing from the cheap seats. For instance, if you've ever watched two people in a conflict, the dynamics between them are often quite clear. When you are in the middle of the action, however, it is a much more difficult exercise. Social judgment requires that you step back and see what is going on around you. Dr. Rebecca Schalm, global practice leader of executive selection and integration at RHR International, describes this unique talent as "peripheral vision." While you are reading this book, your eyes are focused on these words; yet you still take in and process information from your periphery. If something outside of your primary visual focus moves or doesn't seem quite right, you'll notice it. In the same way, some extraordinary leaders have the ability to not only focus on what they are doing, but also to meta-process what is occurring around them. They are able to see how they fit into the storyline and how the plot is playing out.

HOW DO YOU GET IT?

The social dynamics within any organization change continuously. People enter and exit the scene. The business climate changes. Roles and responsibilities shift. Any effective leader must, therefore, be a continuous student of their immediate environment and also be willing to adapt accordingly.

Earlier in the chapter, I talked about the importance of being able to understand not just people, but situations—the way people interact with one another in a certain context or environment. This is referred to as process knowledge. The ability to capture and use process knowledge can enrich an executive's social judgment immensely, helping her manage issues and people with great success. But it starts with knowing what to look for.

Process observations fall into five categories: physical behaviors, decision processes, emotional dynamics, meeting dynamics, and interpersonal dynamics. Let's talk a bit about each one.

Pay attention to physical behaviors

Physical signals such as eye contact, movement of feet and hands, and voice control (or lack thereof) can all reveal useful information about someone's motivations, their goals, and their emotional state. Less subtle cues—leaning forward, inviting further interaction, crossing the arms, and getting up and leaving the room—are likewise telling, although even these indicators can be missed if you aren't accustomed to looking for them. Make a study of people's physical behaviors, think about what they mean and act accordingly.

Watch how decisions are made

Understanding the decision-making norms of a group reveals the direction in which the group needs to change in order to make quality choices. Sometimes, a leader's most effective move is to sit back and say nothing so that she can observe the group dynamic that emerges when she isn't holding forth. A little fake laryngitis can go a long way. Keep it zipped for a meeting or two and you'll quickly see who among the group tends to take over the discussion, who tends to upset the flow, who is disposed to question, and who is inclined to automatically agree. Who accelerates the discussion? Who bogs it down? Who provides the insight that opens new doors? Who has trouble breaking out of previously held assumptions?

Let's look at this from another angle. If you never allow yourself to just sit back and listen, you never actually hear, or are able to integrate, the views of others, a fatal blow to good social judgment. Consider this: Virtually all CEOs purport to be highly appreciative of input from their executive team and describe themselves as participative. But observations of how some CEOs conduct meetings reveal something very different. Many self-reported participative CEOs actually give their conclusions first, and only then begin "listening" to others. These same CEOs may subtly cut short any input that diverges from their view and support only input that reinforces it, further handcuffing their ability to practice effective social judgment. Make it a habit not to consume all of the available airtime and you'll be surprised at how much you learn.

Interpret the emotions behind behaviors

The office, we all know, can be an emotional hotbed. Being able to recognize issues of emotion and address them can go a long way toward running an efficient, transparent office that doesn't get derailed by anger, resentment, jealousy, sabotage, or any other of a number of all-too-human tendencies. Take time to observe the emotional cues that arise when those within your charge interact. These cues can often act as a magnifier for unresolved conflict, personal anxieties, or hidden agendas. Does a certain person act deliberately bored around the conference table? Is another individual particularly vociferous in their opposition to a certain issue everyone else supports? There are deeper questions to ask in connection with these emotional behaviors and the answers have ramifications that will eventually become critical, if they haven't already. Become a careful observer of the emotions in your office. Address the ones that you think warrant discussion; don't delegate those discussions to other people if you don't have to. Let everyone know you're real.

Step back and observe meeting dynamics

Earlier in the chapter I alluded to the way even the briefest meeting can speak volumes about the dynamics among the members of your team. Meetings are a veritable fount of process data, which an executive ignores at great risk. Even when you are the one leading the meeting, try to keep your antennae up so you can attend to the signals that arise when you *aren't* speaking. These cues can tell you an enormous amount about how to proceed on a specific content issue or how to lead a group so that it functions more effectively. The pace and flow of the discussion provides important clues as to what the group cares about most, which topics it is most comfortable with, and on which issues it needs the most guidance.

Pay attention to how people interact with each other

A skilled process observer learns things about people by watching them interact with others and can capitalize on this knowledge to improve a group's ability to function. One can infer a certain degree of respect among team members by the confidence shown during their collaboration. The deduction is that these people know how to function as a team. Using similar process observations, one can gather extensive information about any group, which can be put to productive use in future meetings and interactions.

Process observations aren't the only way to nurture social judgment. Here are three more techniques you should incorporate into your routine to develop an ongoing pulse-reading of the interpersonal dynamics in your environment.

Find a taxonomy of personality that works for you

When attempting to size up others, many people have a hard time knowing where to start. They often go by their gut feel, with no way to really structure their impressions. One of the best ways of getting better at characterizing others is to find a system—a taxonomy—to describe them. There are many available. In terms of the publicly packaged taxonomies, they go from the very basic, such as the Myers-Briggs Type Indicator (MBTI) or DISC Assessment[1] (both of which describe people in terms of four dimensions), to the complicated Strengthsfinder,[2] which yields thirty-four "talent themes."

On a more scientific level, psychologists have known for decades that stable personality traits all roll up under one of the "Big Five" categories: conscientiousness, extraversion, agreeableness, emotional reactivity, and openness to experience. The idea, then, is to be able to describe people in terms of these Big Five. For example, how conscientious is Bill? Is he outgoing or shy? Does he get along with people or is he a rebel? Is he calm or abrupt? Does he invite or avoid risk? There are tests, of course, that can measure these traits directly and, therefore, help you build an understanding of the taxonomy. The Hogan Personality Inventory is an excellent tool to understand these (and more) dimensions in greater depth. Understanding these will give you a framework to describe other people.

When trying to read others, reflect on your own successes and failures

One of the best ways to determine the powerful social influences in your environment is to think about your recent wins and flops when it comes to assessing people. In terms of the wins, last time you made a good hire, what was it that you saw in the person that told you he or she would likely do well? What questions did you ask to probe into the person's character? What did you pay particular attention to? In terms of the flops, think about the last time you were surprised by someone's behavior. Maybe you hired someone you had high hopes for, but he ended up being a complete dud. Maybe outside of work you trusted a contractor and he scammed you. What mistakes did you make in your assessment of these people? What didn't you ask? Did you pay too much attention to one aspect of the person and fall prey to the halo effect? Write down these self-observations and see how they affected your decision-making process in the different situations. This will help expand your awareness of the things you need to pay attention to next time.

Understand, but don't play politics

Organizations are not static environments. They change constantly, politics riding freely across the winds of change. Keen social judgment does not exist in a temporal vacuum. You must treat it as a continuous endeavor, one that demands regular time and constant refreshment. There's only one way to avoid ever being blindsided—always know what's going on. Kathleen Reardon's book, *The Secret Handshake*, is an excellent resource to help you understand politics. Reardon describes several political games people play and she characterizes the types of political players, including such colorful types as "The Street Fighter" and "The Maneuverer." While I believe strongly that your best bet is to avoid politics at all cost, they sometimes can't be avoided and having a strategy to deal with them begins with becoming politically savvy yourself.

Testing Your Read

You may have a good read on someone or you may not. Sometimes, our initial experiences of people cloud our ongoing perceptions of them. First impressions shape how we think about others, yet they don't always tell the full story. Therefore, you need to calibrate your assessments of people.

Start with your team. Take some time and write a one-pager for each person who reports to you. Don't treat this as a performance review or succession plan. Instead, write down each person's strengths, weaknesses, and the way you characterize them in general. Add a few statements about their career trajectory. Where do you see them fitting into the organization down the road?

*Once you have gone through each of the members of your team,
share your insights with someone who knows them well. It could be
a trusted HR leader or someone who just has good social judgment.
See how your perceptions of the people on your team line up with
others' perceptions. You may find some startling differences. Once
you've been able to calibrate your insights with others' perceptions,
take note of the areas you may have misread. Are there patterns in
your assessment mistakes? This is how you really build the social
judgment muscle.*

WHY IT MATTERS

Most leaders spend the bulk of their time trying to influence or negotiate.
Well-developed social judgment enhances one's ability to do both. Leaders
who possess this intangible have a deeper appreciation of what is motivating
the person on the other end of the line or across the table. Knowing what an
individual cares about most and what they are willing to take or leave enables
one to more often elicit "yes" responses, thereby moving the organization
forward more swiftly and with stronger support.

At a more granular level, the executive who is able to synthesize the
words someone is saying with the way those words are being said is able to
understand that individual at a deeper level. He can then motivate them
more effectively. He can more easily help them get the most out of themselves. He can cut straight to the heart of any issue around which they may
be tap-dancing.

The same is true of managing groups. Through careful reading of how a
group behaves over time, an executive can determine which actions will move
it in an appropriate direction. This applies to one's staff, clients, the board of
directors, and any other stakeholders. Business acumen and functional expertise may get someone to the top, but social judgment will keep them there.

Ice Time: Part Two

They were only two days into the journey when the Endurance
*encountered pack ice, forcing the captain to maneuver the ship. A week
later, the ice became thicker yet—thick enough to halt progress for a
full day.*

Three days later, the Endurance *was stopped in its tracks once
again. "I had been prepared for evil conditions," wrote the captain,*

but the dense ice they were facing now was, he felt, of "very obstinate character."

When the ice loosened and pathways opened up a few days later, the ship resumed its slow advance southward. After several weeks, it had reached its first important destination, Antarctica's merciless Weddell Sea, and then, soon after the calendar had turned to 1915, the 100-foot ice walls of Coats Land.

But the ice was simply too thick—and it was everywhere. Soon the Endurance was immobilized again, this time for more than a week. The captain ordered the ship's fires banked to save fuel. He sent the men onto the ice with chisels, saws, and picks to try and force a passage, an effort that proved fruitless. Though he hadn't abandoned all hope of breaking free, he was now contemplating "the possibility of having to spend a winter in the inhospitable arms of the pack."

Possibility became certainty, and the ship's interior was converted to winter quarters for the twenty-eight officers, scientists, engineers, and seamen aboard. The ice surrounding them continued to thicken, alerting the captain to the chance that, should the Endurance be caught in the wrong spot, she would be crushed. Nonetheless, he wrote, they had no choice but to wait.

Until a few months later, that was. The captain had made sure to keep spirits buoyant during the cold, dark months despite the ship's hull being squeezed frequently by the ice. He had encouraged the men to take moonlight walks; sketches had been performed inside the ship; holidays had been celebrated. But now it was October—spring—and as the ice began to break apart, the ship, helpless in the ice's twisting and writhing, began to succumb. The hull begun to bend and splinter, and water from below the ice began to pour in. Sounds like gunshots accompanied each instance of timber giving way to the unstoppable pressure.

The captain was forced to give the order he most despised: Abandon ship. Over the following weeks, the crew salvaged provisions while watching the ship slowly disappear into the jaws of the ice. His transcontinental plans abandoned, the captain now had a new mission: Get his crew home alive.

For months the party lived in makeshift camps on a large floe, hoping they would drift toward a favorable location. But when one of these floes broke in two, the men assembled in their lifeboats and, after five harrowing days at sea, landed on bleak Elephant Island, the first time they had stood on solid ground for more than a year.

It was now that something more than their physical exhaustion was preying on them, the captain realized—it was the dipping of their morale. Choosing five companions and the strongest of the lifeboats, he decided to risk an open-boat journey to the distant South Georgia whaling station, where help could be found. He packed supplies only for four weeks, knowing that if they did not reach their destination within that time, supplies would no longer make a difference.

After sixteen days, the lifeboat, though pounded and tossed by the ocean's storms, came to rest on the island's unoccupied southern shore. The captain, along with two of his companions, then walked thirty-six hours over mountainous terrain to reach the whaling station. Rescue parties were sent out and his men were saved.

Soon fellow explorers and the public learned that Ernest Shackleton's leadership had been largely responsible for his men's physical and emotional survival during their two years of hardship. Shackleton's methods and philosophies became legendary. When someone had been sick, he had ordered extra rations for all in order not to isolate or alarm the ailing individual. He had remained calm and confident in the most dire of circumstances. He ignored the predominant class system of the time, making university professors take their meals alongside Yorkshire fishermen. He organized games on the ice, encouraged nightly sing-alongs and toasts to loved ones, and had the men all shave their heads as a gesture of solidarity. To help the crew get over the trauma of having to abandon their ship, Shackleton literally served them, rising early to make hot milk and hand-deliver it to every tent.

The captain's spirit of equality and humanity was infectious. When First Officer Lionel Greenstreet spilled his much-needed milk on the ice, one by one, the seven men who shared his tent silently poured some of their equally precious ration into his mug, refilling it. Numerous such acts occurred during the time these twenty-eight men spent together in the most dismal of circumstances. They were reflecting their captain's moral fiber and his sailor's guts.

Shackleton's good judgment had not been born during the Imperial Trans-Antarctic Expedition; it had existed before. During the *return trip of the Nimrod Expedition several years earlier, he had given his one biscuit allotted for the day to his ailing shipmate, Frank Wild. Wild wrote in his diary that day, "All the money that was ever minted would not have bought that biscuit, and the remembrance of that sacrifice will never leave me."*

THE BOTTOM LINE
Be a student of behavior. Understand people as a means of leading them.

Presence

Look famous. Be legendary. Appear complex. Act easy. Radiate presence. Travel light. Seem a dream. Prove real.

—Anonymous

The Quiet Little Girl: Part One

Anna was born on October 11, 1884, at her parents' West 37th Street apartment in New York City. She was a shy, sweet young thing. After a few years, those around her began to wonder if she'd ever break out of her shell. Despite the world of fortune she grew up in, she was so subdued a girl that her mother called her "Granny"—at least until she died from diphtheria when the girl was eight. When her father, an alcoholic confined to a sanitarium, also died less than two years later—her brother Elliott Jr. was also now dead from diphtheria, like their mother—the girl was taken in by her grandmother.

What she lacked in sociability and ease, she seemed to make up for in maturity and insight beyond her years. "No matter how plain a woman may be," she wrote while still only fourteen—a time during which she felt insecure, ugly, and neglected—"if truth and loyalty are stamped upon her face, all will be attracted to her."

After she'd been privately tutored, with the encouragement of her father's sister, Aunt Bamie, the family decided to send her to a private finishing school outside London. The headmistress was a noted feminist educator who sought to cultivate independent thinking in the young women in her charge. There, the young woman learned to speak French and her self-confidence slowly began to blossom. In 1902, at the age of seventeen, she came back home and, after her splashy debutante party, entered the real world, becoming a social worker in the East Side slums of New York.

That same year, she met her father's fifth cousin, Franklin, and was pleasantly surprised when the suave twenty-year-old Harvard man showed interest in her. After a White House reception and dinner with her Uncle Theodore, the president, on New Year's Day 1903, Franklin affirmed his attraction and began courting the young lady in earnest. She later took him along on her rounds of the filthy tenements. The privileged young man was moved in a way he had never been before.

By November, the pair were engaged, and on St. Patrick's Day in 1905, married, with her uncle Teddy giving her away. Married life, however, was not the blissful time she had anticipated. Franklin's mother, Sara, lorded over the couple, dominating in all domestic matters, insisting that the young woman become a proper wife to her son.

In addition to living under the thumb of her mother-in-law, the young woman, though always favored by Uncle Theodore, often found herself at odds with his eldest daughter, Alice. She was not blind to the irony: Alice was beautiful, photogenic, and well suited to the family's place in high society. Yet Uncle Theodore felt (Anna) Eleanor's conduct to be far more commendable—in short, more Rooseveltian—and he would ask the narcissistic Alice, "Why can't you be more like your cousin Eleanor?"

Her lovely relationship with her uncle, unfortunately, could not withstand the widening political abyss between the Hyde Park and Oyster Bay sides of the family. As Franklin's political star began to rise, the young woman was forced to campaign against her cousin, Uncle Theodore's son and namesake. When Theodore Jr. lost, due in large part to the young wife's influence, relations between the two family branches only became more tense. But Eleanor was just hitting her stride.

Imagine yourself walking into an important meeting. The room is filled with a mix of people, some who know you, some who don't. When you pass through the doorway, do people sit up and take notice or does your entrance cause barely a ripple? When you speak, do people listen intently or frequently interrupt? Do you command attention or blend into the background? When a decision needs to be made in a group, do all eyes turn to you or not?

The answers to these questions should tell you whether you possess a central leadership intangible: presence.

Presence is, in fact, often directly equated with the existence of leadership itself. When we see someone with presence, we automatically assume she is a leader. Because presence is such a powerful intangible, people often overestimate the abilities of those who possess it. Charismatic people sometimes reach positions of authority undeservedly—they look like executives, so we think they must make good ones. However, the history books are filled with examples of charismatic leadership going terribly awry—Jim Jones and David Koresh were both charismatic leaders.

Presence is essential, but it must be backed up by real substance—it is a vehicle for good leadership rather than a proxy for it. Nonetheless, your ability to have impact as a leader will be dramatically increased by strong executive presence. Extraordinary leaders understand their impact on others and utilize their presence to inspire others and generate followership. Let's talk further about what defines presence and how you go about creating it for yourself.

WHAT IS IT?

The first time I met a certain CEO of a public company in my consulting work, I was tongue-tied. Despite my preparation for the meeting, which included having learned as much about him as possible, as soon as he walked in the room I flubbed my words and undoubtedly came off as even more junior than I was at the time. There was something about him that made me shrink psychologically. I felt like I was cowering in my chair, like my brain was clouded over. He was a big guy, not overwhelmingly tall, just big in stature. He had huge hands that dwarfed my own in a handshake. He had a booming voice that jarringly disrupted the quiet of the room where I was waiting for him to arrive.

It's not that he was scary—quite the opposite, really. He was, in fact, extremely charming and affable. I had heard about him for years from colleagues and from reading about him in newspapers. I was well aware of his formidable successes and authority in the industry. I was, to say the least, very impressed.

On reflection, I see that what I was really witnessing was true executive presence. This intangible is talked about a lot, often in different ways. In the entertainment industry, people talk of the "X" factor; in federal politics, of some individuals appearing "presidential."

I think that latter one is particularly interesting. What makes someone look presidential? I'll never forget a moment that occurred during the last presidential election, while I was casually watching television with my seven-year-old son. It was one of the first Democratic debates, so there were about ten candidates lined up at individual podiums. Since it's hard to turn off the psychologist in me, I asked my son who he thought looked most like a president. He pointed to Barack Obama and said "him." I asked Brandon why he thought that particular man exuded presidential quality. He couldn't articulate it—there was just something about him that made him look like a president, he said.

The following week, during the Republican debate, I asked my other son, who was five, the same question I'd asked Brandon. Aaron pointed to Mitt Romney.

The two choices fascinated me. Even before they were ten years old, my sons had developed an archetype—a cognitive representation—of what a leader is, and then had compared each of the candidates they saw on the screen to those archetypes. At their early ages, they could perceive executive presence, or at least what they felt was the intangible manifestation of it.

Executive presence is the outward expression of power and authority. We all recognize power intuitively, though we have a difficult time defining it within specific boundaries. Power, of course, comes from a variety of sources—money, status, fame, attractiveness, and persuasiveness. Among psychologists, power is often defined as the ability to influence others and promote one's goals. People with power seem to have an invisible aura, an indescribable magnetism.

From the perspective of executive leadership, presence requires a number of specific ingredients, including reputation, identity, charisma, superior verbal and nonverbal communication skills, and—as my sons unintentionally demonstrated—correspondence to people's leadership archetypes.

Reputation

The basis for someone's executive presence exists before you even meet him. In the example I used at the beginning of this chapter, I was well aware of the CEO's reputation before he walked in the room. He had worked hard, over many years, to forge a track record of success. In this particular case, there was even a kind of myth that surrounded the individual. Some of this reputation was positive and some of it wasn't; he was recognized as a strategic genius, but also something of a tyrant. The strategic background was legendary: He had reshaped his organization almost single-handedly through some brilliant maneuvers that perfectly anticipated market shifts. However, he also had a penchant for publicly dressing people down. It was known that if you didn't have your stuff together, you could expect to hear from him. No doubt, my experience of his executive presence was influenced by my preconceived expectations. His reputation had produced an anticipatory psychological reaction in me—I was anxious before I even met him.

Identity

While reputation is critical, it alone does not elicit executive presence. The next ingredient is identity. By this I mean knowing who you are, being comfortable in your skin. Yale psychologist Sidney Blatt has described identity as "defining oneself as a separate and autonomous individual, different from others, yet at the same time understanding of how he relates to those around him."[1] This occurs over the course of one's life, with some people at a more accelerated pace than with others.

A well-formed identity is highly evident. When I see people who are *not* displaying executive presence, what I usually see in its place is someone *trying to impress*. They try desperately to look and act like someone else. Sometimes it shows up in how they dress: I knew a young emerging leader who wore a suit two sizes too big for him in an organization where few people wore suits. Although he was trying hard to increase his presence by dressing up, it had the effect of making him look more junior than he actually was. It seemed like he just wasn't comfortable—it looked like he was wearing his dad's suit—and didn't have a fully formed identity of his own.

Sometimes, this same sense of discomfort will come across in what people say. They will try to use words that are too complex or esoteric, achieving the opposite effect to what they intend. What happens when people do this? They appear as though they're trying to be someone they're not. To establish executive presence, you must have a strong identity, be comfortable with it and act in a way that is consistent with it.

Charisma

Often, people with strong identities are described as having "charisma." According to organizational psychologists William Gardner and Bruce Avolio, "A strong sense of identity is a main characteristic of charismatic leaders because they have explicit motives and values that they are able to easily articulate to their followers."[2]

Charisma is a fascinating concept and an enduring, elusive one to psychologists. The actual term is derived from an ancient Greek word meaning "gift." It was later used by the church to describe gifts from God—*charismata*—that would perform special acts such as prophecy and healing. The first time it was used in the context of leadership was in the early twentieth century, when German sociologist and economist Max Weber wrote about social authority and how people follow leaders with character. According to Weber, the charismatic leader "is set apart from ordinary men and treated as endowed with supernatural, superhuman, or at least specific exceptional powers and qualities . . . (which) are not accessible to the ordinary person but are regarded as of divine origin or as exemplary, and on the basis of them the individual concerned is treated as a leader."[3]

Occasionally, when the topic of charisma or executive presence comes up in my conversations with clients, people ask me if it's something you are born with or you learn. Without going into a full discussion of nature versus nurture, I believe there is good evidence that genetics determine whether one has the capacity to express personality characteristics (such as charisma); however, certain conditions must be in place in order for those characteristics to be expressed. I believe, in other words, that charisma is a combination of biology and experience.

What conditions or experiences, then, can enable charisma to be expressed?

The answer might surprise you. It turns out that our ability to create psychological bonds with other people, often developed early in childhood, is a necessary factor in the development of charismatic leadership. This effect has been demonstrated in numerous studies in a variety of contexts. In one such study, Israeli researchers looked at the effect that attachment—the type of bond subjects had with their peers and superiors—had on charismatic leadership.[4] In the study, military cadets were described by superiors on their attachment style according to four types—secure, anxious-preoccupied, dismissive-avoidant, and fearful-avoidant—and given ratings on charismatic leadership. Results showed that military cadets who were more securely attached were also more likely to be perceived as displaying charismatic behaviors.

In childhood and early adulthood, the bonds we have with our parents are particularly important. Longitudinal studies consistently show that teenagers who have secure relationships with their parents are more likely to express charismatic leadership behaviors than those who don't.[5] Parenting style matters too. Specifically, parents' level of psychological control over their children has a direct link to future charismatic leadership behaviors. It is the father's level of psychological control, in particular, that matters. Teenagers who had more controlling dads were less likely to be seen as charismatic leaders. Mothers' level of control mattered less, which is consistent with my own observation that fathers typically have more influence on our views of, and approach to, leadership than mothers, who typically influence us in most other important areas, such as our approach to social relationships.

Communication

The third main ingredient for executive presence is communication, both verbal and non-verbal. To have presence means to be articulate. You need to have strong linguistic command, a good vocabulary, and the ability to clearly deliver your message. This is a must—and one of the reasons I strongly advocate regular reading, one of the best ways to build vocabulary, to every aspiring leader.

People with executive presence avoid jargon, they speak authentically, and they don't mince words. They also use humor as a mechanism to connect with people and, many times, use curse words freely. Some of the most impactful people I've known have amusingly filthy mouths behind closed doors. Humor and swearing serve to surprise the audience and keep them off-kilter. Used properly, they can be effective tools.

Beyond *what* people say, it's important *how* they say it. Leaders with executive presence speak with a captivating voice, they have animated facial expressions, and they show confident body movements. They don't fidget. They don't put their hands in their pockets or fumble with their pens. I mentioned voice as an important factor: Ever notice how people with low-pitched voices have more impact? Bill Mitchell, CEO of Arrow Electronics (a Fortune 200 multi-billion-dollar company), has a voice that is, in my view, nearly identical to that of NBC news anchor Tom Brokaw. Bill has a deep, booming voice that simply exudes executive presence. It turns people's heads and makes them sit up and listen.

Voice aside, leaders with presence also exhibit very direct eye contact—sometimes to the point of making others feel uncomfortable. Watch the eye contact of someone with executive presence—you will see them blink less and hold their direct gaze longer than the person they are talking to. In fact, you can often observe the power differential between any two people in conversation by the amount of time they respectively hold eye contact.

Archetypal fit

The final ingredient in executive presence is more related to everyone else, rather than the leader himself. As a society, we have mental models of what leaders should look like, called archetypes. The extent to which a given leader fits society's archetypes of leadership plays a strong part in determining the amount of executive presence she has. That is, we have certain expectations of what leaders look and act like and, therefore, executive presence is fed, in part, by the extent to which a leader fits this assumption.

Researchers in Austria have identified four of these archetypes, based on Max Weber's taxonomy of charisma that I alluded to earlier in this chapter: the hero (heroic charisma), the father (paternalistic charisma), the savior (missionary charisma), and the king (majestic charisma). I would add others to the list, including the mother (maternalistic charisma) and the oracle (visionary charisma).

Each of these six archetypes is characterized by specific behaviors and appearances. If you don't fit any of them, people most likely do not automatically see in you strong executive presence. Pay close attention to the granular characteristics of archetypes, things such as manner of dress and physical stature.

Height, for example, matters. For the most part, we equate height with power and, as a result, with executive presence. Tall people disproportionally occupy C-level positions in public companies. Taller people also earn higher salaries, reach higher-status occupations, and win more presidential elections. Does this have anything do with the tall people themselves and their skill levels? Of course not. It has everything to do with our preconceived, psychological link between "tall" and "power."

This link extends to other facets of life as well. We say someone has *high* status or is *high up* in the chain of command. Conversely, we say someone is *down* on their luck or has *lower* status.

Research in cognitive psychology provides an explanation for this. In our brains, power is represented as a vertical dimension in physical space.*

Biology and evolution are likely contributors to this tendency. Simply enough, taller animals are considered more dangerous than smaller ones. Likewise, children quickly learn that their parents and taller siblings have more physical power and, therefore, rank superiority. So, our brains automatically process high things as more powerful and low things as less powerful. Why do you think a judge sits on a bench raised above the level of everyone else in the courtroom, or why we call kings and queens "Your Highness"?

HOW DO YOU KNOW IT WHEN YOU SEE IT?

Although presence is difficult to define precisely, damned if you don't recognize it immediately when someone with presence enters a room. Or walks into a party. Or strolls down the street. Among all leadership intangibles, presence is the one with perhaps the greatest power to seize our attention, take us by surprise, and intrigue us when we may not even be sure what we're reacting to.

Still, like all leadership intangibles, there are specific qualities and behaviors that those with strong presence exhibit. One can learn a lot from studying these. Here are some.

They are masters of the first impression

Managing the first few minutes of any meeting is essential and those with presence are remarkably good at creating chemistry with people. They are open and approachable, and they take in information more than dole it out at the outset of the conversation. They are adept at building rapport, because they actively and conscientiously listen. They make others feel comfortable and at ease. They show warmth and acceptance. They have a firm handshake and a deliberate sparkle in their eye. By creating a strong connection, an open dialogue, and a sense of mutual comfort, they maximize the potential for the interaction before it's even begun.

---

* When presented with an identical image, like a picture of an animal, alternately placed on either the top or bottom of a computer screen, people describe the higher one as being more powerful.

It looks like they aren't trying

When someone exerts a commanding presence, it's often accompanied by an apparent lack of effort. They have an easy way of talking, moving, and processing information. You don't see them sweat; they're in control. The more people appear to us as if they are trying to achieve a particular result, the more junior they seem. Truly masterful leaders create the opposite impression. They produce outcomes regularly and people are always left scratching their heads at the ease with which they seem to get it done.

They exude warmth

People with executive presence exude both energy and a sense of calm at the same time. How do they do this? First, they make sure their voice lacks tension. Yes, they are enthusiastic, what they have to say is interesting, and they can hold a room like nobody's business, but they don't do this by screaming at the top of their lungs or maintaining rapid-fire patter. Quite the contrary: They speak in an even, relaxed tone, thereby putting at ease all of those around them.

They also tend not to generalize or use absolute, blanket statements. Instead, they focus on words that fit their audience and they deliver those words from the heart.

They smile—but not too much. (Yes, smiling too much can be off-putting, because eventually it comes off as artificial, or worse. A certain client of mine habitually over-smiles, often making it look as though she's hiding something. I'm pretty sure that's not the impression she's after.) They look at you directly, radiating their power and cordiality in parallel.

And they say your name. People love hearing their own names—it's a natural point of connection. Of course, they know when to stop, too. Twice in a sentence does get to be a bit transparent.

They tell good stories

The most exceptional leaders I know are also great storytellers. They use stories to subtly build the case for their opinions rather than just making declarations or verbalizing conclusions. Filmmaker Robert McKee was once quoted in *Harvard Business Review* as saying: "A big part of a CEO's job is to motivate people to reach certain goals. To do that, he or she must engage their emotions, and the key to their hearts is story."[6]

How true. Top leaders build narratives to support their visions and ideas. They use case studies. They often say, "Let me give you an example. . . ." They embed anecdotes into presentations and meetings to ground the business content in accessible, real images or metaphors. People remember stories more than they remember facts, after all. If you've ever sat in on a series of interviews with multiple candidates, you know this to be true.

They focus on the bigger picture

Want a quick test to determine executive presence? Listen to the words people use. Those without it tend to use words that keep them at a safe level, squarely within their sphere of influence and not beyond, or focused on the task at hand and no further. Those with executive presence have a keen way of elevating the conversation in exciting, inspiring ways. They talk about strategy, vision, and long-term goals. They refer to big issues rather than getting mired in the minutiae. They use grander—though not necessarily more complex—words and operate on a bigger, more global scale. This isn't the same as hyperbole or overstatement. I'm talking about the difference between "We're tracking to solid results this year" and "I want this organization to break out in twenty-ten. We're going to knock it out of the park and set the stage for unprecedented growth over the next five years."

HOW DO YOU GET IT?

One of the greatest historical examples of presence is former U.S. President Bill Clinton. He currently tours the world, giving paid speeches on a variety of topics. A friend of mine went to one of his sessions held at a large sporting arena and described the experience to me in detail. Prior to the speech, the place is buzzing. It's packed to the brim with a cross-generational audience eagerly anticipating Clinton's arrival. Suddenly the lights dim and an announcer says, "Would everyone please rise and welcome former United States President William Jefferson Clinton." At that point music begins, and the electricity in the arena is palpable.

Clinton takes the stage looking incredibly well put together and sporting a slight tan. He looks magnetic; people are in awe. Clinton starts the speech by revealing a personal, heartwarming story, then proceeds to take the audience through the journey of his fascinating life and his vision of the future. Most remarkable to my friend was that, although Clinton was speaking to an audience of thousands, it was as though he was speaking to him personally, to the point where he was moved emotionally. Clinton was smart, funny, warm, and utterly charming. In a number of ways, he defines leadership presence.

Presence is both a mindset and a set of behaviors. To show it, you must think like an executive and act like one too. Let's talk about how.

Mental Aspects
Play hard to get

We like things more when they are rarer or more difficult to acquire. You know this from your dating life: the sooner the challenge goes away, the sooner you feel like moving on. (It's okay, you can admit it. Other people are just as bad.)

The same goes for leaders. When interviewing candidates for leadership roles, interviewers subconsciously consider two questions: (1) How difficult will it be for us to get this person; and (2) How badly would other companies want him? As a candidate (or date, for that matter), you tread a very fine line: You want to represent a challenge to the other party, but you don't want to be seen as cold, distant, or arrogant.

> *With respect to executive presence, my advice is to play it cool. Don't be the first one to initiate the conversation or chime in during a team meeting. Don't be too eager. Let the conversation unfold and then create a strong impression by being the one who pulls together the main points of the discussion. During an interview, be sure to be engaging and warm, but don't be overly forceful or eager—let them come to you. The charismatic person waits until the other person is interested. The power of playing hard to get is no lie.*

Challenge the status quo

A sure way to stand out is to somehow take on the established way of doing things. You want people to think, "Wow, that was a breath of fresh air" or "She really brings something different to the table." You must be unique. Have a point of view and stick to your guns. Tell people how you would do things differently than they are already being done. Don't be invisible. Assert your position on issues you feel strongly about. Subtly reinforce the idea that you can be an intelligent voice of change and you will see your presence rise.

Be fluent in business

You can't be myopic about your business and have presence at the same time. To be seen as having presence, you must have business intelligence. You must understand the language and the levers. That means understanding your company's big-picture strategy. If I were to ask you right now what that strategy is, could you do it (without pulling out a giant binder from your bookcase)? You must have at least basic finance knowledge to be taken seriously. I know several HR and IT leaders who don't have great presence, because they simply don't get finance. If you want a seat at the table, you'd better be financially literate. The point is not that every CEO must come from a finance background. Instead, for you to stand out and make an impact on your environment, you need to start by boosting your business intelligence.

Be confident in what you know

Earlier in my career, as a younger management psychologist, I recall being slightly hesitant when I had to go toe-to-toe with a senior leader. I discussed this trepidation with a senior colleague of mine, who looked me straight in the eye and said, "Just remember: You know much more about human behavior than he does. You are the expert and he needs your expertise. Yes, he is much older, more experienced, and makes a lot more money than you do, but he needs you." It was an important revelation. I could hold my own because I had this in my back pocket. I knew what I knew and what I didn't know, and I didn't have to pretend otherwise. This advice has served me well over the years and I always advise others the same. Be clear about what you know and be confident in that knowledge. It can be a small domain of expertise or a large one. The key is to walk into any ambiguous situation with the knowledge that you know more about your area of expertise than anyone else in the room.

Find your story

A few pages ago I noted that leaders with strong presence always have at their fingertips a selection of stories to substantiate or illuminate the business point they are attempting to articulate. Think about what your stories are.

In his recent book *Executive Presence*, communications consultant Harrison Monarth reveals five very helpful storytelling techniques that enable people to convey complex ideas. First, he says, pick a theme for your story—all good stories have one. The theme might be "Winning against the odds" or "Why the customer is king." Second, Monarth asserts, brevity rules. Be brief, make your point and move on. Don't over-explain part of the story or give more detail than is necessary. People usually "get it" faster than you think. Third, use understatement. Just as you don't need to fill in all the blanks for your audience, you needn't overdo your story by exaggerating its outcome. Using understatement, you can add humor and leave it up to your audience to resolve the message. Fourth, in storytelling, you must transport the listener. Tell your story in the present tense so that those in your audience can experience the events themselves. Create a scene that people can imagine inserting themselves into. Your story will be that much more captivating. Lastly, says Monarth, keep it simple. Avoid overly complicated words. Use straightforward metaphors to summarize concepts. Why are children's fairy tales so forceful and enduring? Because it is the simplest stories that have the greatest impact.

Be known for something

To have presence, you must establish a reputation that comes to precede you. Building up such a reputation can take years and, hopefully, it has already happened for you. However, it doesn't happen on its own. You can be intentional about building your reputation. Think of building your reputation as being akin to building a brand, for which you need, of course, a marketing strategy.

Start by clearly formulating how you want to be known. You need to champion a project or a strategy. Find something you believe in strongly. It doesn't need to be the ideal fit, just a good fit. Many people wait too long to do this. Think of something that you could be known for in a year from now—where people might say, "Oh, yeah, her, she's the one who led that important IT initiative" or "I know him, he pushed that big product when no one else thought it would fly."

What can you use to make your mark? Once you have this in mind, start talking about it to others and don't stop. In every team meeting, mention it. Plug your brand. The more repeated exposure people have to it, the more they will associate you with it. Of course, hitting a home run on the initiative itself helps too.

Physical Aspects
Make a powerful first impression
Presence begins the moment you step into a room. You need to shape what those first few moments look like. Make an entrance, be noticeable. I'm not saying barge into the room like a bull in a china shop, but at the same time you shouldn't slink in unnoticeably and slide into your seat. Crack a joke when you come in or say people's names. Whatever it is, be visible. Look people in the eye. Eye contact is a power technique and presence is a reflection of power. Try not to blink a lot; it dilutes your impact. Don't stare at people, but don't look down every time someone looks at you. Eye darting is a sign of deference and will dilute your presence. Lastly, have a firm handshake. It really does matter—people remember weak handshakes and generally don't like them. A firm handshake communicates confidence and executive presence.

Walk tall
You'll often hear that strong leaders "carry themselves well" or have "good stature." These observations may sound figurative, but look closer. The fact is, leaders consciously maintain a physically strong deportment, and others around them detect it and respond to it.

I'm not talking about being tall or big or physically remarkable in any particular way. I am, however, talking about occupying your own space vibrantly. The best way to accomplish this is also the simplest: have good posture. There are several tricks you can use. Pretend someone is gently pulling up on an invisible string attached to the top of your spine. Pull your shoulder blades back and your chest out. Point your toes forward. Don't slouch—people who slouch are seen as slouches. Honestly. Take your hands out of your pockets—it is a decidedly weak pose. Walk with energy and vitality or you'll be perceived as having none.

Good posture applies all the time, whether you're walking, standing, or sitting. Even the stance you take when speaking with others affects their perception of you. It's been shown, for instance, that the optimal "power pose" for males has the feet shoulder-width apart and toes pointing forward, or that sitting up straight and leaning forward when sitting across the table from someone is a reliably effective way of engaging them.

Look good

Being physically attractive on its own doesn't constitute strong presence—but it certainly doesn't hurt. In fact, I'm understating the fact. It can help. A ton.

There are two reasons—one superficial, one somewhat less conscious. Superficially speaking—and we humans do make a lot of our decisions based on outward appearances—those who look good position themselves more successfully than those who look, well, *less* good. Don't feel bad for agreeing. Come on—don't you prefer being around someone who looks good? Fit? Energetic?

Let's start with physical fitness. Being in good physical condition creates a number of positive side effects that contribute to a sense of persuasive over-all presence. First, when you're fit, you naturally exude more vigor. Others pick up on this; it's contagious. Your energy literally translates to the rest of the organization. Second, when you appear physically strong, people will auto-matically extrapolate that quality to the way you will lead the business. Finally, a fit person is assumed to have a certain degree of self-discipline and, again, people in the organization will instinctively follow someone who seems to possess this quality rather than someone who does not.

Beyond fitness, looking good means putting yourself together well. You need to look the part of an executive, whatever that means for your industry. If you're male and you work on Wall Street, the pinstripe suit is a no-brainer. If you work in the media industry, a different look is probably more appropriate.

For women, the task of finding the right thing to wear is much more complex. I will not attempt to advise anyone on appropriate women's wear. My advice for both genders is to dress slightly more conservative than others. It's not that you should dress in a way that's not you. By all means, express yourself and who you are. But at the same time, realize that your clothing reflects your executive presence. My colleague, Debra Hughes, suggests hiring an image consultant or a professional shopper to review how your current look fits with what an executive should look like in your field. Work with them to create the image that you'd like people to have of you. If that doesn't feel com-fortable or it's out of your budget, do your own due diligence and find cloth-ing that presents the image you're after. Dress for the job that you'd like, not necessarily the one that you have.

Say it strong

We've all suffered from "Meek Voice"—that syndrome that tends to overtake people when they're presenting at the front of a room, unsure of themselves in conversation, or suddenly caught in the spotlight—and we've all been upset with ourselves later for being so timid in the moment. If you aren't aware of how you speak, Meek Voice can strike frequently and it can leave a strongly negative impression on others. And since our words are the second thing people judge about us—our appearance being the first—that kind of impression can have a lasting effect you don't want to leave.

The ability to speak well, on the other hand, can have many positive implications. When you're a compelling speaker, people enjoy listening to you. They go out of their way to introduce you to their friends and associates. They stay in conversations with you longer, leading to a greater information exchange. Plus, they trust you more if you seem to know what the heck you're talking about.

Extraordinary leaders are amply aware of how they speak. They understand the importance of enunciating clearly, for example. They know how to use pauses. They don't put emphasis on big words to make themselves sound more impressive. And they don't rush. (This last point is worth repeating: People with presence speak, for the most part, slowly. This may seem like an awfully simple factor as a distinguishing element of leadership, but take a minute to picture a leader you admire, and then ask yourself whether that person speeds through his words like a nervous fourth-grader or delivers them at an easy, relaxed tempo.)

You must be able to articulate well and sound compelling. The words are important. There are two ways to make this happen. First, read. Read every day, whether it's the newspaper or Tolstoy. Second, surround yourself with people who speak well. Your vocabulary will improve by osmosis. Find people who have a knack for artful communication and spend time with them. By the way, this doesn't mean that you should be using the most intricate, complex words available. Often, the most forceful way to communicate your point is by using simple language. Develop a large working vocabulary so that you can shape your message according to the needs of the situation.

Enhancing your leadership communications skills isn't difficult—it simply requires time and commitment. Arrange for formal media training. Get a speech coach. Enroll in Toastmasters. Even the slightest uptick in your ability to communicate effectively can have an enormous effect on the people you lead. It's simple. You need to be able to let them know what you're thinking.

You need to be able to do it in an expressive, convincing way. You need to respond to what *they* think. If you can do this well, people will ask you to lead them. If you can't, your voice will simply get lost in the shuffle.

When training your voice, be aware of the opposite syndrome to Meek Voice: Power Voice. There are those people who so desperately wish not to be perceived as diffident that they've ratcheted their voice up to a volume level that seems unnatural and, therefore, off-putting to others. A good voice is clear and confident—not loud.

General
Study yourself

None of us see ourselves accurately or completely. The gap between how we perceive ourselves and how others perceive us can sometimes be staggering. We have habitual mannerisms we don't detect—for example, we overuse certain phrases without realizing it or we overstep boundaries without recognizing the fact.

If you want others to pay attention to you, you need to pay attention to yourself. After meetings, conduct an after-action review of your own participation and performance. In retrospect, does it feel like your contribution was seen as effective? Did it seem to garner positive, or any, reactions? Why or why not? After being out with friends, think about the conversations you had and the stories you told. Did your anecdotes keep people interested or did they tend to fizzle? Think about the way you spoke, your inflection and cadence, your pacing.

When reflecting on these situations, identify certain individuals as standard bearers and compare your own effectiveness with theirs. Make mental notes about what kinds of things those people do that causes an uptick in the attention they're paid by others. Ask yourself whether you do some of the same things.

Get feedback

The most direct and objective way to assess your own presence is also the simplest: ask people you trust. Before a big meeting, ask a colleague or someone whose opinion you trust to keep an eye on you, particularly to observe the impact you have—or don't have—on other people. Tell the person that you're working on enhancing your impact and leadership presence and that you want direct, blunt feedback. Tell them that getting objective feedback is the only way you'll be able to move the needle on this, so they'll be doing you a disservice by sugar-coating.

Theatrical Leadership

It was a moment early in his career that alerted Stephen Foster to the importance of presentation. He was fairly junior in his career as a hospitality leader, when he found himself in the office of the big boss, who happened to be visiting his property that day. The boss made a small comment about how the drinking glasses on the table smelled funny. Without thinking about it, Stephen had ducked out of the office and replaced the glasses with new ones. It was a tiny thing, a barely conscious act, but one that struck a chord. "Someone around here gets things done," remarked the senior exec. Or maybe it was, "Someone around here is aware of the small things."

Stephen—now senior vice president of operations for Starwood Hotels & Resorts Worldwide—doesn't remember precisely the words, but he remembers the moment vividly, since it taught him a valuable lesson about leadership: Leaders have presence. When a leader speaks, you react.

I sat down recently with Stephen to discuss his approach to leadership and was reminded about how much impact he has as a leader. He talked about the fact that leadership sometimes involves an element of theatrics. Theatrical leadership, he said, doesn't mean being fake; it means being aware of the symbolism of leadership. As a leader, he said, you can't ignore the fact that you're on stage. You're on stage all the time, and if you aren't using that stage to positively influence people and situations, you're limiting your leadership impact.

Stephen comes off as rather informal, but all the same, when you speak to him, you feel instantly that you're in the presence of someone both important and interesting. This isn't accidental. I know that Stephen is aware of the small details. He has refined his delivery in order to shape the way others experience him—right down to the words he uses (he can speak equally effectively with the Wall Street CEO or the cleaning staff in his hotels), the way he dresses (he's always impeccably groomed), the humor he employs (which puts people at ease—not to mention that he simply cracks me up), and the honesty he shows (which allows him to connect with others on a truly personal level).

Stephen is a tall guy with a big, booming voice and a strong personality. He is very sharp, well-read, and highly experienced. He's seen a lot in his career and really knows how to lead people. Yet he doesn't make you feel intimidated. Quite the opposite, actually. He makes you feel comfortable and connected right away. I asked him about how he creates this feeling. You have to be "on" all the time, he tells me—and being "on" means being "present." It's about listening and relating to others in a way that is authentic and honest. It's also about the impact you create when you're not *in the room. "You can't be in two different places at the same time," he said. "So you have to symbolically create a presence about you." And when we said goodbye and he left the room, I fully understood what he meant. It felt like he was still there.*

WHY IT MATTERS

People with presence are a lot more quickly noticed and a lot less easily forgotten. But it isn't simply because they have power; it's because they know how to use it. An executive I know was recently promoted to president of his organization. He was stunned to find that people suddenly wanted to know everything about him and began acting differently toward him as well. They would greet him in the hallway, laugh at all of his jokes, and behave around him in ways they never had before. He was uncomfortable embracing this new level of influence and authority, and unaware of its implications—so much so that, one day, when he made what he thought was an innocuous comment about a matter they were discussing, it suddenly sent the entire organization into a full research initiative to fully flesh out the small kernel of an idea he'd floated.

After some time, this executive came to understand the quality of presence that now surrounded him all the time and he eventually figured out how to use it effectively. He grasped that the symbolism of leadership is large and complex. He realized that everything he now said and did mattered to a far greater extent than it ever had before, and that this was a good thing. It could be used positively and powerfully. Before, his actions might have caused a few minor ripples and then dissipated. Now, he finally realized, those same actions had almost endless ripples, extending all the way to shore. It was an essential lesson.

Another senior individual I came across, a vice president at a national transportation company, was perceived by those in her work environment in a relatively gender-discriminatory way—that is, as unemotional, harsh, demanding, with no time for others. But when I asked people what she was like outside the office, the answers were stunningly divergent: They described her as warm, involved in charity work, a wonderful mother, and so on. It was as if, as soon as she walked through the corporate doors, she became some-one different.

In talking to this woman, I discovered that indeed she was trying to be someone different. The effort was intentional. She felt she was *supposed* to be someone different at the office. We talked at length about this and I gave her some coaching around a very specific point. Strong presence is never artificial; people immediately see when someone is putting on an act. Those who assert themselves powerfully do so because they know how to leverage the authentic parts of themselves. Ultimately, she figured this out and became not only a successful executive, but a real person at the office who others felt they could understand and relate to.

As a leader, understanding the impact of your presence is crucial to run-ning a successful team. If you aren't aware of how you carry yourself, you run the risk of accidentally using presence in the wrong manner and alienating people instead of rallying them. But if you make a conscious effort to under-stand the nature of your own presence and its effect on others, you can max-imize your position to achieve great things.

The Quiet Little Girl: Part Two

By the time Franklin suffered a paralytic illness in the summer of 1921, Eleanor had already begun to evolve into a different person. When she'd found the letters in his suitcase in 1918, the suspicions she'd harbored about him and her social secretary had been con-firmed, and she'd told him she would insist on a divorce unless he ended the relationship immediately. Knowing how a divorce would look, Franklin had complied. But the damage was done. The couple would remain friends living in the same house, a move agreed upon for the sake of their five children and Franklin's political career, but never again would they be anything more.

Now, as his illness continued, she became a more prominent face among Democratic women and an increasing force in the political arena. She found she had a unique ability to connect with people. She discovered that she had specific, strong views on certain issues, prompting Franklin to tell her that, though he respected her sincere desire to change the world, she should be more politically supple. "Your back has no bend," he told her.

But the crowds ate her up. She started working with the Women's Trade Union League, raising funds in support of a forty-eight-hour workweek, minimum wage, and the abolition of child labor. She taught literature and American history at the Todhunter School for Girls.

As Franklin's health improved and he put more energy into his career in the early '30s, Eleanor despaired—she would be forced back into a ceremonial role, a showpiece. To a close friend, she wrote about her feelings of uselessness. But she was to become far from useless. In March 1933, she became the First Lady of the United States. Franklin and his campaign aides recognized her indefinable ability to touch people. They asked her to address the Bonus Army, unemployed war veterans who had marched and encamped in Washington demanding payment of the bonuses promised to them for their service. President Hoover, viewing them as dangerous, had sent the army under MacArthur to drive them out with tear gas. Now Franklin sent food, greetings, and the magical effect of his wife.

However, now that she was First Lady, Eleanor still fretted. When she'd been a child, when Uncle Teddy was president, she had observed the strictly circumscribed role and traditional protocol of her Aunt Edith. Eleanor resolved to fill the role differently. Despite criticism, she did not sink into the role of a quiet, smiling appendage to Franklin. Instead, she continued with the active business and speaking agenda she had begun. She held weekly press conferences. She launched a widely syndicated newspaper column, "My Day." She maintained a heavy travel schedule, frequently making appearances at labor meetings to assure workers that their plight was known to the president.

She became a vocal supporter of the African-American civil rights movement. She used her weight in the media to connect with women who found themselves in domestic isolation. She banned men from her press conferences, because they discriminated against women, especially female journalists. She wrote articles for Woman's Home Companion.

The fourteen-year-old who had felt like an ugly duckling was becoming a figure of strength, compassion, and inspiration throughout the world. In 1941, when the U.S. entered the war, Eleanor co-chaired a national committee on civil defense, frequently visiting civilian and military centers to boost morale. Two years later, she traveled to the South Pacific and visited thousands of wounded servicemen through miles of hospitals. A Republican serviceman insisted to a colleague that he and the other soldiers who'd encountered her warmth would gladly repay any grumbling civilians for whatever gasoline and rubber her visit had cost. In 1944, she embarked on a tour of Latin American countries.

And, in 1945, when her husband finally succumbed to death, she was appointed by the new president, Harry S. Truman, as a delegate to the United Nations General Assembly, where she helped draft the UN Universal Declaration of Human Rights.

Later in the decade, Eleanor would be courted for political office by Democrats in New York and throughout the country. "I heard that I was being offered the nomination for governor for the United States Senate in my own state, and even for Vice President. And some particularly humorous souls wrote in and suggested that I run as the first woman President of the United States! The simple truth is that I have had my fill of public life of the more or less stereotyped kind."

But Eleanor Roosevelt had enshrined herself a legacy that was anything but stereotypical. The girl who had found herself plain and affection-starved as a child had, in the end, transcended the image of a First Lady, bringing comfort and hope to millions. In one of her final speaking engagements, at Ball State Teachers College, she conveyed to 1,500 students, faculty, and community members the urgency to strive to understand other peoples of the world. "This is what it means to face world leadership," she told them. "The government cannot do it for us. Many of us do not even know the whole of our own little communities. It would help us all over the world to under-stand people."

Soon after, she was gone physically, struck down by tuberculosis. But the impact of her presence would never fade. "The United States, the United Nations, the world, has lost one of its great citizens," said UN Ambassador Adlai Stevenson. "Mrs. Eleanor Roosevelt is dead, and a cherished friend of all mankind is gone. What other single human being has touched and transformed the existence of so many?"

THE BOTTOM LINE

Your reputation will always precede you. Think, act, and speak like the executive you want to be.

Self-Insight

It's not only the most difficult thing to know one's self,
but the most inconvenient.

—Josh Billings, American Humorist, 1815–1885

A Divine Message: Part One

The century had not been kind to France. It had been decades since the beginning of war, a seemingly eternal period that extended long back before she had even arrived on this Earth to begin serving the son of the Lord. Battle, it seemed, was the only constant, and nearly all of it on French soil. She wondered when the raids on her village would end, whether it would be burned a second time. What could they want with Domrémy, this little isolated patch in the Northeast? Why could they not just be left to live?

The enemy, she supposed, must want it all—every last corner of France. They would not stop until it was nothing more than half of a dual English Monarchy. Scorched earth was everywhere, the economy in ruins. The Black Death, though decades old, still hung like a pall over the country, its merchants cut off from foreign markets, its legacy of demise still manifest in every house. She was young yet, but she heard the frequent laments and saw the wistful expressions in the eyes of those who had lived in, those who remembered, the blissful, holy kingdom that had existed, it seemed, only yesterday. As the young peasant girl stood in the field and looked out over her parents' modest fifty acres, she realized that yesterday must seem long ago indeed.

It was then that the visions came.

Ask any great leader what it was that made them who they are today, and you'll likely hear an insightful story connecting early experiences to current success. Ask them what advice they would give to a younger version of themselves and, again, you'll receive a thorough, honest, meaningful response that shows how they've integrated personal learning over the years. Extraordinary executives have a deep awareness of not only *what* critical events happened in their lives, but *why* and *how* they happened. They understand who they are, how they've become that person, and what they stand for today.

At an executive level, self-insight manifests in multiple ways. Good leaders must be aware not only of their own motivations, but also how those motivations influence their behaviors. They must be alert to their strengths and weaknesses and know how to leverage the former while working on the latter. It is a vital element in the path to success.

WHAT IS IT?

In every leadership assessment I perform, I look for self-insight as a key indicator of effectiveness at a senior executive level. The presence or absence of this trait often swings my recommendation one way or the other.

I define self-insight as perspective on oneself: knowing your strengths and weaknesses, understanding your hot buttons and blind spots, recognizing your impact on others, getting what motivates and drives you, and seeing how your life experiences have impacted who you are today. Why is it so important for a leader to have self-insight? It's really the only way you can change. In order to grow and develop as both a leader and an individual, you need to be able to reflect—to have perspective on your experiences. And if you're not able to grow or develop, you're not going to cut it as a leader.

A number of forces impede our ability to both get an accurate read on ourselves and then do something with it. In fact, a large body of evidence suggests that we're actually pretty lousy at it.

As an example, most of us are poor at estimating our own intelligence. Multiple studies have shown that when researchers ask people to guess how smart they are and then give them an IQ test, their estimates and scores are largely unconnected. We're also pretty hopeless—no better than a chance guess, in fact—when it comes to estimating our ability to detect when others are lying to us. In short, we think we're much better detectives than we actually are, with most of us grossly overestimating our ability to realize when we're being fooled.

We even come up short evaluating how competent we are at work. A recent study showed that nurses' estimates in their abilities to perform basic life support tasks fall short of their actual performance, and doctors' beliefs about their understanding of thyroid disorders fall short of their actual knowledge.[1]

While we may have a fuzzy picture of ourselves, others see us more accurately. In one interesting study, a group of students (the "reporters") were asked to enter a room and read a simple weather report while being videotaped. The entire scene lasted a minute and a half. The students then took an IQ test off-screen and were asked to guess how they had done on the test. A group of other participants (the "raters") then watched one of the videotaped scenes and rated how smart they thought the presenters were. Sure enough, after viewing each presenter for just those ninety seconds, the raters were able to predict the presenters' IQ scores only as accurately as the raters had predicted their own.

Probably the most widespread research on self-insight has been conducted by David Dunning, a professor of psychology at Cornell University. His pioneering work in the areas of self-judgment and eyewitness testimony has shed new light on how we see ourselves. "The notions people have about their skills and knowledge are far from perfect indicators of their actual proficiency," says Dunning. "Those with the most vaulted beliefs of their competence are not necessarily the most competent; those who denigrate their skills are not necessarily the least skillful. Impressions of skill are somehow decoupled from reality—perhaps not completely, but to an extent that is surprising."[2]

Some of this inability stems from overconfidence, an effect that has been studied in a variety of contexts. For example, older drivers tend to think they're better drivers than others of similar age. People think that they're less vulnerable to getting the flu than others. Entrepreneurs and business owners think their businesses are more likely to succeed than other businesses. Even bungee jumpers have a skewed perception of reality: The typical one believes he's less likely to have a dangerous incident than the next guy who tries it—not unlike motorcyclists who, on average, are pretty confident that some other biker might get in an accident, but they themselves probably won't.

Here's the even funnier thing. Even if you acknowledge the frequency of overconfidence and believe you, therefore, aren't disposed to it, you're *still* probably mistaken. When specifically asked, people overwhelmingly say that they are uniquely able to overcome the overconfidence bias that others prevalently fall prey to. Guess what? Those people still, for the most part, overestimate their own abilities.

Dunning published numerous studies demonstrating just how far off the mark we often are in our self-assessments. In one such study, he and a Cornell colleague, Justin Kruger, brought students into their lab and asked them to do a basic intelligence test focused on logical reasoning. After completing the tests, the students were asked to estimate how their own logical reasoning skills matched up against other participants. They were also asked to guess their own test scores. Dunning and Kruger then split the participants into four quartiles based on their actual performance and compared how each group thought they did with their actual scores.

The results were fascinating. First, the vast majority of students estimated their own logical reasoning skills were higher than average (above the fiftieth percentile). Second, Dunning and Kruger found a very small correlation between perceived performance and actual performance. In other words, most people got it wrong. Third, people in the bottom quartile were, by far, the most inaccurate in estimating their own performance.

Dunning and Kruger found this third observation to be particularly interesting: people who are at the bottom end of any performance measure tend not to realize how bad they are. This finding has been replicated in a number of other contexts as well. For example, students in the bottom quartile of a debating tournament estimated that they were winning 61 percent of their matches when, in reality, they were winning less than a quarter of them. Likewise, people seen as having a poor sense of humor will tend to dramatically overestimate how funny they are to others.[3]

The phenomenally successful *American Idol* recognizes this effect and, for ratings' sake, milks it for all it's worth. Not long after the show's debut, viewers began watching in droves—not only to see highly talented performers do their thing, but in equal measure to watch the clips of train-wreck auditions: truly awful singers who butcher their way through thirty seconds of musical horror and then are asked mercifully to stop. The particularly perverse attraction for audiences is the frequent indignation of these people after they have been rejected. By and large, it's the worst singers who are the most upset. Despite millions of people recognizing from their sofas at home how dreadful these people are, the singers themselves are genuinely shocked to hear that they aren't worthy of a recording contract.

What accounts for this phenomenon? Now known as the Dunning-Kruger Effect, it has four basic tenets:

1. Incompetent people tend to overestimate their own level of skill.
2. Incompetent people fail to recognize genuine skill in others.

3. Incompetent people fail to recognize how extreme their inadequacy is.
4. It you train people to improve their skill level, they come to recognize and acknowledge their own previous lack of skill.

It is a landmark finding, pertinent in nearly all facets of life, and especially in leadership. Those who lack leadership potential tend not only to overestimate their own leadership capabilities, but also to have a diminished sense of this same ability in others. If you ask this type of person why a given leader is successful, they'll likely have a hard time coming up with an answer. An absence of perspective prevents them from recognizing both their own shortcomings and others' strengths.

Fortunately, even if you don't have deep insight into yourself, it isn't a lost cause. Research has provided evidence that people can actually gain perspective over time. In other words, they can come finally to acknowledge what they *don't* know. And recognizing what you don't know is half the battle.

HOW DO YOU KNOW IT WHEN YOU SEE IT?

You know that friend you have? The one who always tells those awful jokes and aimless stories, but doesn't know they are awful jokes because no one has ever told him, since he's otherwise a nice guy? He probably isn't going to lose any friends due to his lack of self-awareness, but he probably isn't going to gain many new ones, either, and it's highly unlikely anyone is ever going to ask him to take on any prominent social function or one with important consequences, like emceeing their wedding or partnering in a new business venture. There's simply too great a risk that, because he does not know himself well, he'll ruin things. I mean, don't get me wrong—the guy's pretty smart, actually. But the risk that he might pull out one of those awful jokes is just so high, you'd rather keep him out of the way where he can't do any harm.

The guy described above has, yes, some lessons to learn, or at least one big lesson to learn, about himself. He has plenty of good qualities going for him, but his inappropriate humor and pointless storytelling are serving as a major barrier for him socially. The poor guy just doesn't know it.

The biggest problem is that he won't change until he realizes his shortcomings. Self-insight is the catalyst for growth. You need to understand yourself and how others perceive you *in order* to develop as both a person and a leader. This is the major reason why people go to therapy: to improve their mental functioning through self-knowledge. The same goes for executive coaching, especially when it's done well: Learning how you, as a leader, impact others will enable you to improve your leadership skills. Without this knowledge, you have blind spots and your ability to lead is diminished. Don't be the guy described above!

There is only one way to really develop as a leader, and that is through self-awareness. There are a number of ways we can identify people with self-insight. Here are some.

They talk about themselves accurately . . .

How well someone can answer the question "How would others describe you?" says a great deal about a leader's self-insight. Some leaders struggle to come up with an answer or are unable to answer the question at all. But those with self-insight will reply elaborately, commenting on their strengths, their limitations, how they are perceived by others, and the reasons behind those perceptions. Most important, their answers align closely with others' opinions of them, rather than diverging due to personal bias or delusion.

. . . but they aren't self-focused

Extraordinary leaders turn the lens on themselves to a constructive degree, but stop short of compulsive narcissism, which can torpedo leadership instead of enhancing it. These individuals understand that those who wish to lead others must first get to know themselves. They get to know and work on themselves, not as function of self-absorption, but for the purpose of developing more powerful leadership.

They understand the importance of knowing themselves

Most of the time, those with deep self-insight did not come to it through serendipity or feedback from a life coach. They've come to it following an experience that truly brought home its value.

My colleague at RHR, Steven Gilbert, worked with a company president a few years ago—let's call him Harold—whose career came perilously close to stalling permanently due to his lack of self-insight. After having run a very successful retail division of a large company, Harold received news of a promotion. His new position would mean a tenfold increase in scope and responsibility. "No problem," he said, embracing the opportunity.

Before, Harold's position had been driven by figures and spreadsheets; now, for the first time, he had to manage relationships, liaise with the parent company on a regular basis, direct and delegate tasks to those on his team, and maintain a constant flow of information up, down, and laterally. It was in this new role that suddenly his lack of self-insight became a serious detriment. His business results had always been dazzling, but in his new leadership shoes he needed more than business expertise. Now he wasn't running a business so much as he was leading a large group of people. Without effective people techniques, his ship started to sink, and fast.

With his permission, Steven sat in on Harold's team meetings and observed him in various other circumstances. Later, Steven reflected with Harold on his behaviors during these interactions. There were a number of ways he was coming up short interpersonally, mostly, it seemed, because of three factors. First, he wasn't aware of his own behavioral patterns and tendencies, particularly with reference to his impact on others. He came across far too forcefully while also seeming to dismiss people without realizing it. As a result, he dominated conversations, preventing others from ever getting a word in edgewise. Second, he didn't seem to pay attention to those same patterns and tendencies in others, resulting in mutually incompatible behaviors. And third, he seemed unaware of, or indifferent toward, the cues other people were giving him.

Steven sat down and had a talk with Harold. To his credit, Harold accepted the feedback willingly and pledged to get to know his own character and manner better. Eventually, Harold developed a very strong sense of self-insight. He became much more effective on an interpersonal level and vowed to help those in the company feel more connected with him and one another. Today, Harold's teams describe him as the best leader they've ever had. And all because he took the opportunity to get to know himself better, and then do something about it.

They want you to give it to them straight

Had Harold rejected Steven's observations, he certainly wouldn't have been the first person in history to get defensive about his own traits and behaviors. It's seldom easy to hear feedback from others, even when that feedback is honest, objective, and from people we trust and respect. There's nothing pleasant about being told you aren't a good speaker, you aren't as funny as you think you are, you don't listen well, you need to dress more appropriately, your colleagues see you as a ruthless corporate climber, or the thing that's making people uncomfortable around you is your breath. See—I wasn't even talking about you and that list still made you kind of uneasy, didn't it?

Sure, it's a lot easier to ignore feedback than to undertake the often-arduous effort of really listening to it, internalizing it, and then turning it into new behavior. It's the easier choice, but not the better one. The best leaders aren't just open to feedback. They actually seek it from multiple sources, and on a regular basis.

A Look Inward

Tim Spencer is the type of guy who has always trusted his own instincts—and those instincts have usually turned out to be right. Growing up in a small town south of Ottawa with his two siblings and being raised by a single mom and his grandmother, Tim had a desire in his heart that he knew pointed toward the big city. The vast majority of those in his town stayed right where they were after graduating high school. They worked in the factories, got married, raised their families, and led typical small-town lives. Which was fine for them—but not for Tim. He wanted to leave, go to university, and establish himself beyond the limits of his town.

With few role models to look up to, knowing how to break out wasn't easy. He did, however, have an uncle named Albert who took Tim under his wing. Albert had been successful in business, at one point serving as regional head of sales at Sony.

During the summers, Tim would visit his uncle at his office in Toronto. Tim had shown an early interest in computers and technology, and he knew he had a knack for IT. Albert would tell Tim to follow his dreams, to be kind, to be loyal and to test his wings. He would tell Tim he could do whatever he wanted in life if he set his mind to it and was willing to put in the effort. So, when Tim graduated high school and all of his closest friends stayed in town and went to work in the factories, Tim headed for Toronto.

After university, Tim landed a job at Bell Mobility, an upstart division of Bell Canada. He was the seventh person they hired. By the end of a successful eight-year stint, Tim felt that the entrepreneurial spirit that had attracted him initially to the company had been lost. It was difficult to let go but, again, it was time to trust his gut. He had to move on.

Tim then joined a start-up company called Sigma Systems, which offered customers various business software products. A couple of weeks after coming on board, Tim had lunch with an old friend at the Canadian cable giant Rogers Communications. The friend spoke about the trouble his company was having automating the provisioning of its data services. These services were complex, he said, but should feel seamless to customers. They needed a product that activated services automatically.

Tim challenged himself to design such a product. He went back to the team at Sigma and laid out a variety of strategies for solving the problem. The product Tim and his colleagues conceived was ultimately purchased and implemented by Rogers.

But Tim saw that the same kind of solution might appeal to other companies too. So he sold a license for the product to Rogers, but not the intellectual property. It turned out to be a brilliant move. When the Silicon Valley-based company Excite@Home became Rogers' data network provider, they liked Sigma's solution so much that they deployed it across their own international network.

Out of nowhere, Sigma was accelerating, fast. Around the same time, Silicon Valley was taking note. Notable venture capital firm Kleiner Perkins teamed up with Cisco Systems to purchase Sigma for $36 million. About a year later, Sigma was sold again, this time to a strategic buyer—Liberate, a vendor in the cable market selling interactive TV middleware.

But about eight weeks after the deal closed, disaster struck. The SEC and the FBI launched a joint investigation into Liberate's accounting practices. The company went into freefall.

There was no blueprint for this kind of situation. Tim had no guide other than his intuition. "I pulled everyone into a room and told them the truth. I reassured them we had a good business." The investigation dragged on for over a year.

Soon, an investment banker swooped in, bought enough shares of Liberate to gain control of the board, and installed himself as the CEO. Then he started selling off Liberate's assets. "Sigma was the first to go," Tim says. And this was a seminal moment in his leadership journey, because as he worked with the new CEO to help put the company up for sale, a thought occurred to him.

"What if I buy it?"

Tim approached some investors he knew and suggested a management buyout. It was the right time and the right decision. With Tim now at the helm of the company he had built, Sigma Systems became profitable within half a year and grew by 20 percent annually for the next five years.

It was around 2006 that I got a call from Tim. Business was good, but he wanted to enhance his own leadership and get his team to perform better. I was immediately impressed with his depth of thought and willingness to embrace outside leadership advice. When we first met, Tim told me he expected to have a discussion about operational processes—how to optimally structure and better manage the team. But the chat soon took a different turn. We talked about whether Tim felt he had a firm grasp on the ways he influenced those around him and the techniques he could use for encouraging higher performance.

"I quickly realized I didn't know enough about myself and how I impact people," Tim told me during our interview for this book. "Getting a better understanding of that suddenly became important." I conducted a half-day assessment of Tim, including a battery of tests, and then went through a full 360-degree process, meeting with each of his reports and soliciting their insights about him.

Tim's leadership growth as a result of this assessment process was distinct and immediate. He took in the feedback, processed it, challenged me, asked difficult questions, and talked about his own career trajectory and overall plan. He had always been so busy putting his head down and charging forward that he'd never taken the time to sit down and talk about himself. We especially dug into how his behavior led his team to feel as though they were being over-managed. He over-engineered and often controlled decision making. He had been applying a technologist's approach to management—structured and detail-focused—instead of a more versatile leader's approach that would get the most out of his people and raise everyone's game. As a result, his people weren't developing their own leadership capabilities; they merely took on more work as they progressed at the company. Together, we reframed Tim's leadership mindset and focused on talent development as a priority.

His self-insights started a dialogue within the organization about how everyone could become better leaders. "That hadn't been the *focus before," Tim said. "It had been on performance management. This process put the mirror up on me and also on my people. I made some hard decisions about people that I had been putting off, but which, in retrospect, should have happened much earlier. We started talking about the talent we had in the organization and how to really develop it."*

Today, Tim is a stronger, more flexible leader with a keen sense of his impact on others. He is a true chief executive, no longer needing to fall back on his technology roots in leading others. He understands how to influence without exerting his authority and how to build leaders in their own right. He has a framework for assessing people, making talent decisions, and coaching others as he'd been coached.

The credit doesn't go to me; it goes to him. You must know yourself in order to be an effective leader. Tim's greatest self-insight was to seek self-insight in the first place. He'd be the first to tell you he's still a work-in-progress, but he feels he now has the tools to go as far as he wants to go. Just like his Uncle Albert always said.

HOW DO YOU GET IT?

Since those around us provide us with a regular stream of feedback both explicit and subtle, opportunities for self-insight are abundant. To take advantage of these opportunities, however, we must be able to hear it, be willing to absorb it, and be committed to using it.

It's perfectly natural, after all, not to feel the instinct to self-reflect. First, we lead busy lives. We spend so much time trying to manage others—our colleagues, our spouses, our kids—that our own selves are usually the last thing we might see as deserving of a little examination. Second, there is usually no great apparent negative consequence resulting from a lack of self-reflection. I may be thoroughly satisfied with my life just the way it is, thank you very much—I don't do "soul searching" and all that. Leave all that Zen-type stuff to the shirtless old guys who do tai chi on the beach every morning. Finally, self-insight may tell us things about ourselves we don't necessarily like. As in any kind of analysis, self-insight can lead to valuable change and can unlock new opportunities for gratification and achievement, but we aren't always guaranteed to like what we find when we turn over the rock, so leaving it in place sometimes seems like the more convenient option.

Once you've opened yourself up to the value of taking a good, hard look at yourself, how do you go about finding the insights you seek? Sometimes we have self-discoveries that hit us like a brick, but usually the experience is much quieter than that. Insight into ourself may occur passively or intentionally, but the latter accelerates the process dramatically. If you think of self-insight not as an accidental gift each of us is allotted, but as something you continuously, actively pursue, you are more likely to arrive at it more quickly and more meaningfully. Here are some ways to dig for it.

Solicit feedback the right way

Can you gain self-insight through introspection? Seems plausible, but in fact there is a substantial body of research that suggests that introspection alone may not work. Your ability to perform effective introspection depends largely on your abilities in a given matter. If you are competent in a particular area and have the necessarily cognitive skills to integrate social feedback from others, you will be able to self-reflect on your experience and grow from it accordingly. However, if you lack competency in that area and do not have the general ability to integrate data, self-reflection will simply not work.

People who have committed crimes and chronic social deviants often come to psychotherapy seeking to understand why they do the things they do. It's not that they haven't thought about it (often *ad nauseum*), it's that they don't have sufficient resources themselves to consolidate their thoughts. So, in the absence of being able to perform self-insight alone, one needs the help and support of others. What I'm talking about is feedback. The best ways to really generate self-insight is to (a) treat your work like a science experiment, making hypotheses and then testing them out, and (b) seek feedback from others who are equipped to guide you effectively through the process.

Once again, feedback alone is insufficient. In fact, Dunning goes into great detail in his wonderful book, *Self-Insight*, about why feedback typically doesn't work. The reason it doesn't work, however, is because people generally don't give us true feedback, and we aren't intuitively wired to hear the *kind* of feedback we need to increase our self-awareness. We have mental processes that shield us from hard feedback. As Dunning puts it, and I agree, sometimes feedback can be useless or even counterproductive to real growth. If done properly, however, feedback is undoubtedly the key to self-insight and personal growth.

For starters, you need to ask for feedback from the right people. They need to be:

- credible themselves;
- willing to give you honest feedback even if it doesn't align with your current self-concept;
- good at observing behavior themselves; and
- willing to deliver the feedback in a way that is challenging, yet palatable and constructive.

Let's return to the *American Idol* example. If I was looking for feedback on my singing abilities, I wouldn't ask Kara—she wouldn't challenge me enough. I wouldn't ask Simon, because his feedback would be difficult to stomach. I would, however, be glad to hear what Randy had to say (and I have a pretty good idea what he'd say about my singing, but I'd invite the feedback nonetheless).

There is a large body of evidence supporting the notion that managerial self-awareness has a direct link to success as a leader. This is often done through 360-degree feedback. Several researchers have noted that a higher level of congruence between self- and other-ratings on 360-degree feedback is associated with a wide variety of managerial and performance outcomes. Likewise, the research clearly shows that 360-degree feedback is a much better predictor of one's actual performance than self-assessments alone, and it also leads to better developmental outcomes. You are able to change more effectively when you receive insightful feedback from people around you than you would be able to with your own self-perceptions.

> This issue is further exacerbated by one's level within an organization. Ask any effective CEO about feedback and they will typically tell you they never get enough. This is mainly because people are either telling the CEO what she wants to hear or there are not enough built-in mechanisms for honest feedback to be solicited, organized, and shared. This problem is borne out in the research: Higher-level employees are more likely than lower-level employees to have an
>
> *(continued)*

> *inflated sense of their own competency, and high management's 360-degree scores typically show less congruence between self- and other-ratings than those of their more junior counterparts. Clearly, the higher up you are in an organization, the less in touch with your own reality you are. You need to change this pattern. No matter how high up in the organizational chart you are, get feedback from people you trust—and listen to it.*

Do something with the feedback

So you go through a 360-degree feedback exercise and some things are identified. You have a pretty good idea of how people perceive you—what your strengths and weaknesses are. Chances are, you agree with certain parts of the feedback and disagree with other parts.

What do you do with the feedback? Most leaders I know take their 360-degree feedback, file it deep in their drawer so that no one can accidentally catch a glimpse of it on their desk, and then move on to the next task. They don't take the time to leverage the feedback in any meaningful way.

Feedback is data. It's a gift that people have given you and you need to respect that gift and do something with it.

First, be very clear about the main messages. Categorize the feedback into three groupings: 1) what people want you to start doing, 2) what people want you to stop doing, and 3) what people want you to continue doing. Then, come up with a few action steps that you will do to address those opinions.

Don't make it a long list of activities. Stick with a few key follow-up actions that will target the areas identified in the feedback. Then, do what most leaders don't: share the outcome of your 360-degree feedback with your team. It is seldom done, and yet such an easy win. Do this at a team meeting or as part of one-on-ones with each member of the team. Let them know that you believe in feedback and that you're thankful people have taken the time to provide their insights on your behavior and performance. Tell them you take the feedback seriously and you are determined to continue your own self-development. Then, proceed to tell them the highlights of the feedback and what you plan on doing about it. Ask them to give you input going forward on your progress in these areas.

This may sound like a reversal in roles. Isn't it your team members who should be sharing their own feedback with you and isn't it you who should be monitoring their performance?

Exceptional leaders know this is not true. They engage their teams to help them grow as leaders. Not only does this increase employee engagement (people feel special when you solicit their input in your own development), but it also creates a culture of feedback. When it comes time to give them feedback on their performances, you'll be in a much better position to do so.

Reach out to an old friend or family member, or go to your high school reunion

To truly understand your impact now, it's enormously helpful to have a retroactive lens on yourself, as you were earlier in life. With years of experience under your belt, you will have substantially more perspective. Most people hate going to reunions, but they can be enlightening in a variety of ways. They can shed light on what kind of student you were in high school or what your social life was like. At a reunion, you not only talk about it, you feel it, as you warp back in time and experience the same kinds of fears and emotions.

Don't feel like going to your reunion? Give an old friend a call. Do a mini-interview. Ask what you were like then—what kinds of behaviors or tendencies people tended to associate with you. What did people like most about you? What didn't they like? Were you aware of what they didn't like? Was your personality static during the entire period that person knew you or did they observe any change in you?

Members of your family are also helpful in building an accurate profile of yourself and understanding your tendencies and patterns. Ask your parents what you were like as a kid. Talk to your siblings or cousins about how they remember certain events. Ask them what they thought of you as a child. What was your general behavior like? Did you fit in easily or did you prefer to stick to yourself? Were you shy or outgoing? Were you a ball of fire or as cool as a cucumber?

Family members are incredibly valuable sources of data about you, and you will benefit from real conversations with them about your background— who you take after most, what traits have been passed down generation to generation, what area of the world your descendants came from, the cultural traditions they brought with them, the rituals that have served to bond the family together over the years, and your perceived "role" in your family. And so on. Learning the detailed story of you—and by you I don't mean you, but everything that led up to and influenced you—can be a powerful eye-opener.

Keep a diary of your thoughts

Keep a running diary of your thoughts and experiences. Something important occurs when you put pen to paper. Your thoughts become crystallized—clarified—making it easier for you to articulate them to others later. In addition, using a diary is a way to preserve your thinking at a moment in time. Great development occurs when you are able to later reflect on how you were thinking at a given period in your career. You are able to see how you matured, the basis for decisions you've taken, and the accuracy of your predictions. I recognize that some people love this technique and others hate it. While I find it quite difficult to journal my thoughts with any sort of discipline, I have clients and acquaintances who swear by it. It does work. By taking the time to put your thoughts down on paper, you are recording them and learning about yourself at the same time.

A journal is unique in that it functions as an ongoing conversation with yourself. Apart from the occasional pep talk in the mirror, rebuttal to a talk show host while behind the wheel, or aimless murmuring while preparing a meal, there are few instances in life where we actually *talk to* ourselves. And talking to yourself can really help you explore feelings, work through problems, answer questions, and recognize insights.

Finally, even when you don't know you're learning about yourself through journaling, you really are. When you put pen to paper (don't do a journal on a computer), you're recording your thoughts and experiences. It's the reason people have always written, even when they didn't have an audience. C. Michael Curtis, long-time fiction editor at *The Atlantic*, says we are compelled to write stories because "they teach us how to be." Extracting your thoughts and feelings from inside your head and transforming them into something tangible causes you to contemplate your own disposition, your behaviors, and your responses to things. And that kind of reflection can only help.

Speak to a management psychologist

I realize that I'm biased towards my own profession, but the truth is, what I do helps people become more reflective leaders. Management psychologists, by virtue of our education and experience, are skilled at helping executives build self-awareness. Especially when the management psychologist is familiar with the work behavior of the executive, he or she can help the executive probe and find the revealing links between early experiences and on-the-job behavior patterns. The management psychologist has a suite of tools to assess leadership capabilities in a reliable and valid manner, so that you can truly trust the accuracy of the results. He or she can also help construct a plan for development that is linked to the patterns that have been identified. Our ties to the past can be strong. Understanding the origins of our behavior at work is very useful, and often essential, to becoming a more effective and successful executive. By recognizing the links between what we have experienced throughout our lives and how we function in the professional world, we can arrive at a better understanding of ourselves and build more satisfying, productive work lives.

Oh, and while I'm on this topic, let me take this opportunity to make a suggestion. Leadership assessments are very, very important events. Your chances of having a positive experience are greatly improved if you utilize a licensed management psychologist (also called industrial psychologists, organizational psychologists, I/O psychologists, or occupational psychologists, depending on what part of the world you live in) who is bound by a code of ethics, accountable to a professional college, and has the necessary training and insight to provide you with the data you need.

Do something outside your comfort zone

When was the last time you pushed yourself beyond your usual limits? Really stretched past what you think of as your capacity?

I'll bet those times stand out in your mind as being particularly profound moments in your development. You've probably learned a lot about yourself by stepping into the unknown. The more entrenched a person's routine becomes, the more opaque his line of sight into himself becomes as well. You must break the habit of routine in order to better know your boundaries.

I have seen many executives take on roles outside their area of expertise. One retail leader I know was on the fast-track to the executive suite. She had a background in finance and had always been ranked at the top of her peer group. She had shown up on every High Potential list since joining the company and was already being considered for promotion to multiple officer roles.

This leader, however, recognized fairly early on that none of the senior executives in her organization came from finance. They all had operational experience—they had been in the field and had the battle scars to show it. So, in a rare move, she sought out a role in the operations field.

She landed a role as a regional manager and began to learn what it meant to really be accountable for the bottom line. This was a huge leap of faith for her and well outside the typical career path for those in finance. Yet in the end, it was a brilliant move: She proved to be wonderfully successful in her field role, driving profitable growth in her region in ways that hadn't been done before. She took a real learning approach to managing her new portfolio, and once she got her head around the operational side of things, she brought in her finance expertise and hit a home run.

Two years later, the organization recognized her success by promoting her to senior VP of operations, a position she still holds today. This superstar leader is a great example of the tremendous value of searching within yourself, recognizing the gaps in your knowledge and experience, taking on roles that fill those gaps, and reaping the rewards.

WHY IT MATTERS

One of my clients—let's call him Theo—is a senior leader in the high-tech sector. To his very core, Theo is a future-focused, action-oriented individual. He is optimistic and entrepreneurial. He has tremendous energy and drive. He's passionate, almost to a fault. The swiftness with which he rose in the retail world was a surprise to no one—these elements are all part of the profile for success in that industry.

At a certain juncture, however, Theo's meteoric rise seemed to stall. He had reached a level in the organization that now required him to take on more strategic responsibilities, and he had been placed in charge of multiple operations across several regions. The next target in Theo's sights was a senior VP role, yet suddenly he was having difficulty gaining traction.

My assessment of Theo revealed the following: The very trait that had formed the keystone for his success to date, a bias for action, was now tripping him up. To succeed at the most senior levels, one must constantly self-reflect, invite feedback, and consider multiple viewpoints—all while maintaining a penchant for action. In his indiscriminate rush to act, to achieve, to get things done, Theo simply wasn't allowing himself the time or headspace to think about, and improve on, his past experience. His *modus operandi* was to keep churning forward, no matter the circumstances. If there was a problem, his solution was to bury the hatchet and move on—the proverbial addressing of the symptom while ignoring the underlying issue. He paid little heed to feedback since it was, to him, a waste of time, something that only chewed up valuable hours which could otherwise be used to *get stuff done.*

Despite his impressive track record of results, Theo's lack of self-insight at this level of responsibility was now blinding him to the negative perception his behavior was creating. People found him defensive and lacking depth. His constant sense of urgency was overwhelming to others. He came across as aggressive, in your face, and *too* passionate.

Most important, with regard to Theo's career aspirations, was the fact that people did not believe he could possibly succeed as a strategic leader when he was always so abrupt. People want to see a leader as someone willing to take charge, yes—but they also want to see him as someone who takes a moment to stop and think. When people see someone as action-obsessed as Theo, they automatically interpret him as lacking perspective.

When I told Theo about the existing perception others had of him, he winced. "Sure, I can be a bit curt in my delivery," he said, "and sometimes people can't keep up with me. But I don't think I'm *that* bad." It wasn't that he was intentionally rejecting the feedback; it was that he couldn't process it since he hadn't paid attention to the signals in the first place. I tried to help him think about certain negative reactions people sometimes had to his behavior. I asked him, already knowing the answer, how often did others turn to him for help?

Finally, Theo started to get it. It took him a long time to really change his behavior—habits are hard to break, after all—but once he started down the path, it was amazing to observe how far he came and how much he improved. I felt that I was literally watching him achieve self-insight before my eyes, as if a light that was never there before had been switched on.

To become a truly versatile and effective leader, it's necessary for you to achieve the kind of breakthroughs that Theo eventually reached. You must be able to recognize your own strengths and weaknesses. You need to understand your hot buttons and blind spots. You have to know what motivates you, what your impact is on others, and how your life experiences have impacted who you are today.

Self-insight isn't just a critical ingredient to help you assume leadership status; it is also the primary tool for leadership growth and development. If you do not have the ability to see yourself objectively, it is impossible for you to recognize what a given situation requires of you or what qualities you can leverage at certain times. If you aren't well attuned to both your abilities and your habits, you will find yourself dealing with a wide variety of circumstances in one of only a few possible ways. But if you know where your strengths lie and what your weaknesses are, if you've studied your own tendencies and patterns of behavior, if you get *why* you usually do what you do and are also willing to try altering those habits, you thereby allow yourself the possibility of becoming the most effective type of leader: strong and focused, yet adaptable and self-aware.

A Divine Message: Part Two

She had cried when the voices left. How beautiful they were, how imbued with clarity and truth. She had petitioned the garrison commander for permission to visit the royal court, only to be met with sarcasm. She had returned the following January, earning an escort to visit Chinon after news from the front confirmed her vision of a remarkable military reversal; she made the journey through hostile territory in male disguise, but finally reached the court. Now, here she stood before the uncrowned king, insisting that Saint Michel, Saint Catherine, and Saint Margaret had visited her, instructing her to drive out the English and bring the Dauphin to Reims for his rightful coronation. Here she stood, asking permission to travel with the army and wear the equipment of a knight. She had looked inside herself and discovered why she was born, no matter how daunting a purpose it might be. She knew her duty and her destiny.

Charles looked at the girl, all of sixteen years old. What other choice did he have? It was a time of utter despair. The dual monarchy was nearly accomplished, the French command nearly vanquished. Its army had won no major victory for a generation. When he granted an illiterate farm girl's request to lead his country at the behest of God, it may have seemed irrational to some. But to most, it was simply a last resort. The girl, having seen into her own soul, stood proud.

Soon the decision began to seem no less than prophetic. Sent to the siege at Orléans, the only remaining loyal French city north of the Loire, the girl appeared infused not only with the spirit of the Lord, but also his strength. After nine days, the siege had been lifted. Joan of Arc was co-leading the army and imploring the leaders of England and its ally, Burgundy, to "settle their debts to the king of heaven" so that no more blood need be shed. But the English did not believe in the insolent young girl's visions. Its appetite for war was far from sated.

The English chose poorly. Over the succeeding months, they fell prey, battle by individual battle, to the French, to the girl moved by

*the insight of divine guidance. In a matter of months, the English
army was devastated and most of its commanders captured or killed.
"The Maiden lets you know that she has chased the English out of
all the places they held by attack or other means," wrote the girl.
"They are dead or prisoners or discouraged in battle. Believe what
you have heard about the earl of Suffolk, the lord la Pole and his
brother, the lord Talbot, the lord Scales, and Sir Fastolf; many more
knights and captains than these are defeated."*

*The peasant girl had hardly watched these battles from a
remove. She was acknowledged as a heroine in battle whose
resilience was godlike indeed—an arrow to the neck on May 7th
while assaulting an English stronghold; a stone cannonball to her
helmet as she climbed a scaling ladder during the recovery of Jargeau
on June 12th; a crossbow bolt to her leg on September 8th at Paris,
just before the royal order to finally withdraw. Her series of swift
victories had crushed the English. Soon, the coronation of Charles VII
took place at Reims—just where Joan of Arc had vowed it must—and
the kingdom of France was restored.*

*Eventually, Joan of Arc was captured by the Burgundians, sold to
the English, tried by an ecclesiastical court for heresy, and, at the age
of nineteen, burned at the stake. After she expired, the English raked
back the coals to expose her charred body so that no one could
claim she had escaped alive, then they burned the body twice more,
reducing it to ashes to prevent any collection of relics. Her remains
were cast into the Seine.*

*The Hundred Years' War, an inheritance feud between monarchs,
would persist for twenty-two years after Joan of Arc's death. Two
years after that, in 1456, Pope Callixtus III reviewed the decision of
the ecclesiastical court, found Joan innocent and declared her a
martyr. She was beatified in 1909, canonized in 1920, and, today, the
peasant girl stirred by an awesome moment of self-revelation remains
one of the patron saints of a country that owes its independence to
her as much as to anyone in its history.*

THE BOTTOM LINE

Figure out what makes you tick. It's the only way you'll get better at what
you do.

8

Self-Efficacy

*Believe it can be done. When you believe something can be done,
really believe, your mind will find the ways to do it. Believing a
solution paves the way to solution.*

—David Joseph Schwartz

A Little Belief Can Go a Long Way: Part One

In 1970, when the Catholic, male-dominated, conservative (even by
South American standards) country elected a self-proclaimed Marxist
as president, he ushered in sweeping socialist reforms, started daycare
centers, provided milk to schoolchildren, and nationalized the banks,
farms, and copper mines. (The country produces more copper than
any other country in the world.) But because it was the height of
the Cold War and the United States had a vested interest in the
mines, Richard Nixon was determined to see this new brand of
socialism fail. His administration used its influence to ensure that no
foreign government loaned the new president the money needed to
support his programs. Simultaneously, the CIA covertly gave the
truckers' union in the country the funds to go on strike, halting the
flow of goods throughout the nation.

The effects were profound indeed. In the first years of the
1970s, inflation in the country shot up from 35 percent to more than
500 percent. Then, on a September morning in 1973, the country's
army and its proud general seized control of the presidential palace.
The president committed suicide to avoid capture, and the military

took over the government. At the time, many people in the country were so poor and hungry that they welcomed the coup. But they couldn't have foreseen the horrors to come: Over the subsequent decade and a half, the general would toss aside human rights, murdering at least 2,200 civilians, and torturing 30,000 more.

One of those tortured was a young girl whose father, an air force general, had remained loyal to the former president and, as a result, was imprisoned and tortured for months. Like her father, the girl was an active member of the Socialist Party. She played protest music in a popular band called Las Clap Clap, covering songs by Bob Dylan and Joan Baez. A year after her father's death in 1974, the twenty-three-year-old student and her mother were arrested. The secret police took them to Villa Grimaldi, a luxurious estate with an indoor pool, marble staircases, and torture chambers. There, the girl and her mother were blindfolded and abused by guards who were later exposed as notorious for meting out rape and electric shocks among their preferred torture methods.

Despite his brutal methods, the president pulled his country out of poverty—for a time. To make it rich again, he enlisted a group of economists who had been educated at the University of Chicago. The Chicago Boys, as they were known, instituted a number of free-market policies that cut the previous leader's social programs and privatized industries, dramatically increasing trade and investment in the country. But when a recession hit in the 1980s, the government had no safety net. With the population starving, the despot allowed himself to be voted out of office in 1989 to avoid a civil war. Democracy was restored the following year and the new government kept the best of the new economic initiatives, tempering them with modest social programs. The country emerged with the fastest-growing economy in South America over the next decade.

However, the tyrant had left in his wake a legacy of fear. For more than a decade, victims of torture lived alongside their torturers in a state of quiet tension. Meanwhile, the young woman, who had survived, decided to study medicine because she saw it as a "concrete way of helping people cope with pain," a subject with which she was keenly familiar. After specializing in pediatrics, she spent much of her time volunteering with groups that helped the children of those imprisoned or missing. The experiences moved her *deeply, and she made it her goal to bridge the gap between civilians and the military. However, the odds were stacked against her. In the first place, the country's civilians were still terrified of its soldiers. In the second, she was a woman. Still, she felt in her heart that she could make a difference.*

I meet all kinds of fascinating people in the work I do. Some are shy, some are outgoing, some are strong, and some are meek. Some had great childhoods and others dysfunctional ones. I can tell you that many people have incredibly low levels of self-esteem. They are sometimes psychologically fragile and defensive when facing a perceived threat.

But nearly all extraordinary leaders have a deep faith in their own ability to do the job. They fundamentally believe that they will be successful in the task facing them and they know that they are the most capable for the role they occupy. This self-efficacy is usually not unfounded, as most of the people I assess are already successful in their own right. However, that core belief in their ability to achieve is a very powerful intangible of leadership that, almost without exception, characterizes the best of the best.

WHAT IS IT?

It may sound simple to say that one must believe one can get the job done in order to do it, but in fact, self-efficacy is a complex trait influenced by several factors. Beyond self-esteem—a global characterization of one's self-worth—self-efficacy is the underlying belief in an individual's ability to attain a set of objectives.

When Albert Bandura, Stanford University's famed psychologist, realized that children learn more from observing others in action than anything else, he changed the face of psychology forever. It all started when he put a bunch of kids in a room and asked them to play with whatever toy they wanted, in whatever way they wanted. Then, an adult came in and proceeded to savagely knock around one of the toys, a blow-up Bobo doll (you know, the kind that never fall down). When the adult left the room, it turned out that the kids inevitably took some swipes at the doll too.[1] The children Bandura observed weren't necessarily persuaded to act a certain way by being told to act that way—or even, to Bandura's surprise, by being positively reinforced for it. They were most influenced by just seeing someone else act a certain way or perform a certain task, whether that person was actually trying to model behavior or not. They mimicked adult behavior regardless of whether it was consistent with what the adults were telling them to do. This, Bandura said, is how we learn behavior.

Bandura immediately recognized the generalizability of his findings and characterized them in what he called social cognitive theory. This theory argues that we automatically observe the behavior of those around us, process it, reflect on it, and then integrate it into our own behavior. Although to the casual observer it may often seem like monkey see, monkey do, this isn't the case at all; it's monkey see, monkey process and reflect, then monkey act accordingly. Of course, all this psychological gear work occurs in the blink of an eye.

For most people, their parents provide a convenient example for understanding Bandura's theory. Think about your politics for a moment. Are they similar to your father's? For most people, they are. But this doesn't mean your dad sat you down every night and explained his political views to you. It means that, whether you were consciously absorbing it or not at the time, you heard him discussing world events, commenting on issues of the day, making pronouncements at the dinner table about this bill, that government, or whatshisname who just got elected to office and how in the world did such a *putz* ever get enough votes he'll never know. In other words, your dad, directly or indirectly, taught you politics.

And, directly or indirectly, you decided either to espouse those politics or take a contrasting view. Based, at least in part, on your agreement or disagreement with dear old Dad's views, you decided where you would eventually land on the political spectrum. That's social cognition—the reciprocal relationship between our observations, thought, and, ultimately, behaviors.

How do you relate to people and interact with them? Did you consciously sit down one day and decide you were going to behave toward others in a certain way or did it just seem to happen naturally? Social cognition argues that it wasn't natural at all, but an unconscious response to your early observations of the way your parents, primarily, and others, secondarily, behaved toward the people they came in contact with. You watched other people do their thing in the social arena, then you reflected on it, integrated it into your own behavioral mix, and finally turned it into a certain type of social style that, more likely than not, persists today.

Learning something new, then, isn't easy, since to do so we have to struggle against deeply ingrained behaviors we've adopted in response to our observations of others. Those behaviors have taken solid root over time and guide virtually everything we say and do. If you think about your own actions and behaviors in day-to-day life, you'll probably come to find they're highly predictable, as are the behaviors of others you know well. Breaking out of these patterns is, to put it mildly, an effort.

Bandura argued that learning a new behavior requires a few key ingredients. The most important of these, he believed, is self-efficacy, which he described in the following way:

> *[Self-efficacy is] people's beliefs in their capabilities to perform in ways that give them control over events that affect their lives. Efficacy beliefs form the foundation of human agency. Unless people believe that they can produce results by their actions, they have little incentive to act.[2]*

In lay terms, of course, Bandura was simply saying that to be able to do something, you need to believe you can do it. But how do you create that confidence? Does it just occur?

No, said Bandura—there are four main ways of developing it. The first and most effective way of building a strong sense of self-efficacy, he said, is through positive experience. "Successes build a belief in one's efficacy," said Bandura. "Failures undermine it." But he took this a step further: "If people have only easy successes, then they are easily discouraged by failure. Development of a resilient sense of efficacy requires experience in overcoming obstacles through perseverant effort." In other words, it isn't just experiencing success that enables one to believe in one's own capability; it's having success in the face of barriers to that success.

I have seen this notion play out countless times in the leadership arena. Many high-potentials I've encountered have all the goods to be successful leaders, but can't seem to progress at the pace they think they should. What they don't always realize, or have a difficult time hearing, is that they simply need experience.

Bandura's second source of self-efficacy is social modeling—seeing others do something—the basis of his social cognition thesis. "If people see others like themselves succeed by sustained effort," he wrote, "then they come to believe that they, too, have the capacity to do so. Observing the failures of others instills doubts about one's own ability to master similar activities." Seems almost absurdly obvious, perhaps, but take a moment to consider your own experience and think about how many times you've seen someone else achieve something and thought, "If she can do it, I can do it, too."

When I ask my clients about the leaders they've modeled themselves after, they often describe an influential figure from early in their life or career. And, inevitably, they don't just describe that person's qualities; they talk about watching them carefully to see how and why their success occurred. A colleague of mine at RHR, Joanna Starek, often employs the concepts of self-efficacy to enhance the performance of executives she works with. "Performance psychology," she says, "is about helping people break their own mental barriers around success. When I'm coaching, I try to figure out the things that are blocking the executive from being even more successful. The key is to help them see themselves as a different type of leader. It's the most exciting coaching you can do, because you see the direct link between one's psychology and his or her actual performance."

In terms of social modeling, Joanna highlights the importance of *who* the model is. She says it should be someone who is similar to the individual. The model has to be relevant, that is, someone the individual can identify with. "It can be extremely powerful," Joanna says, "to see someone similar to you learning an important skill or overcoming a barrier. Much more powerful than just seeing someone complete a task."

The third source of self-efficacy is what other people say to us—or, in social cognition terms, *social persuasions*. I don't know about you, but I've certainly never encountered anyone whose psyche is immune to the opinions of others. A few choice words from someone else can build us up just as easily as they can bring us crashing down. Words are enablers and they are deflators.

I remember my first real crush, at the age of twelve, when I was just starting to learn about how to interact with girls. I was just as awkward at it as most boys are at that age. One of my classmates had a dance party. At the party, I took a deep breath, steeled my nerves, and told the girl I liked how I felt about her. Then I waited what seemed like an eternity for her to respond. To my horror and humiliation, she told me that she felt, um, slightly different than I did, crushing my hopes.

Ultimately, I recovered, but today, a wife and three kids later, that moment still sticks out in my mind, as vivid as if it happened yesterday. It's no exaggeration to say that a single moment affected my confidence in that area for a significant period of time. A little bit of discouragement made me question my ability to ever master the task. Good thing I was only twelve (and that no man ever *really* masters the task of fully understanding women—just ask my wife).

The final source of self-efficacy, asserted Bandura, is one's physiological and emotional state. How we feel physically and emotionally guides our self-perception. If you don't believe that, ask yourself if your behavior today has anything to do with how you thought you looked or felt this morning, or whether you got a good sleep or not last night. Of course it does.

Consider what happens to most people when they have to get up in front of an audience to speak. They have butterflies, sweaty palms, shaky knees, and dry mouth. Most of us experience these symptoms, but it's the difference in how we interpret them that provides the telltale sign of our belief in ourselves. Those with low self-efficacy for the task of public speaking will see those physiological reactions as a sign of their inability to speak publicly, decreasing their self-efficacy further and creating a vicious cycle. In contrast, those with high self-efficacy for the task will feel the butterflies, regard them as just part of the experience that usually precedes a successful speech, and then take the stage brimming with confidence. It isn't the actual physiological responses themselves that influence our ability to learn or perform—it's our interpretations of them.

I've seen numerous friends, associates, colleagues, and clients become extremely emotional and highly anxious in demanding situations. Some interpret it as passion and positive energy, something that can be turned into productivity and success. You know the kind of person: When asked if they're nervous, they say, "Just nervous enough" or "Yep—lots of good nervous energy to turn into a great performance." Others view emotionality as a sign of personal weakness. The physiological responses are the same, but the way they're construed are very different, leading to highly dissimilar results.

Self-efficacy versus self-esteem

It's important to make the distinction between self-efficacy and self-esteem. The former is one's belief in their ability to succeed in a specific situation or task; the latter is one's overall sense of self-worth. Self-esteem is pervasive and enduring—it runs across everything we do and builds upon itself over time. If you are a person with high self-esteem, you have a strongly positive global sense of yourself. You have pride. You regard yourself highly. You believe you're a good person.

Self-efficacy is more targeted—it gives you the belief that you can get a specific thing done. I see it in a number of my most successful clients. Throughout their lives they have carried with them, for many different reasons, a deep sense of confidence that they are able to accomplish anything they set their mind to.

Naturally, the belief that you can accomplish a certain task, or the absence of that belief, can affect our behaviors in several ways. First, it affects our motivation. If you believe you have the ability to accomplish something, you're going to work harder to make it happen. (Or, on the other side of the coin, if you don't think you're going to pass the exam, you don't study, and, therefore, you fail the exam. This was a little piece of logic a high school classmate of mine used to cite. He didn't get far.)

Second, it affects the choices we make. Faced with a difficult choice between two tasks, which will you most likely choose? The one you're more confident in. This has implications for career decisions, investment decisions, and one's general willingness to take risks, often a critical determining factor in success. Consider that the optimal level of self-efficacy is slightly *above* one's actual ability. Yes—those who believe they can do something a little more difficult than they actually can will probably work hard enough to eventually make it happen. On the other hand, those at the low end of the self-efficacy spectrum will, in general, perceive tasks to be harder than they actually are, preventing them from ever really testing themselves.

Perhaps most crucially, our level of self-efficacy affects the way we perceive obstacles or failures and our hand in them. People with high self-efficacy attribute failures to external factors, whereas people with low self-efficacy blame themselves and their lack of ability.

I once worked in an outplacement firm where I observed this contrast all the time. It was especially noticeable in those going through the career transition process, a time which is always fraught with emotional ups and downs. One guy I came across, a pharmaceutical executive, maintained a relentlessly positive attitude about his job prospects. I touched base with him after he'd fallen short on a few interviews. He said he felt as though he'd been authentic in his presentation and that, although he may not have been a perfect interviewee, if none of these opportunities worked out, then they simply weren't meant to be, and he would find the right fit sooner or later—which he did, only a few months after our conversation.

Contrast that with a finance executive I know. Though fairly successful in her career to date, when between jobs, she is emotionally reactive and severely anxious about her chances. I watch her constantly prepare for the worst, rather than setting herself up for success. During her most recent period of transition, she went on a few interviews and, like many, struck out. The difference between her and the pharma executive was that, when I met with her, she focused entirely on what *she'd* done wrong and how it was *her* fault that she had "failed." Although she did eventually find another position, it took her many more months than the man with high self-efficacy, and she was exhausted from the emotional roller coaster she had kept herself on. Two people, same set of circumstances and events, different interpretations—and, ultimately, hugely different results. These contrasting examples help illustrate that self-efficacy is a form of expectancy—it shapes what we expect to happen. Your level of self-efficacy is like your internal probability calculator. When staring down a task, you subconsciously estimate what the probability of success is, and that internal calculation guides your subsequent behavior.

The impact of self-efficacy is very real and has been studied in a wide range of contexts, from driving to weight loss to marriage. In particular, it has been shown to be especially important in coping with health issues. Chronic pain, diabetes, cancer, obesity—in all such cases, those with high self-efficacy had better health outcomes. Nearly three decades of studies in health psychology show a clear link between self-efficacy and the ability to quit smoking. Yep, you've got it right: If you want to quit smoking, you need to believe you can. The same applies to alcoholism.

And especially to sports. Why do professional teams hire sports psychologists? To help strengthen athletes' belief that they can sink the three-pointer at the buzzer or kick the winning field goal with time expired. Self-efficacy has been shown to be one of the most relevant psychological factors in determining athletic performance, including being a discriminating factor between qualifying and non-qualifying Olympic gymnasts and successful and unsuccessful college wrestlers.

Speaking as a hockey dad, I can tell you this is relevant for me. I was particularly interested in a recent study that looked at collegiate hockey teams in the Midwest. The researchers recruited the athletic trainers on several teams to administer two self-efficacy questionnaires before each game across a sixteen-week season. The first questionnaire involved team self-efficacy; it asked players to rate their confidence in the team in the following seven areas: being able to (1) outskate, (2) outcheck, (3) force more turnovers, (4) bounce back from performing poorly, (5) score on power plays, (6) kill penalties against the opposing team, and (7) have an effective goaltender who could block a high percentage of goal attempts. The second questionnaire, concerning individual self-efficacy, asked players about their confidence in their own ability to (a) outperform their defensive opponent, (b) outperform their offensive opponent, and (c) bounce back from performing poorly. Survey scores for the team questionnaire were averaged together and compared with individual scores, and then, ultimately, team performance.

The results provided evidence that, while both types of self-efficacy—individual and team—predicted performance, team efficacy was even more important than the extent of self-efficacy felt on an individual basis. When one player believes in his own ability, he's well positioned for individual success; but when an entire team believes in itself as a unit, the opposition had better watch out.

Interestingly, the researchers also looked at whether self-efficacy can be fluid over time. They found that, indeed, the team's past performance did affect its overall sense of efficacy. It's what Bandura was saying all along. Belief in oneself affects performance. Performance affects belief in oneself, which affects performance—and so on. So, the next time you hear one of your friends say a team is gaining momentum, you can reply, "No, they're just acquiring more collective self-efficacy."

HOW DO YOU KNOW IT WHEN YOU SEE IT?

People with self-efficacy are not hard to recognize. It isn't because they walk around telling others just how fantastic they are. Self-efficacy is a highly influential trait, but a quiet one, emanating powerfully from within. Look at the people in your organization. See who exhibits the following behaviors. They're the ones who possess this crucial leadership intangible.

They have an external locus of control

In 1954, a psychologist named Julian Rotter discovered that people differ in what he called "perceived locus of control"—the extent to which they believe that they can control events that affect them. One's locus can either be internal or external. Those with a high internal locus of control believe that events result primarily from their own behaviors and actions—they'll tell you that they are in control of what happens to them. Those with a high external locus of control believe that powerful others, fate or chance, primarily determine events—the stuff that happens is basically out of their hands. This internality and externality, Rotter argued, represented two ends of a continuum, as opposed to being an either-or typology. In other words, we have a range of self-beliefs and sometimes we believe that we have more control than at other times.

We do, however, tend to naturally default to one end of the internal-external continuum. One's place on the continuum has enormous implications for his or her career. High internals, since they believe things are within their control, manage their own behavior better, are more active in seeking information to help them execute, are more interested in gathering knowledge to help them understand the situation they're in, will try harder to influence other people, and, in the end, simply work harder to achieve the goal they've set for themselves.

High externals, on the other hand, prone as they are to attribute results to outside influences, will tend to expend much less effort trying to make something happen, since they don't believe it matters much what they do anyway. They have low motivation to achieve and strong beliefs in the influence of fate, luck, and chance. High externals, since they believe outside forces are more powerful than their own efforts, show not only higher stress levels, but also a greater incidence of clinical depression.

> *Those with self-efficacy possess a strong internal locus of control. Think about the conversations you have at work. Certain people around you will be wont to say things such as, "Our ability to win is a function of execution—we do it right and we'll win" or "We control our destiny, let's do this." Then there are others who can always be heard spouting declarations like, "Our fate is in the economy's hands" or "Regulatory restrictions limit how successful we can be." We can move mountains, say people in the first group. Nothing we do is going to make a lick of difference, say people in the second. Which type of person are others going to follow?*

They want the ball

Because those with self-efficacy have a strong internal locus, they also have a strong quarterback mindset. "Give me the ball," they say, "and I'll run with it." Not only are they up for the challenge, they want to lead the charge.

In the 1991 World Series pitting the Minnesota Twins against the Atlanta Braves, the Twins entered game six down three games to two in the series. Before the game, Kirby Puckett, the five-foot-eight sparkplug and eventual Hall of Famer, went to the clubhouse, gathered his teammates, and said, "Guys, I just have one announcement to make. You guys should jump on my back tonight. I'm going to carry us."

In the first inning, Puckett hit a triple, driving home a run, and then also scored himself. In the third inning, he made one of the greatest catches in World Series history, leaping above the fence and snaring a fly ball that would have been a home run and given the Braves the lead. In the fifth inning, Puckett delivered another run for the Twins with a sacrifice fly. The Braves tied the game again, and the two teams were still tied after nine innings.

In the eleventh inning, Puckett came up again. And with two balls and one strike on him, he spotted a hanging changeup and belted it over the left-centerfield wall, ending one of the most dramatic post-season games in history and transforming the Minnesota Metrodome into instant pandemonium.

They inspire others to want the ball too

The Twins would go on to win the seventh game of the World Series by a score of one to nothing, the result of a masterful, gut-wrenching, ten-inning pitching performance by Jack Morris. In interviews after the game, Morris would say, "I said to myself, Kirby did his job. Now it's my turn." In the introduction to this chapter I talked about Albert Bandura, the famous psychologist whose theory of social cognition includes the important finding that children internalize behavior not so much by receiving instruction from others, but by seeing them do things themselves. It would appear this works on adults too. Those with self-efficacy, by demonstrating the connection between self-faith and consistent success, inspire others to adopt the same kind of belief in themselves.

They face things head on

One of the cardinal rules of powerboating is to "turn into the wake." That is, when a wake created by another craft is rolling toward your boat, you do not align your boat along its length—an instinct most people have. You turn your boat nose-first into that swell, absorb the impact, and then continue on your merry way.

Those with self-efficacy always turn directly into the wake. You never see them skirting responsibility or passing the buck. They don't exhibit fear in the face of even the greatest obstacle, because they believe it's fully up to them whether they get past it or not.

They aren't derailed by setbacks

Self-efficacy leads to natural optimism, because it simply feels good to believe that you're responsible for the outcome of your actions. Think about those you know who, after they've given something their best shot but come up short, still feel good. That feeling comes from the fact that they gave it their best. It's this type of person who is going to try just as hard next time, since they still believe in their ability to succeed. By contrast, those who believe that the outside forces of the universe are more potent than their own abilities will constantly be deflated by failure, because they attribute it to factors beyond their control. There are few things more disheartening than the belief that nothing you do matters, and there are few things more empowering than the belief that you can accomplish just about anything if you put your mind to it.

They're focused realists

It's important to remember, however, that those with strong self-efficacy don't believe any goal is automatically within their grasp or that they can conquer the world simply by closing their eyes and wishing it. It means they believe they have the specific blend of talent and ambition to achieve the particular aim of conquering the world if they only work hard enough to do it. Yes, extraordinary leaders are often optimists by nature. However, self-efficacy is not blind optimism; it's powerful self-confidence with regard to a particular task or goal.

They disdain arrogance

You know that associate of yours who's always trumpeting his latest achievement, taking credit for the team's success, or delivering messages whose not-so-subtle goal is to convince others of his talent? That's not the guy with self-efficacy. Understanding the distinction between self-*assurance* and self-*importance* is essential, because one tends to inspire people and lead to great results, while the other tends to drive people away and lead to excuses for poor results.

People with self-efficacy aren't driven to sing their own praises, because they believe that it's their own ability, not validation from others, that determines success. They are seen by others as confident but not arrogant, ambitious but not entitled. They want to work hard because they like seeing the positive results of hard work, which further reinforces their belief in the power of their own efforts.

Self-efficacy often does correlate with a high degree of confidence. But this confidence should not be confused with a sense of superiority or privilege. The confidence is internal; it is not broadcast. When I talk to self-efficacious leaders, they are always only too pleased to talk about their goals—what it will take to achieve them, the tools they have to leverage—the concrete and execution-focused initiatives. People more driven by arrogance than self-confidence will, though they probably won't realize it, be more inclined just to talk about their accomplishments, the skills they boast, and the challenges they can overcome. "Throw whatever you want at me, I'll nail it," this person might say. It's an empty comment, specific to nothing and impressive to no one. The difference between this person and the self-efficacious one is that the latter displays both confidence and humility at the same time.

They see the road ahead clearly

An internal locus of control is like a feather duster constantly sweeping away cobwebs in order to allow a clear picture of one's goals and the steps necessary to achieve them. I always find it interesting talking to leaders with strong self-efficacy when they are about to take on a new role. A major part of RHR's work concerns executive integration and transition. We support and accelerate the onboarding of leaders into their new roles, whether they are internal promotions or new hires. Our model includes several success factors that are critical to attend to during the first year of one's transition, in order to hit the ground running. Beyond these success factors, I'm also interested in the types of people who are able to transition smoothly time and again. According to my observation, self-efficacy is a major trait of these people. Those who believe in their realistic ability to get the job done are very clear about the objectives to be met, the challenges they're likely to face, and the gaps they'll need to address. They are objective and level-headed in their perspective. Their attitude isn't colored by outside influences. They are able to address the organizational landmines that inevitably arise in the early stages of a transition. To them, it's very simple: They have the goods to make it work, so it's entirely up to them whether success happens or not.

A lack of self-efficacy works against the transitioning executive. Individuals lacking assurance in their own abilities tend to get a little more "freaked out" about what they perceive to be giant challenges or daunting obstacles. They experience more self-doubt and insecurity, often leading to hesitancy in getting what they need to be successful and ultimately compromising their performance. They externalize early bumps in the road, such as organizational politics, insufficient resources, or difficult people, seeing them as insurmountable obstacles rather than leadership challenges.

In the Palm of Her Hand

Is it a surprise that Mary Jo Haddad moved from being a nurse for twenty-three years to CEO for The Hospital for Sick Children, a world-renowned health and research facility? Not to anyone who knows her. When I spoke to Mary Jo and asked her to reflect on her own leadership journey, I was struck by the force of her own self-efficacy, both as an early catalyst for her success and a sustaining quality today. "I never hesitated to take on opportunities," she said. "Doors kept opening and I kept stepping through them." It is with characteristic modesty that she describes these doors as opening on their own. It was Mary Jo's passion and self-belief that made those doors open.

I asked her where this confidence comes from. She named four things. "One—knowing who I am. Two—being able to say 'I don't know.' Three—respecting others. Four—always learning."

Then she added something else, which I believe speaks more directly to her success than anything else: "I always take seriously the opportunities that present themselves." Mary Jo has indeed seized every opportunity that has presented itself.

This lesson, she says, comes most directly from her father, a Lebanese-born butcher shop owner who somehow managed to raise and educate six kids. It was he who taught Mary Jo to "shoot for the moon," she says, because "even if you miss, you'll land among the stars." Having someone instill this kind of self-faith in her early on has had a clear, powerful impact in her life and her career. I don't think even she realizes how often she refers to traits like passion, possibility, and sheer tenacity when she speaks. And what I find most admirable about Mary Jo's leadership approach is that, despite her steadfast belief in her own abilities, she's always working to make herself better. "Greatness and talent," she says, "are really just a combination of instinct and preparedness."

I am equally impressed by the way Mary Jo consciously spreads the "can-do" feeling to others around her. She makes declarations like, "I'm very hard-working" and "I deliver," but in the same breath says things like, "I'm affiliative" and "I bring people together, rather than necessarily being the one to solve the problem." Good leaders believe in themselves, but exceptional leaders have the ability to make others believe in themselves. "At some point, I became a change agent," Mary Jo told me. "When I started in the CEO role, I arranged focus groups and asked people what it is we value here." When she was invited by the Women's Executive Network to speak about leadership, one of her first remarks was, "It's about recognizing and nurturing the potential of others."

Words like "nurturing" pepper her conversation more than that of most leaders, and it's easy to see why. When Mary Jo speaks to you, she somehow combines a soothing bedside manner with the feeling of someone you know just gets things done. You can't take the nurse out of the CEO, one might say.

And she concurs. It was Mary Jo's experiences as a nurse that ignited her enduring passion for health care. She tells the story of a premature baby named Sheldon, so tiny he weighed less than a pound and fit in the palm of her hand, as the person who more than any other taught her the importance of courage and desire. Though Sheldon never made it out of the hospital, it was his ability to fight, Mary Jo says, that made the most permanent impact on her, making her deeply compassionate and, at the same time, incredibly tough. As a result, her self-efficacy is two-pronged. She has a strong belief in her ability both to deal with people's emotions and to operate effectively in a demanding environment. In fact, the week I spoke with her, a big crisis arose at the hospital that made national headlines. Mary Jo dealt with it expertly, in a grounded, focused, and strong manner, defusing the situation.

She is able to deal with these types of situations because she never takes her eye off the ball. As the leader of a 6,000-plus staff, Mary Jo knows that success will happen only if she and everyone around her share a belief in their ability to create change. Her ultimate goal, she says, is to "create a climate that recognizes the potential for greatness." Now that's something that would make any patient, employee, or citizen proud.

HOW DO YOU GET IT?

Belief in your own task-specific competence depends on a host of factors. Obviously, one's background plays a big part—though not always in the way you might assume. You may not realize how deeply ingrained some of the early messages you heard as a child became. Whether it was positive reinforcement from your parents, a positive nod from your strict ballet teacher, or a pat on the butt from your football coach, it had an effect on you. It's part of the mental recording you play over and over again in your mind.

Yes, self-efficacy is formed by way of a highly iterative, incremental process over time. Self-efficacy follows the path of a yo-yo being played by someone walking up stairs. How many championship athletes or award-winning performers have you heard admit that they still become nervous wrecks before the big game or that they become nearly crippled by stage fright before putting a smile on for the crowd?

Every one of these accomplished people tend to say something else too: that, eventually, after the blood starts flowing or they've sung a few bars, they remember something critical—they've been in this situation before. And they've succeeded. Here are some ways to develop your own sense of self-efficacy.

Ask for help

Many people feel too proud to ask for help. Although it's easy to understand why, this is a major error in one's growth as a leader. Every extraordinary leader I've worked with seeks help. It often comes in the form of a mentor, role model, or trusted advisor. Resist the inclination to figure everything out on your own. It will only lead to you giving yourself the wrong advice.

Giving yourself advice or encouragement sometimes feels false, because (a) you don't know what base this advice is founded on and (b) you don't necessarily believe the stuff you're telling yourself about your own ability to create success. Having an advisor can really help you achieve the kind of self-efficacy that feels genuine and that you truly believe. It doesn't need to be part of a formal mentoring process; that can feel phony and it often doesn't work. Find someone whose career you'd like to emulate or who simply impresses you. Someone who is similar enough to you in terms of age and industry that you can relate to them, but more experienced than you in areas that you find particularly challenging. Ask the person if he'd mind grabbing lunch or dinner with you. Tell him you've always been impressed by him and would love to pick his brain. Odds are, he will feel flattered and gladly accept, even if he may not be able to schedule it in for a few months. That's okay—what harm has really been caused? Challenge your own self-assumptions here about the cost of being rejected. It's probably a great deal less than you realize and there is a good chance that you will not be rejected. The key is to spend time with someone you look up to and to feed off of his excellence. Build confidence through osmosis. Extraordinary leadership is contagious and you need to get the bug. Recall Bandura's social cognition theory again: It isn't being told that you're great that leads to a sense of personal potency, it's seeing evidence of other people using their skills to do great things that makes you realize you can do it too.

On a simpler level, a mentor can be objective about your abilities and help you see them for what they are. Someone who observes you closely and knows you well can help you not just identify your true strengths and weaknesses, but also maximize the former and mitigate the latter.

Place your own stamp

At RHR, we once encountered a particularly memorable CEO candidate. When my colleague Guy Beaudin, the firm's VP of International Operations, first met with this well-regarded leader, he was in a 2-IC (second in command) role at a large consumer goods company. Though he knew he was being groomed to take over the top spot when the current leader vacated it, he didn't believe he had the skill to succeed in the role, this individual said. Guy was taken aback. How could someone with such experience, such potential for greatness, not believe in his own ability to succeed?

The answer is this: It's more common than you think. One's self-assurance, even if it has been historically strong, may be overwhelmed by the feeling of having big shoes to fill, of having to match a great track record, of having to replace a beloved figure, or of having to bring everyone onside when they were quite happy with the way things were. We can often observe this phenomenon with star high school athletes who go on to university to discover that, suddenly, there are hundreds of people with abilities that match or, in many cases, surpass theirs. This revelation isn't always easy to process. It requires that they swallow hard and accept a serious dose of reality.

And it causes them, hopefully, to realize that they are special in their own unique ways. When the executive I referred to above finally did get tapped for the CEO position, Guy encouraged him not to try to be version two of the previous leader, but instead to develop his own personal style, his own distinct point of view, and his own organizational philosophy. As he undertook this exercise, he began to see his own particular strengths and talents in a new light. And he slowly came to decide that maybe, just maybe, there was a reason they wanted him for the role. Yes, he probably could handle it quite well after all. And he did.

Visualize success

An extensive body of research has shown that visualizing—literally picturing yourself achieving a certain goal—corresponds to higher levels of success. By envisioning ourselves having achieved a certain goal, we are then unconsciously forced to think about which of our abilities must have been responsible for that achievement, which, in turn, produces in us the growing belief that, hey, maybe we really can do it. Athletes go through extensive training in visualization to enhance their self-efficacy. Next time you are watching an individual sports event like swimming, golf, diving, ski jumping, or track and field, take a moment to observe the athletes before the race, shot, dive, or whatever. Watch the mental rehearsal they do—they are actually visualizing success in their minds. Not only are they seeing themselves perform successfully, but they are mentally experiencing the sights, sounds, and smells of what that victory will be like.

This has been shown to have a powerful effect. For example, most Olympic athletes work with sports psychologists to enhance their performance through visualization. Perhaps one of the most memorable and dramatic Olympic moments in modern history happened back in 1988, when U.S. diver Greg Louganis hit his head on the springboard doing a reverse two-and-a-half pike, producing a large gash on his head. Remarkably, he was able to come back the next day, conquer his fear of the springboard, and, ultimately, win the gold medal. He later attributed his ability to bounce back from disaster to visualization. He was able to disregard distraction, focus, and then mentally rehearse—and execute—the perfect dive.

Recognize your own self-defeating patterns

Even Superman has kryptonite. Those with strong self-efficacy also have particular triggers that serve, on occasion, to disrupt their self-assurance and ability to succeed. Learn what derails you. What situations cause you to question yourself? What scripts do you play in your head that work against you? You must understand these self-defeating patterns of behavior in order to re-record those scripts and create a more positive picture of your ability to succeed.

Give yourself a good swift kick in the posterior

Role models, personal stamps, visualization, and recognition of your own personal derailers aside, sometimes you just have to tell yourself to get off your butt, jump in with both feet, and let the chips fall where they may. If you don't possess strong self-efficacy, and you don't know that you don't, then thinking about whether you can accomplish a certain task may only cause you to worry that you can't. On the other hand, forcing yourself to take personal risks and just *try* without thinking about whether you're likely to succeed enables opportunities for success. Hockey great Wayne Gretzky famously said, "I miss 100 percent of the shots I don't take." By applying your skills and talents instead of focusing on your fears, you realize how good you really are. Or, if I may quote Yoda: "Do, or do not. There is no try."

Be slightly over-optimistic about your abilities

It is important to have a realistic perspective on your strengths and limitations. You can start by reviewing previous performance appraisals or 360-degree feedback reports, or even asking people directly for their feedback on your capabilities. Make sure to really listen to what they're telling you—not just the good, but the bad too. Think about objective indicators of success. How would you *know* that you're good at something? What markers tell you so? (Have you been promoted quickly through the ranks? Do you have the most sales of any of your peers?) Once you have an accurate read, know that you are capable of at least one order of magnitude better than you currently believe you are. The optimal level of self-confidence is slightly above one's actual capabilities. You must believe that. It's okay to have a slightly inflated sense of your abilities.

However, don't fall into the trap of believing you are dramatically better than you really are. You will get arrogant and cocky, and those around you will find you lacking in self-awareness. Instead, stretch your current self-efficacy slightly beyond what it should be, and work your butt off to meet the corresponding objectives.

WHY IT MATTERS

Leaders lacking self-efficacy tend to make safe decisions, rather than taking well-considered risks. Instead of planting a flag and leading by example, they adopt a CYA approach, making no waves and inspiring no followers. Extraordinary leaders put risk in context with their abilities. They know their boundaries of competence and masterfully exploit them. By doing so, they accomplish more than anyone expects of them and motivate others to do the same.

A Little Belief Can Go a Long Way: Part Two

The young woman went back to school to study military strategy and graduated with the highest honors. Then she joined the army's commander-in-chief to issue a proclamation of nunca más—never again. Together, the pair declared that the days of military dictatorship in the country were over. At the same time, she encouraged public trials for the perpetrators of crimes against humanity during the general's regime. "I'm a doctor, so allow me to use a medical analogy to explain the problem," she said. "Only cleaned wounds can heal, otherwise they'll keep opening up again, and will likely become infected and begin to fester. It's clear to me that the truth must be brought to light." She knew these were the kind of words that had gotten others assassinated, but the goal she had set for herself had become too important to keep silent, and her faith that she could spur change too strong.

By the time the 2006 election arrived, Michelle Bachelet had become a beloved symbol of hope and change in Chile. Choruses of The Beatles' "Michelle" could be heard at her rallies. Her warmth and compassion won over skeptics. The fact that she was a single mother of three made her popular with struggling families. And then, on election day, she became the first female president in the country's history. She had imbued Chileans with the same belief she herself had always maintained: the belief that things don't have to stay the same if only we're willing to do something about it.

THE BOTTOM LINE

Believe you can do more than you have the ability to do, and you will.

9

Fortitude

Guts are a combination of confidence, courage, conviction,
strength of character, stick–to–itiveness, pugnaciousness,
backbone and intestinal fortitude. They are mandatory for
anyone who wants to get to and stay at the top.

—D.A. Benton

The Long Struggle: Part One

His roots stretched back to a cadet branch of the Thembu dynasty,
whose people his paternal great-grandfather had ruled as king. One
of the king's sons was given a first name that would eventually
become the boy's own surname, but because he was the product of
one of the king's wives from the Ixhiba clan, the so-called "Left-Hand
House," the descendants of his particular branch were not eligible to
succeed to the throne.

Obstacles seemed to be almost part of the boy's genetic make-
up. His father, Gadla Henry Mphakanyiswa, served as chief of the
town of Mvezo, but after alienating the colonial authorities, he was
deprived of his position. His mother, Nosekeni Fanny, was a daughter
of Nkedama, of the Mpemvu Xhosa clan, the dynastic "Right-Hand
House"—but boys will be boys: his given name, Rolihlahla, meant "to
pull a branch off a tree"—or, more colloquially, "troublemaker."

But the boy defied expectations, becoming the first member
of his family to attend school. There his teacher, Miss Mdingane,
assigned him an English name, which he would use for the rest of

his life. When the boy was nine, his father died of tuberculosis and the regent, Jongintaba, became his guardian. He was enrolled in a Wesleyan mission school located next to the regent's palace. Following Thembu custom, he was initiated at age sixteen and attended Clarkebury Boarding Institute. He showed promise, completing his Junior Certificate in two years instead of the usual three. Designated to inherit his father's position as a privy councilor, in 1937 the boy, now a young man, moved to Healdtown, the Wesleyan college in Fort Beaufort, which most Thembu royalty attended.

His physical restlessness he expressed in boxing and running; his intellectual curiosity led him to the pursuit of political justice and personal freedom. While studying for his Bachelor of Arts at Fort Hare University, he joined in a Students' Representative Council boycott against university policies. The penalty was an order to leave. Later, after he and the regent's son both fled to Johannesburg to escape the marriages that had been arranged for them, the young man was fired from his new job as a guard at a mine when his employer learned that he was the regent's runaway ward.

Then, for at least a brief period, trouble took a temporary leave from his life. He articled at a Johannesburg law firm, completed his BA degree at the University of South Africa via correspondence, and began law studies at the University of Witwatersrand.

But a person born political never becomes less political, only more. The 1948 election victory of the Afrikaner-dominated National Party, which supported the apartheid policy of racial segregation, prompted the aspiring lawyer to dive actively into affairs of state in opposition of apartheid and everything it stood for. While maintaining a law partnership providing free or low-cost counsel to many blacks who lacked representation, he found time to help lead the African National Congress's (ANC) 1952 Defiance Campaign and the 1955 Congress of the People, whose adoption of the Freedom Charter provided the fundamental basis of the anti-apartheid cause. He and 150 others were arrested in December 1956 and charged with treason, leading to a trial lasting five years, at the end of which all defendants received acquittals.

Free again to pursue his political ideas, in 1961 the man, now mature, co-founded and assumed the leadership mantle of the ANC's armed wing, Umkhonto we Sizwe (meaning "Spear of the Nation" and abbreviated as "MK"). Committed to methods of non-violent resistance, he coordinated sabotage campaigns against military and government targets, making plans for a possible guerrilla war should the sabotage fail to end apartheid. His goals were to bomb symbols of apartheid, places such as passport offices and native magistrates courts, while ensuring that no one would be hurt or killed. The move to armed struggle, he told his partners, would be a last resort. Non-violent protest was the intended method, but ending years of repression and violence by the state was, at whatever cost, the ultimate goal.

After living on the run for seventeen months, the man, now a political target, was caught and imprisoned in Johannesburg Fort following a tip to security police in South Africa by the CIA. Charged with leading workers to strike and leaving the country illegally, he was sentenced to five years in prison.

Soon after, when prominent ANC leaders were arrested and charged with the capital crime of violent sabotage, the man revealed all, explaining that, after using peaceful means to resist apartheid for years, the ANC had only witnessed the country's situation become worse, leaving as their only choice acts of sabotage or outright submission. "During my lifetime," he said, "I have dedicated myself to the struggle of the African people. I have fought against white domination, and I have fought against black domination. I have cherished the ideal of a democratic and free society in which all persons live together in harmony and with equal opportunities. It is an ideal which I hope to live for and to achieve. But if need be, it is an ideal for which I am prepared to die."

The man, along with his compatriots, escaped the gallows, but they were sentenced to life imprisonment. With them safely out of the way, apartheid was allowed to prevail, unhindered. He spent the next eighteen years on Robben Island, a tiny oval-shaped mass just off the coast near Cape Town that had previously been used as a leper colony and animal quarantine station.

The man worked, suffered, and endured. When not performing hard labor in a lime quarry, he took a correspondence course with the University of London, eventually obtaining a Bachelor of Laws degree. Meanwhile, his incarceration became a lightning rod of controversy. Without his knowing it, his reputation outside the prison walls grew, among both those who admired him and those who resented his influence. A plot devised by the country's elite to rescue him from Robben Island only so they could shoot him during recapture was foiled by British Intelligence. Local and international pressure mounted on the government to release him. He became known as the most significant black leader in South Africa.

And, in 1982, possibly to prevent his swaying the new generation of young black activists on the island, the man was transferred, leaving Robben Island for Pollsmoor Prison, a maximum-security facility housing the country's most dangerous criminals and gangsters. There he would remain for another six years. Halfway into his stay at Pollsmoor, he was offered a deal by the country's president: conditional release in exchange for his group's total renunciation of armed struggle. He spurned the offer, releasing a statement that read, "What freedom am I being offered while the organization of the people remains banned? Only free men can negotiate. A prisoner cannot enter into contracts." While the man continued to endure his circumstances—including prostate surgery in 1985—the government continued its attempts to cajole him, arranging meeting after meeting, offering proposition after proposition.

In 1988, he was transferred again, to Victor Verster Prison, a low-security prison near Paarl in the Western Cape. As outside pressure on the government escalated, restrictions on the man were lifted. The following year, when the country's president suffered a stroke and was replaced, the new head, Frederik Willem de Klerk, reversed the ban on the ANC and other anti-apartheid bodies, and announced that the man—now 71 years old—would be, at long last, granted his release. On February 11, 1990, the world watched as he re-entered society with a smile on his face.

What the world didn't know was what might lie behind the man's smile. Though publicly he showed an ambassadorial face, what might he be planning? Would he incite riots, re-organize for sabotage, plot to take down leaders of the apartheid rules, both explicit and tacit, that remained? After all, the man had been imprisoned for nearly three decades. You could hardly have blamed him for being angry.

Few leaders achieve success by having things handed to them. In the hundreds of executives that I have assessed, I have observed an interesting phenomenon: Most extraordinary leaders have overcome at least one major trauma or setback in their lives. In many ways, this challenge, as well as the way they beat it and the lessons they derived from the experience, still define their leadership style and continue to inform the decisions they make.

This resilience, this strength of character, is the basic element in a critical leadership intangible: fortitude. Grit, guts, determination, and endurance—however you might choose to define fortitude—is tremendously powerful as a leadership determinant. Leaders with fortitude are known by everyone around them to be determined when the going gets tough, and they are the people others are happy to turn to when a crisis arises. Let's talk about what it means to possess fortitude, how this trait makes itself apparent in leadership situations and why, even if you haven't had to deal with anything particularly traumatic in your life, you can still be seen as someone with the guts and spirit to rally others toward a common goal.

WHAT IS IT?

In 1962, General Douglas MacArthur made a historic speech to cadets at the U.S. Military Academy in accepting the Sylvanus Thayer Award. His address was based on the Academy's motto: *Duty, Honor, Country*. Among the inspiring words he uttered that day were the following:

> *Duty, honor, country: Those three hallowed words reverently dictate what you ought to be, what you can be, what you will be. They are your rallying point to build courage when courage seems to fail, to regain faith when there seems to be little cause for faith, to create hope when hope becomes forlorn.*
>
> *Unhappily, I possess neither that eloquence of diction, that poetry of imagination, nor that brilliance of metaphor to tell you all that they mean. . . . But these are some of the things they do. They build your basic character. They mold you for your future roles as the custodians of the nation's defense. They make you strong enough to know when you are weak, and brave enough to face yourself when you are afraid.*
>
> *They teach you to be proud and unbending in honest failure, but humble and gentle in success; not to substitute words for actions, not to seek the path of comfort, but to face the stress and spur of difficulty and challenge; to learn to stand up in the storm, but to have compassion on those who fall; to master yourself before you seek to master others; to have a heart that is clean, a goal that is high; to learn to laugh, yet never forget how to weep; to reach into the future, yet never neglect the past; to be serious, yet never*

to take yourself too seriously; to be modest so that you will remember the simplicity of true greatness, the open mind of true wisdom, the meekness of true strength.

They give you a temperate will, a quality of the imagination, a vigor of the emotions, a freshness of the deep springs of life, a temperamental predominance of courage over timidity, of an appetite for adventure over love of ease. They create in your heart the sense of wonder, the unfailing hope of what next, and joy and inspiration of life. They teach you in this way to be an officer and a gentleman.[1]

The Thayer Award is given to American citizens who exemplify the values and ideals wrapped up in those three words. Other recipients of this award include such prominent leaders as Dwight D. Eisenhower, Neil Armstrong, David Packard, Barry Goldwater, Henry Kissinger, Ronald Reagan, Colin Powell, Sandra Day O'Connor, and Ross Perot. These extraordinary leaders have something in common beyond the award. All of them have, throughout their lives, shown extraordinary fortitude. They have "strength of character"; they are "people of substance." Many words and phrases have been used to portray fortitude and its significance in executive leadership over time, yet it remains an intangible, elusive to capture.

* * *

I point to the great Greek philosopher Plato to illuminate the underlying nature of fortitude. Plato described four fundamental virtues: courage, justice, temperance, and wisdom. I believe these are the basic muscles that constitute one's strength of character. Let's delve into each of them in more detail.

Courage is probably the aspect most people think of first when they envision fortitude. To have fortitude means to be hardy and persistent, to stand up in the face of obstacles. Courage doesn't necessarily come from being fearless. I know plenty of people who are seldom scared, though I wouldn't describe them as courageous. Courage comes from standing up against something—defiance despite the odds.

There is courage in battle. There is courage against illness. Whatever the source of the challenge, the outcome is influenced by strength of character. I mentioned the interesting and important pattern I've observed in my work with senior leaders: that there are a disproportionate number of them who have faced, and overcome, some trauma or crisis. They have stood tough in the face of cancer, family deaths, abuse, alcoholism, and a long list of other personal tragedies—and, despite the odds, have bounced back. Mustering up the courage to deal with tragedy, it would seem, is a proximal accelerator of leadership effectiveness.

Why is this so? Whatever the industry, whatever the business model, there will be challenges. Those with the courage to stand strong in the face of such challenges are, undoubtedly, better leaders. We look to them as sources of strength during these times.

Courage also means audacity. As a leader, you need to be willing to do more than others, to think beyond normal thinking, to optimistically focus on future success. Of course, the most recent example of this is Barack Obama's ascension to the presidency. Early in his campaign, he wrote the book *Audacity of Hope*. It showed his courage to think of overcoming the insurmountable, to dream of a better tomorrow. Such is the making of a leader with fortitude.

The second of Plato's virtues is justice. By this he meant knowing, and doing, the right thing. He meant caring for those who are less fortunate and being egalitarian. He meant being lawful and fair. Beyond that, he also meant other aspects of "doing the right thing," like not gossiping, not being unethical, and not winning at the expense of others. He meant helping others and being an honorable member of society.

Justice is as fundamental to fortitude as courage is. A few years ago, I worked with a small, but rapidly growing, manufacturing company headquartered in a quiet town on the U.S. eastern seaboard. The company had been spun off from a much larger company. A few years earlier, the CEO and a small team had gotten together, raised some capital, and undertaken a management buyout of the division they were in, creating the new organization.

Along with a colleague, I met the company's senior team fairly early in its evolution. Our assessment process included both an in-depth conversation about personal histories and a small battery of psychometric tests.

What I found in assessing the CEO was that he had immense strength of character. He was a solid guy with extraordinarily strong values. He lived by them. He had already walked away from doing a huge deal with someone whose values he questioned. He wouldn't do business with anyone he didn't feel comfortable with. He was the kind of leader who inspires trust and faith. I got the very strong sense that he would go to bat for his people—and, in fact, that's exactly what he did. When push came to shove a year later and the company could have sold out and the management team could have made a small fortune, the CEO stopped the deal because he found out that the acquirers would have dismissed two members of his team after the deal was completed. He was an extremely equitable leader, with a firm belief that everyone ought to contribute equally and share accordingly in the profits. His was a true "we're in this together" culture, one in which it was made clear to everyone that fairness—justice—was paramount. Seems like he had the right idea: That small team ended up being a leading company in its space, amassing huge profits for shareholders, and the original team, now quite flush, is still intact and energized for the next phase of growth. I attribute a great deal of the company's success to the CEO's strength of character and sense of justice.

Another characteristic of this CEO was his controlled demeanor. He was gritty and passionate, but in a mild-mannered, unpretentious way. He took in information, processed it, and responded in a resolute, even-keeled manner. I would find it very surprising if anyone could throw him off his game. Not that he was robotic; he was just in control. This describes the third of Plato's virtues, temperance. By this he meant moderation, in both the way one presents oneself and the life one leads.

People with fortitude rarely get seduced by temptation, because they don't believe in excess. They believe in doing things rationally and conservatively. You don't often see such leaders with flashy cars (although I've known a few auto enthusiasts who allow themselves to indulge in only this area) or other personal effects that deliberately call attention to them.

A well-known example of temperance is Warren Buffett, one of the most successful investors in history. One of the world's richest individuals, his personal net worth is somewhere between $40 billion and $60 billion. Yet at the same time, he lives a modest lifestyle. In 2008, Buffett took home a salary of $175,000. He still lives in the same house in Omaha that he bought in 1958 for $31,000. There are rumors that he doesn't carry a cell phone, doesn't have a computer at his desk, and drives his own car. Compared to his net worth, his lifestyle is beyond moderate—it is downright frugal.

(continued)

Buffett is also well known for his assertion that he will not pass down his wealth to his children. He doesn't believe in "dynastic wealth," and once told TV host Charlie Rose, "I want to give my kids just enough so that they would feel that they could do anything, but not so much that they would feel like doing nothing." He is a major philanthropist, single-handedly making the largest donation ever, Berkshire Hathaway shares valued at over $30 billion, to the Bill & Melinda Gates Foundation. This is clearly a man of fortitude.

The final of Plato's virtues is wisdom. The topic of executive wisdom is dealt with in much more detail in Chapter 1, which is dedicated to that subject. However, the main point here is that people who possess fortitude utilize their virtues to make good decisions. They have good judgment about business and about people. They use their experiences, courage, sense of justice, and wealth to make good decisions, and that's why they are so successful.

Wisdom is, in part, an artifact of experience, especially when that experience challenges one's outlook on life. The link between fortitude and wisdom is painfully demonstrated when young people get sick. Think for a moment about Ryan White, the young boy from Indiana who was a hemophiliac and, ultimately, died of AIDS in 1990 at the age of eighteen, due to a contaminated blood treatment. The unimaginable challenge of living with a fatal disease in a world that, at the time, didn't understand (and greatly feared) AIDS required enormous amounts of courage and fortitude. Expelled from his school, shunned by society, and given six months to live, White bravely set out to change how people viewed the disease. He battled his own school district to get reinstated into his home school, despite the protest from his entire town. For six years he spoke wherever he could on his illness and the misconceptions associated with it. He took his message to a national stage, appearing on television and confronting his fears. It is nearly impossible to comprehend the bravery this took during his final years. The experiences he had during his brief life generated a lifetime of collective wisdom for the rest of us. His words inspired a generation of Americans to be more tolerant and courageous in the battle against AIDS. Ryan's hurdles became our lessons. Ultimately, true wisdom emerges through challenge.

> *Let me point out an important distinction: the difference between fortitude and will, another of the intangibles discussed in the book. While the two may come from similar places, they mean very different things. Will is the ability to get things done or make things happen. Through determination, force of spirit, forward thinking, and action, people with will are able to effect change. Will is the reason that people not only think great things, but do them.*
>
> *Fortitude, as we've been discussing, is strength of character. It refers to the internal resources necessary to tackle challenges and learn from them. It is honor, it has to do with principles, it means doing what's right. It is courage, justice, temperance, and wisdom. It is the ability to endure a trial, face a test, invite a challenge, and come out the other side a better, stronger leader.*

HOW DO YOU KNOW IT WHEN YOU SEE IT?

Ask most people what fortitude means to them and they'll say something along the lines of "toughness." People with fortitude have rhino skin; they'll say they just let things bounce off them as they forge indomitably ahead. They're tough nuts, tough cookies, tough customers.

Or, perhaps, they'll talk about the resilience people with fortitude show in the face of challenge or failure. They fall off the horse and get right back on. Or they stare that horse in the eyes and let 'im know who's boss. Nothing stops them. They press on no matter what happens.

These and other descriptions do indeed describe people with fortitude, but, just as Plato has led us to consider, this is an intangible that we would not do proper justice to by describing it merely as toughness or resilience. And the best way to uncover fortitude's layers is to observe those who do exhibit the trait. Then we can see the different ways it manifests itself and the different attributes that show up in their day-to-day behavior.

They test themselves

Leaders with fortitude don't rest on their laurels—ever. They constantly seek new avenues, new challenges, and new pursuits as a way of consciously building resilience and avoiding complacency. They may instinctively possess fortitude, but they also actively seek to develop it to the highest limit possible.

A high school teacher of mine used to give pairs of students a topic to debate and then ask one of the students to adopt a position he knew was untenable. The purpose of this exercise wasn't to win the debate; it was to teach us to remain strong and focused even when the odds were stacked against us.

They show conviction in their actions

If I were to ask you to picture someone who serves as a good example of fortitude and someone who isn't such a good example, odds are the first person would be the kind who makes strong, clear decisions and second-guesses herself rarely, if at all, while the second person might be characterized by wishy-washiness, fence-sitting, and weakness when they do act. Leaders with fortitude act firmly and resolutely. They always display powerful faith in what they're doing and they give others good reason to do the same.

They take responsibility

If you have fortitude, you aren't just willing to steer the ship into dangerous waters, you're willing to take responsibility for hitting the occasional iceberg. These kinds of leaders are successful not because they always make the right decisions—no one has a perfect score in that regard—but because they accept the possibility of rejection or failure and never pass the buck. They have the strength and character to assume accountability for their actions. When things go wrong, they'll say things went wrong and will search for the reasons why. They won't act defensively.

Consider a scenario in which a VP approves a substantial initiative entailing a big investment for the company and the initiative fails miserably, costing the company huge dollars and resources. One type of VP passes blame to the senior manager who suggested the initiative or looks for another scapegoat, then he has his communications director draft a memo intended to divert the staff's attention to something else. The other type of VP calls a staff meeting, explains the details of the failed initiative, the original reasons for giving it the thumbs-up, the implications, steps that will need to be taken to overcome the setback, and, finally, makes it very clear that it was his decision to give the initiative the green light. Which leader would you say has fortitude?

They go against the grain

In the late 1990s, electronics retailer Best Buy made a decision to go beyond its domestic business in the U.S. market and grow internationally. They saw the first opportunity in Canada, where the market was relatively fragmented with only one dominant player, Future Shop. Best Buy's original plan was to set up its own stores in various Canadian cities to compete directly against Future Shop. They intended to start by opening a few stores in Toronto in 2003 and then follow a three-year expansion program that would lead to about fifteen more store launches in various cities throughout the country. At the same time, Future Shop was planning its own defensive strategy, with the objective of increasing its store count to around 120 over the subsequent four years.

In early 2001, the founders of Best Buy and Future Shop met and decided that they could, ultimately, be more successful if they teamed up, rather than competing against each other. Soon thereafter, Best Buy agreed to purchase Future Shop for $560 million.

The most surprising move came next. After the purchase, Best Buy's management made the unorthodox decision to adopt a dual-brand strategy. They would keep the Future Shop brand and add Best Buy as a second brand into the market. Such a strategy might seem strange, if not downright foolish: One of the main benefits of an acquisition is the ability to generate efficiencies under one banner. Two brands means, obviously, double the costs. With both brands under the same management, marketing dollars would be split in half. Another risk of a dual-brand strategy is the cannibalization of both brands and blurring of their identities in the eyes of customers.

Despite these risks, both management teams felt strongly about the opportunity. Ex-CFO of Best Buy International, John Noble, said the following: "There were four reasons why Best Buy veered towards a dual-branding strategy in Canada. First, the Canadian consumer electronics [CE] market was fragmented with the leader, Future Shop, having only about a 15 percent share. We felt there was room for a second brand. Given that most retail sectors in the U.S. had at least two major players—for example, Home Depot/Lowe's and Staples/Office Depot—we felt that a second major retailer in CE in Canada would be in order. Second, Best Buy had already signed, before perceiving Future Shop as a potential target for acquisition, about eight real estate leases as part of its original greenfield approach. We were committed to those locations. Third, there were operational factors. Conversion of Future Shop stores into Best Buy stores would take a while, particularly in terms of store redesigns and staff transition. There would be a period of time when the two brands had to be managed independently. But, the most important reason was the recognition that Future Shop was a well-established brand, with over 95 percent unaided brand awareness among Canadians. Replacing such a hugely successful brand with Best Buy, which was unknown in Canada, seemed counterintuitive."[2]

Not everyone agreed. Even Best Buy founder, Dick Schultze, was quoted as saying of the dual-brand strategy, "I'm not saying that it can't be done. I'm saying that it has never been done."

Despite the unprecedented move, the strategy was pursued. At the head of the new path was Kevin Layden, a Future Shop executive tapped to lead Best Buy Canada post-acquisition. Widely lauded as the man who spearheaded the dual-brand strategy, Layden and others alongside him had to possess extraordinary fortitude to pull off what they did. As a previous Future Shop employee, he had to persuade his new owners to keep his brand alive. Not an easy feat, to say the least. "Not too many companies would agree to do what we did to begin with," Layden said before moving on to become COO of Best Buy International. (He left the company in 2008.) "What kind of company buys another company, then leaves the existing management team in charge and then says, 'Go ahead and open up our brand and keep your existing company and experiment with two brands?'"

That's exactly what they did, and the strategy paid off in spades. The combined market share of Best Buy/Future Shop stands at around 40 percent, light years ahead of the 17 percent Future Shop held prior to the deal. Both the customer and employee experiences are very different at each brand, thereby representing different value propositions. Consumers appreciate having choices in where they shop, and most Canadians can tell you which of the two brands they prefer. Hindsight tells us that this move also probably kept Circuit City from entering the Canadian marketplace and taking a bite out of the CE pie. All in all, it was a great business decision, executed by a small group of people who showed great fortitude and went against conventional wisdom to achieve phenomenal success.

They don't wilt in the face of bad news

As discussed in the introduction to this chapter, most people will probably describe fortitude in exactly this way. People who display this trait take on the biggest obstacles and find a way to make them positive, or at least productive.

They're people who "keep a stiff upper lip," they're "fighters" and "battlers," they "don't know the meaning of the word quit." Adversity and leadership go hand-in-hand. Reaching a certain level of leadership carries with it the inevitability of taking frequent risks and experiencing regular failures. The leader with fortitude sees the "failure" as a mere stumbling block and continues her forward motion, while taking steps to avoid the same trip-up next time.

They enforce justice within the organization

There's an easy way to identify someone with true leadership fortitude: They stand up not only for themselves and the things they believe in, but also for others in the organization and for the organization's goals, values, and ideals. From these kinds of leaders, strength and pride become contagious. They are the kinds of leaders whose organizations become greater than the sum of their individual parts, because the individuals within the organization exude a collective force and spirit. You see leaders of this type going to bat for others all the time. They tend to spend more energy defending the virtues of the organization than broadcasting their own achievements. Their fortitude is taken up by others, resulting in robust companies that move ahead constantly, often through stormy waters.

They have staying power

Though a difficult intangible to capture easily, fortitude often shows up in an individual's track record as a history of rolling with the punches. Most top leaders, as I said earlier, have been challenged to overcome several hurdles while remaining focused on the goal ahead. I like to call this "leadership stamina." Real leadership fortitude enables those at the top to keep their footing no matter what kind of obstacle arises. Those I've observed as having the greatest fortitude have also exhibited a remarkable ability to "keep their eyes on the prize," even when facing arduous challenges—very often, more than once.

Big Brother

Some people are born with the kind of fortitude that makes them great leaders; others have it thrust upon them. For Todd Soller, today the chief information officer of Best Buy US, it was the latter. Todd was thirteen when his father died. When his mother had to go back to work, he was forced into a new and unfamiliar role: that of caregiver to his two younger siblings. Todd learned responsibility—fast.

Maybe to say he "learned" responsibility isn't accurate—it was burned into him. When I spoke to Todd about leadership, the theme of responsibility came up over and over, revealing itself as nearly a compulsion. "It's hard for me not to take responsibility for things," he says. Today, as the person accountable for keeping Best Buy's systems up and running, Todd carries a huge weight on his shoulders, and he seems happy to do it. During the holiday period, for instance, his mandate is to ensure that not a single machine in any store fails. For a company like Best Buy, the position of CIO is undeniably crucial, and there's a reason why Todd is in that role. He's a rock. In a crisis, he's the guy you'd want in your corner. He exudes strength and courage. And you don't have to know him long to know he's the type who will do the right thing in good times or bad.

In particular, it was Todd's relationship with his little brother Brian that molded his character. Brian was eight when their dad passed away, and it fell to Todd—or, rather, he felt it was his duty—to do the things a father would do. When Todd went away to school in Wisconsin, for example, he would regularly travel the three hours back and forth home to watch Brian's baseball, basketball, and football games so he would have someone there to cheer him on. Todd himself played on baseball and basketball teams, typically as captain—"not because of my physical skills," he says, "but because I worked harder than others."

Todd also became involved in the Boys & Girls Clubs of America early in life—at first, he says, "just to stay busy and keep my mind off things." But through his involvement inspiring and enabling young people, he found real meaning and purpose. At seventeen, he was mentoring other kids, taking them on trips, and teaching them important life lessons. Years later, Todd is still respected in this organization.

The first person in his family to attend college, Todd went to business school at the University of Wisconsin–Whitewater. He paid for it entirely himself. That pattern of self-reliance remained consistent when he entered the workforce, starting with Accenture. There, the same acceleration that had happened to him personally happened to him professionally. He was thrown into challenging situations, situations for which resilience and maturity were required in equal measure.

Again, he had to learn what he was made of, with little time to think about what that meant.

Soon after Todd left Accenture for Best Buy, the company made the mammoth decision to outsource its entire IT function—to Accenture. Though there were many others with more seniority than him, Todd was enlisted by the then-CIO to join a small team whose responsibility it would be to decide the fate of the 800 or so people affected by this decision. It doesn't surprise me that he was chosen for so important a duty. The CIO saw in Todd the same thing that I see in him—unmistakable strength of character. Todd himself didn't know whether he would be outsourced. And, faced with deciding the fates of so many people, he didn't really care. "When my wife asked what was going to happen to me, to us, I reassured her we'd be fine, and rather than direct my energies toward addressing my own fate, I had to focus instead on whether all those other people were going to be taken care of," he says. Thanks to Todd and his team, those people were taken care of, each of them in the best way possible.

Todd is the earliest worker I've ever encountered, routinely arriving at the office at 5:00 a.m. or 5:30 a.m. No, that isn't a typo. I've had meetings with him at 6:00 a.m. Why is he like this? It's simple, I think. He's driven to be the guy who's there to deal with stuff when it happens. The guy you can count on.

HOW DO YOU GET IT?

Fortitude comes from many sources. As with wisdom, experience is a necessary ingredient in developing one's strength of character. You can wait for those experiences to shape your leadership or you can play an active role in building it. Here are some methods for doing so.

List the things you've overcome

This may seem like a sophomoric exercise. It isn't. Most people already probably have more fortitude than they realize and they can help bring it to the surface by literally writing about the impediments they've conquered in the past. It can be big stuff or little stuff—it doesn't matter.

This activity can take any form you like. You could write a few hundred words about the three biggest things you've ever had to overcome in your life, including the details of how you got through them and what you learned when you came out the other side. You can jot down bullet points about the experiences that have struck you as your biggest tests and trials, explaining why, and what you had to do to power through and press on. You can privately solicit input from those closest to you, asking them what they've observed to be the biggest obstacles you've faced and/or risen above. No matter how you conduct the exercise, its purpose is the same: It enables you to recognize your own ability to endure, something that remains hidden from a lot of people until they actually take a look at it.

Face your fears

Maybe you have a sense of your own general strength and durability, but are still sometimes encumbered by particular things that intimidate or unnerve you—possibly things that are serving as specific roadblocks in being able to achieve the next level of leadership.

Enlist help in tackling those fears. Clinical psychologists use a variety of proven techniques to assist people in facing their greatest phobias. Such experiences aren't typically easy and they often take time, but they can result in an enhanced feeling of hardiness and the justified belief that you can take on any personal challenge directly and come out on top.

Embrace the tough battles

When there's a sensitive or "big" issue to deal with, don't shy away from it. Take it on. Test yourself. See what you're made of. Chances are you'll discover that you're made of a lot more than you think.

The more you force yourself to invite such challenges, the more confidence you'll develop in your own ability to conquer them. Few acts garner the respect of others more than stepping to the front of the pack does.

Choose a mantra

This one, too, may seem juvenile—but it works, and plenty of top leaders I know use it on themselves. I even found myself doing it recently. Last year, I set out to train for a half-marathon. Although I've run shorter distances throughout my life, I hadn't ever run more than eight miles or so. Over the course of four months, mainly in the snow and cold, I trained. If you've ever prepared for a half (or full) marathon, you know it's not easy. What got me through those long runs was a simple mantra that popped into my head during one of these training sessions: "Good things come to those who run." I'm not sure where it came from, and it doesn't even rhyme very well. Nonetheless, I repeated it over and over, and sure enough, it helped me get through the tough runs and, ultimately, reach my goal. A few inspiring words can work wonders when you require a bit of courage or daring. And there's no one better to deliver those words to you than yourself.

Embrace new endeavors

To build fortitude, you must do things you've never done before. Whether it's running a marathon, traveling to a foreign country, or taking on a role that stretches you in an unfamiliar area of the business, you need to reach outside your comfort zone. To use another exercise analogy, in weight training there is a phenomenon called the plateau. You can lift the same weights using the same exercises until you are blue in the face, but at some point, your ability to build more muscle mass will level off. Your body automatically shifts to cruise control.

The only way to break through this plateau is to change things up. Use a different type of exercise or do it at a different angle or with a different level of resistance—anything. Some popular exercise programs call it "muscle confusion." In other words, by constantly surprising your body, you train it to respond in positive ways. You can develop fortitude in the same way—by never accepting a personal status quo or inadvertently settling into a rut. Do new things, push yourself, and explore outside the boundaries. Along the way, you will build a level of fortitude you never knew was possible.

Absorb the lessons of others

Often, getting up close and personal in places where people have overcome truly enormous barriers can lead to powerful inspiration and a deep sense of personal fortitude. I know of one tremendous training program, originally conceived at Best Buy but now being offered elsewhere, in which executives are taken to historical American battlegrounds, where they learn what others endured and overcame. The leaders who attend this program are truly changed by it. Not only are their perspectives enduringly altered; they are also inspired to test the limits of what they themselves can overcome. As William James put it, "Compared with what we ought to be, we are only half awake. Our fires are damped, our drafts are checked. We are making use of only a small part of our possible mental resources . . . men the world over possess amounts of resource, which only exceptional individuals push to their extremes of use."

WHY IT MATTERS

In a recent collaboration by researchers at the University of Pennsylvania, the University of Michigan, and the United States Military Academy at West Point, an interesting trait was looked at: grit.[3] Given the well-established importance of intellectual talent to achievement in all professional domains, the researchers were more interested in asking the same question I present in this book: What about the other, more subtle individual differences that predict success?

They defined grit as perseverance and passion for long-term goals—working strenuously toward challenges, maintaining effort and interest even in the face of failures or adversity, looking at achievement as a marathon requiring that the runner stay the course rather than be derailed by disappointment or boredom.

The findings are noteworthy for anyone aspiring to be a true leader: Grit proved as much a predictor of success as talent or IQ. Yes, the sustained and focused application of effort over time showed itself to be an important differentiator of leadership.

In a related study of the development of world-class pianists, neurologists, swimmers, chess players, mathematicians, and sculptors, it was found that just a handful of the 120 subjects in the sample had been regarded as prodigies by teachers, parents, or other experts. The study showed instead that the most accomplished individuals in these fields had worked day after day, for a number of years, to reach the top.[4] The researcher's conclusions were as logical as they are powerful in implication: In every field examined, the general qualities possessed by high achievers included a strong interest in the particular field, a desire to reach a high level of attainment, and a willingness to put in great amounts of time and effort.

Putting it more plainly, in almost any field you can point to, it isn't just brains or innate talent that propels people to the top. It's drive, energy, grit, and persistence. It's fortitude.

The Long Struggle: Part Two

On the day of his release, the white-haired former agitator spoke these words to a spellbound nation: "Our resort to the armed struggle in 1960 with the formation of the military wing of the ANC was a purely defensive action against the violence of apartheid. The factors which necessitated the armed struggle still exist today. We have. no option but to continue. We express the hope that a climate conducive to a negotiated settlement would be created soon, so that there may no longer be the need for the armed struggle."

These words made two things abundantly clear: Nelson Mandela's attitude toward injustice had not changed during his twenty-seven years in prison and that his present approach was likewise unchanged—hope for peaceful reconciliation, but a commitment to stamping out apartheid no matter what the means.

His strength and forbearance became palpable touchstones for a country still divided. Despite frequent racially fueled clashes, Mandela maintained both his audacity and his diplomacy. When the leader of the ANC was assassinated in 1993, the country braced, fearing an eruption. Mandela appealed to the nation: "Tonight I am reaching out to every single South African, black and white, from the very depths of my being. A white man, full of prejudice and hate, came to our country and committed a deed so foul that our whole nation now teeters on the brink of disaster. A white woman, of Afrikaner origin, risked her life so that we may know, and bring to justice, this assassin. The cold-blooded murder of Chris Hani has sent shock waves throughout the country and the world. . . . Now is the time for all South Africans to stand together against those who, from any quarter, wish to destroy what Chris Hani gave his life for: the freedom of all of us."

Mandela's words were enough to pacify the nation. While some riots did occur, stepped-up negotiations led to an unprecedented milestone in the country's history just over a year after Hani's assassination: multi-racial elections, in which the ANC won a majority, and Mandela, their leader, was inaugurated as South Africa's first black president.

During his guidance from 1994 to 1999, Mandela led a transition from minority rule and apartheid to true democracy, winning international respect for his tireless efforts. Perhaps the most telling influence of his fortitude came at the 1995 Rugby World Cup, when the Springboks, South Africa's very white national rugby team, won an epic final over New Zealand. The Springboks had historically been scorned by black South Africans. After the final, Mandela presented the trophy to team captain Francois Pienaar, an Afrikaner, wearing a Springbok shirt with Pienaar's own number 6 on the back—once again, even after all this time, showing the way.

THE BOTTOM LINE

Your leadership destiny will be determined largely by the strength with which you confront challenges.

Fallibility

This is the very perfection of a man,
to find out his own imperfections.

—St. Augustine

The Perils of Perfection: Part One

At this juncture, every word he spoke seemed to carry extravagant weight. The race was that close. He'd been in the small towns and the big cities. He'd addressed the wage earners and the well-heeled, and those whose lives had been turned upside down by a turbulent economy. He'd run a respectful campaign anchored by soft-spoken intelligence and well-articulated arguments, more or less a direct contrast to his opponent's soldier mentality and more blustery discourse. He'd opted from the very beginning not to go in for smear tactics or play the obvious card, the one everybody had been talking about for months now. Yes, if he won, it would be historic. But it would mean little if he emerged the victor not for what people saw in him, but for what they saw on the outside.

These were the things he thought about before every speech, town hall, interview, or forum. People were beginning to exalt him, putting him in danger of starting to believe his own hype. He reminded himself what was getting them so excited. First, they were thrilled about anyone who stood apart from the existing commander. Second, they saw him as someone more relatable-to than his opponent, someone they could connect to. And hopefully, he thought, someone with *genuine ideas, a true passion for the country, and a sound platform from which to lead.*

As he stepped into the historic university's gymnasium and was handed the mike, he looked out at the 3,000 students and local residents, many of whom had spent the night camped out on the university green. They applauded him appreciatively, excitedly, seated in a circle around him like an adoring crowd in a Greek amphitheater.

Perhaps Robert Kennedy had felt the same thing standing in this spot four decades earlier. They'd been making him into a symbol of something perfect, too—a savior, the guy who could do no wrong. He'd risen to the occasion, satisfying their appetite for words that were weighty and profound. He'd said things that made good solid sense, but that also seemed to rise to another level, striking a collective chord within the populace that resonated deeply.

What would he do to meet their expectations? On one hand, it was to be expected that people would be wound up about a new leader after eight years of collective despair. On the other, it carried with it awesome pressure. He took the mike and began. As he spoke about meeting challenges and fulfilling destinies, they whooped and hollered. As he talked of writing a new chapter, they applauded wildly. At his invocation of the words of Dr. King, the ovation nearly blew the roof off the gym. He was rolling. They were behind him. He felt their admiration and appreciated it; this was what he'd been trying to achieve all these months, all these years—but, while admiration was good, exaltation was not.

If you've ever shopped for a diamond, you know that they're defined by the four C's, one of which is clarity. Most diamonds have tiny inclusions—scratches, air bubbles, blemishes, and so on—which is not surprising given the intense amount of pressure necessary for a diamond to be created.

A rare few, however, have no visible inclusions. Even fewer are completely flawless. These diamonds, of course, are the most valuable. In much the same way, we place the highest value on flawlessness in other aspects of life and, often, aim for it ourselves. We try hard to show the world how perfect we are, how flawless our lives are, in an attempt to show value. Think of the typical workplace. If you manage people, you probably expect high performance from your staff and you probably hope for, if not expect, perfection in their work. As a leader, you may also have external pressures to be perfect—from the street, from your employees, from shareholders, and even from your family.

It is under the weight of this pressure that I have seen many leaders derail. In an attempt to appear perfect, they try to cover up their flaws. In my experience, leadership is unlike the diamond. Extraordinary leaders show their flaws rather than hide them. They understand that there is value in imperfection.

You may think there is a dichotomy here. Let me explain. Those in positions of leadership ought to set big goals for their teams and create the conditions for those goals to be met. They should aim to be the best and encourage superior performance and effort.

This is not the same as seeking perfection. Nor is it the same as trying to represent perfection. Fallible leaders are *real*. They do not depict themselves as not having any flaws—they know that would create unworkable expectations. They do not try to convince us their decisions are always right—nobody's are. They don't try to manufacture an unduly lofty perception of themselves. Instead, they maximize their strengths and work on their weaknesses.

Leaders obsessed by the unreachable quest for perfection, on the other hand, often cover up any signs to the contrary. No one in recent memory exemplifies the implications of this fixation more than Martha Stewart. Known for her attention to detail, Martha basically built a brand around being perfect. In 2000, at the height of her success as CEO of Martha Stewart Omnimedia Inc., she said the following in an interview: "I'm a maniacal perfectionist. And if I weren't, I wouldn't have this company. . . . It's the best rap! Nobody's going to fault me for that. I have proven that being a perfectionist can be profitable and admirable when creating content across the board: in television, books, newspapers, radio, videos. . . . All that content is impeccable."[1]

Sure enough, just a few years later, she would be proven wrong. While it's debatable how improper her original acts were, Martha's reaction to the allegations made against her represent, in my opinion, her biggest leadership miscues. In her desire to appear perfect, she made major errors in judgment. She was initially accused of making improper stock trades—a lapse in judgment, perhaps, but one that could have been recoverable from a leadership perspective. In Martha's desire to present herself as perfect, to not admit her mistakes, she committed a fatal error and ended up getting ousted from her role and going to jail.

Over the past few years, we have seen illustrated, in all-too-vivid detail, the problem with executive perfectionism. Consider the downfall of Enron,

WorldCom, Lehman Brothers, Bear Stearns, and Washington Mutual, and the fiasco at AIG, and you will see leaders who try to be *in*fallible—and who fall victim to the consequences.

Here's the problem that ultimately sank these leaders: nobody's perfect. However, wanting—*needing*—to be perfect, they masked errors and orchestrated cover-ups. They held up their reputations as unassailable and came to perceive themselves as above reproach. Nothing, they felt, should—could—bring them or their companies down. Of course, history has shown the fallacy of this idea, sometimes in rather spectacular fashion. There are leaders in every type of company, in every industry, in every period of history, who have clung desperately to a veneer of perfection and, in every case, it has ended badly.

* * *

Let's talk instead about the power of being *imperfect*. Or, rather, acknowledging and embracing your own imperfection. We're all flawed; that's what makes us human. There is inherent beauty in imperfection—in art, in music, and in people. It is because of the differences in our individual perceptions that beauty *does* lie in the eye of the beholder. As a culture, we have socialized the importance of saving face. We want to appear flawless to the world—perfect kids, perfect houses, perfect jobs, perfect leadership. We spend beyond our means and take on excessive credit in order to show the world how perfect our lives are. Children grow up embarrassed of mistakes. We celebrate being number one and irrationally devalue anything less.

How many of today's top leaders ranked first in their college class? None. Yes, you read that right: Among CEOs of all the companies listed on the *Fortune* 100, none ranked at the top of his or her class. Yes, some were excellent scholars. Some won academic awards for their achievements. But not one ranked first.

What does this tell us? That even the best aren't perfect? Maybe being number one isn't the position it's cracked up to be. Maybe we should be aiming for third place or fifth place when we set our goals. I know that may sound shocking. Shouldn't we always aspire to be the best? I don't think so. I believe that being second or third might even be better.

Here's why. It is through the process of not being number one all the time that people are forced to get better at what they do. Our most exemplary leaders became successful *because* they were fallible, not in spite of it. And they certainly never tried to convince those around them otherwise.

We love fallible leaders, and for good reason. We follow them because they seem accessible and human. They listen to others, take in feedback, don't set expectations they can't meet, and show remorse when they blunder. They are humble and, occasionally, vulnerable. They are open to ideas and, because they don't fear failure, they are willing to take risks. They are confident in who they are and don't pretend to be someone else. They delegate because they know that others can do certain things better than they can. Above all, they learn from their experiences, in particular their failures. These are the hallmarks of the fallible leader.

WHAT IS IT?

When leaders incorrectly assume that they need to be infallible, particular sets of counterproductive thought patterns often result. Infallible thinking manifests itself in three general ways. The first is called *self-promotional*, characterized by perceptions such as "Everything I do is perfect," "My assumptions shouldn't be challenged," and "I want everyone to see how good I am."

I once worked with a leader who was completely focused on his ego and reputation. He would do anything to protect both, often at the expense of getting genuine feedback. He had just gone through an assessment process that included a 360-degree exercise. The purpose of the process was solely developmental; there was no threat to his job or compensation in any way.

Nonetheless, upon receiving his feedback, this leader was utterly resistant— at least to the negative parts. He loved hearing the positive feedback and, not surprisingly, agreed with it wholeheartedly, but there was some tough feedback around his weaknesses, and he just didn't get it. He deflected the comments or shifted the blame to others. Like other leaders I've encountered, this individual was so intentionally deaf to constructive feedback, was so obsessively focused on being seen as perfect, that he couldn't fathom any feedback that might contradict this notion. His self-promotional infallibility, ultimately, prevented him from ever hearing real feedback, integrating it, and developing as a leader.

A second category of infallibility, called *avoidant*, shows up in statements such as, "I will not do anything that may show my flaws, expose me as an imposter, or otherwise not result in surefire success." I worked with a CFO of an entrepreneurial company who was, to his detriment, entirely risk-avoidant as a result of his desire to be infallible. Several potential acquisition opportunities had presented themselves to him, but he wouldn't entertain any of them, nor would he ever encourage his company to make the kinds of investments necessary to succeed in the long run.

The consequences of this aversion to risk became dire when a larger, rival organization created a product similar to the type already marketed by the CFO's firm. Instead of improving on its existing product or investing smartly in research and development, the CFO's company had stood pat, opening the door for the rival company to gain a point of leverage with a superior product. It was this product that surged ahead in the market and the CFO's company began a downward spiral.

If only they had been a bit more aggressive—either committing to enhancing the product or seeking out bolt-on acquisitions to pump up their market share—it might have been a different story. I believe a major part of the company's demise was the lack of risk-taking and foresight by the CFO, and the resultant complacency of the entire management team.

Finally, *protective* infallibility involves keeping things close to the vest in order to avoid the perception of failure. "I won't admit my mistakes to anyone," think leaders who fall into this category. "I will report only positive news." These are the leaders who get into legal and ethical hot water. They hide information, cover things up, and even fudge information if they think it's necessary to preserve the picture of infallibility they are so desperate to portray. Then we see them on the front page of the newspaper.

Fallibility Spurs Innovation

Roger Martin, Dean of the Rotman School of Management at the University of Toronto, recently penned an excellent book called *Design Thinking*. One of the book's more interesting assertions is that businesses too often get stuck in a "prove it" mentality, and good ideas and innovations become stifled by naysayers who take a scientific approach to an intrinsically artistic process.

The result of this kind of interference is that few really new things come out. From my perspective, a certain type of fallible mentality is necessary to fully engage in effective design thinking. You must be able to realize that you don't have all the answers and be willing to seek them out.

You must also allow yourself the possibility of failure. Failure, of course, is closely tied to achievement, as we have heard time and again, often from some of our greatest innovators.

One of my favorite such stories is that of Dr. Spence Silver of 3M Corporation. As a scientist at the giant conglomerate, Silver was tasked with finding a strong bonding agent. The initial solution he devised was relatively weak. Instead of being embarrassed by his failure to meet the stated objective, Silver took his thinking further, sharing his finding with some friends and colleagues. It was one of these friends in particular, a man named Arthur Fry, who pointed out to Silver a specific potential application of the sticky agent. Fry, a singer in his local church choir, was eternally frustrated by his bookmarks always falling out of the pages of his hymnal. The recipe Silver had accidentally cooked up would enable him to keep a temporary bookmark in place. Today, thanks to Silver's perseverance in the face of initial disappointment, Post-it Notes are used by, well, everybody.

As this story illustrates, failure has been, in countless cases, the catalyst for landmark accomplishments. This holds true not only in chemical engineering, but also in the arts, science, sports, and leadership. Exceptional leaders acknowledge failure and force themselves to learn from it—because they know that magical things can happen as a result.

Humility and Servant Leadership

Lao Tzu, the father of Taoism, wrote the following:

> I have three precious things which I hold fast and prize. The
> first is gentleness; the second frugality; the third is humility,
> which keeps me from putting myself before others. Be gentle
> and you can be bold; be frugal and you can be liberal;
> avoid putting yourself before others and you can become a
> leader among men.

I love the wisdom of this seeming contradiction: Don't make it your priority to put yourself ahead of everyone else, and pretty soon you'll probably find yourself leading them. Many executives I know share this perspective. The best of them approach leadership as servant leaders: They truly feel they are there to serve their employees, their shareholders, and their communities. They have what I like to call quiet egos, an essential ingredient of which is fallibility. These types of leaders are humble and grounded. They don't prioritize being the most visible, the most prominent, or the most celebrated. Instead, they prioritize openness to different ideas and fresh views. And that's how they become great.

HOW DO YOU KNOW IT WHEN YOU SEE IT?

What's the best mistake you've ever made? It's an interesting question. It requires you to both recognize when you've made mistakes in your life and to understand that these mistakes had value.

Not everyone has a ready answer to this question. Those who do are likely to be reflective and insightful, and well-attuned to their own strengths and weaknesses. They see the world with clarity and are pragmatic about their limitations. Fallible leaders are easy to detect; they stand out in the best of ways. One observes them pursuing new learning continuously, being curious about themselves and the world around them, and regularly asking advice from others—they're quite sure they don't have all the answers and are happy to gather knowledge from other sources. Let's take a deeper dive into the cues that reveal the fallible leader.

They reveal their blemishes

Is there any better way to relate to someone else than through the simple admission of imperfection? Are you more trusting of people who claim they're incapable of making a mistake or of those who readily admit their flaws? The best leaders are more than willing to reveal their imperfections, but they attach to this honesty evidence that they've grown by virtue of their mistakes and misfires. They are not just the kind of people we can relate to; they are also the kind of people we want to emulate, because they don't just sit around bemoaning the fact that they aren't perfect. Instead, they subtly let us know that they are on a continuous mission to identify, work on, and learn from the things that might otherwise hold them back.

They talk about specific moments of failure

Truly successful leaders do more than just confess their generally imperfect nature; they also point to specific moments of disappointment, errors from which they've rebounded, the innate deficiencies they've managed to overcome. Ask yourself this: Do you respond more to a leader telling a story about an incredible success she was responsible for or to one telling a story about an awful mistake she made, the lessons she learned from that mistake, and the way she still uses those lessons to be a better leader today?

They make greater-good decisions

Leaders who view themselves as infallible tend to make choices that frequently raise eyebrows within their organizations. Their choices are often self-serving or, sometimes, made for the sole purpose of covering up a bad call. When such decisions come down, even those not prone to suspicion find themselves scratching their heads to figure out the rationale behind it. Usually this rationale is not communicated or it is tweaked to fit the kind of message the leader thinks people want to hear, which only confuses them more.

Fallible leaders don't usually get themselves in that kind of hot water, because they don't make decisions based on how those decisions are going to affect the way people "see" them. Rather, they make decisions based on specific criteria like alignment with the organization's objectives and risk versus potential reward. They do not include as one of their primary criteria, "How is this going to make me look to everyone?"

They are authentic and comfortable in their own skin

Leaders who strive to achieve an air of infallibility usually come off as, for want of a better word, *unnatural* instead. They often seem skittish, wary, nervous, or a little off-center. Their posture might suggest that they know more than you or, perhaps, that they're somehow humoring you. Something in their physical bearing probably strikes you as odd, as though they're a little uncomfortable in their skin or trying to be someone other than who they really are.

The contrast the fallible leader presents is very often a strong one. Fallible leaders don't try to present themselves as anyone but who they are, because they have a realistic self-concept and are comfortable with it. They speak openly and transparently, and they don't feel the need to pepper their conversations with fifty-cent words. Though they're ambitious and driven to achieve, they're quite content with not being perfect and so they don't spend their time trying to convince those around them of their flawlessness.

If you interview people as part of your role, then you've seen both sides of this behavioral coin. The candidates who come in trying to demonstrate how fantastic they are, how they can do it all, how every decision they've made has been the right one, are the ones who make you hesitate. It's the other type of candidates, the type who speak with honesty about who they are, who acknowledge their failures and poor decisions (and, hopefully, share the lessons they learned) that you're interested in talking to more. In fact, for all you executives in transition who are on the interview circuit yourselves, remember this: Someone, at some point, has told you to "be yourself" during the interview. What they're really telling you is to be fallible.

They don't equate risk-taking with fear of failure

Fallible leaders put themselves out there. They take risks and aim high on behalf of their teams and organizations, acknowledging the possibility of failure, but communicating the reasons why decisions are made. One management motto that has become increasingly popular, particularly in the IT space, is: "Fail Fast." That is, it's important to try and sometimes to fail, but the best results happen when you commit to taking the risk fully and quickly. Plunge in, and then, if it ain't working, get out. Fallible leaders are not afraid, or ashamed, of failing. To them, the shame is in not taking the shot in the first place or, once the shot has been taken and missed, not learning from the experience.

They aren't freaked out by having talent around them

You know the old adage: "You can tell a lot about a man by the company he keeps"? Same goes for leadership. One of the most telling signs of extraordinary leaders is who they choose to surround themselves with or include on their immediate teams. It is awfully easy to become threatened by talented people and, therefore, to *avoid* hiring them, since they eventually might be the ones to push you out of your role. The leader absorbed by her desire to be infallible is content to hire those whose skills and knowledge fall just short of her own. They represent safe bets. I've encountered more than one leader who operates in this way. Why, on the other hand, do fallible leaders so often succeed? Because, rather than being made paranoid by talent, they seek it out. They surround themselves with people whose brains and abilities complement their own or even people whose experiences and insights they themselves can learn from. They're both talent scouts and talent magnets. After all, who wouldn't want to work on the kind of team where everyone's abilities are highlighted rather than stifled?

They're magnets

Fallible leaders are able to connect with others. One observes their ability to create chemistry with people quickly and naturally. Leaders who try to be infallible, on the other hand, keep others at an unintended distance. After all, everyone possesses the natural ability to detect phoniness in others. We often know instinctively if someone is pulling our leg, trying to sell us something we don't need, or trying to present themselves as someone they're not. You know that too-good-to-be-true feeling you get about some people? That's your subconscious antennae telling you to take a closer look. Authentic, fallible leaders elicit the opposite kind of response from us. Around them, our antennae relax. We feel at ease with them, drawn to them, and trusting of what they have to say, because whatever other impression they may make on us, they strike us first and foremost as *real*.

The Right Spin

When you walk into Anton Rabie's office, you notice a bunch of things tacked to his wall—pictures, clippings, mock-ups, the usual stuff. You assume you're looking at a collection of the things that have made him proudest as president of the vastly successful children's products company, Spin Master. You know, the kinds of items most people display in their workspaces—awards they've received, successful campaigns they've been a part of, products they've helped launch, or notes of thanks from colleagues for a job well done.

But here's where Anton's office differs. The stuff on his wall doesn't flaunt his successes; instead, it highlights his failures.

Actually, that's not quite right. All those samples of stalled products and mock-ups of misguided ideas aren't a representation of failure at all. They're more like a reminder of constant learning and adaptability, both for Anton and anyone else who enters his office. Sure, he says, the usual mix of plaques, industry accolades, and press cuttings are a nice way to acknowledge success, but what's critical is to acknowledge what hasn't worked and why—and to broadcast very clearly the point that Spin Master achieves what it does mostly because no one person in the organization believes he or she has all the answers.

Spin Master's success began when Rabie and his friend Ronnen Harary, studying together at the Richard Ivey School of Business at the University of Western Ontario, invested $10,000 in a product called Earth Buddy, a bunch of sawdust and grass seed stuffed into the end of a nylon stocking and shaped to resemble a human head. When soaked, the seeds sprouted grass that looked like green hair. Anton and Ronnen decided to make 5,000 units and so they brought in another classmate, Ben Varadi, to oversee manufacturing. Earth Buddy, which retailed for about $8, sold 4.3 million units. Today, Anton is president and co-CEO, Ronnen chairman and co-CEO, and Ben executive vice president.

To me, the founders' instincts for what makes a good toy and their well-documented marketing savvy are only part of their success formula. Paramount to the company's rise, I believe, is the fact that they recognized one another's complementary skill sets in the first place. With the launch of Earth Buddy, Anton and his partners adopted a philosophy of collaboration and productive risk-taking that still makes up their recipe for achievement. Anton's sense of his own imperfection—his awareness that he has part of the necessary expertise, but not all—pervades the company, creating a highly productive environment in which the talents and contributions of everyone are maximized.

The fallible approach, that magical combination of risk-taking and learning through mistakes, has led to a glittering track record. But Spin Master's amazing success isn't a result simply of blind trial and error. Yes, they're open to possibilities, willing to try lots of different things, and aware that some ideas will succeed and others will fail, but they're also smart about the way they take chances. "Any mistakes we've made," Anton says, "we've never bet the farm. The way we've taken risks is undoubtedly our competitive advantage."

He talks a lot about batting average: it's okay to take risks as long as the wins outweigh the losses. Because of its attitude, Spin Master's batting average is impressive indeed. From its meager beginnings selling Earth Buddies in 1994, the company has become the fourth-largest toy company in North America, behind Mattel, Hasbro, and Lego. Revenues in 2009 were reported to be around the $700 million mark, dramatically lifted by the runaway success of their Bakugan toy franchise (which, by the way, is slated to become an even bigger phenomenon with the release of Universal Pictures Bakugan movie in 2011).

Not only are Anton and his partners smart about taking risks, they're also smart about building on failures. When things don't go as planned, they dissect what happened in order to extract valuable lessons. Or, as Anton puts it, "You gain equity from mistakes. One, you can't regret them—you have to move forward; two, you can't blame anyone; and three, you do a rigorous debrief."

On a personal level, Anton is surprisingly candid about his imperfections. Yes, he is a confident, assertive guy who, at age thirty-nine, seems to enjoy a work-hard-play-hard lifestyle. However, sometimes *success at a relatively early age can give people an overinflated sense of their own abilities and make them resist honest feedback from others. On the contrary, Anton is not only open to feedback from others, he invites it. It's important for a leader to know he's good at what he does and to believe in himself and his company's vision. But it's much more important for him to know that he's not perfect. Anton clearly believes in himself and in the company's products, but by no means does he think he has all the answers. In meetings, he's generally a quiet leader, processing more than talking. It communicates a true learning orientation and shows that everyone's thoughts are welcome and valued.*

As Spin Master continues to grow, its founders continue to seek out people who have the answers they don't. "We pride ourselves on a diversified talent pool," says Anton. "A few years ago we realized we needed to grow rapidly because we were up against the big guys. There were things we knew we didn't know. So we went to where the talent was and got some very seasoned, smart, experienced people."

It's that kind of comment that speaks to the perspective Anton and his partners uphold every day. You know that office wall of his I mentioned? Beyond the pictures of failed products and wayward ideas, it's even been known to hold the results of his 360-degree feedback, for all to see what he's working on as a leader. How many company presidents do you know who do that?

HOW DO YOU GET IT?

Given how exasperatingly flawed we humans are, it may sound funny to ask how one *acquires* imperfection. But that isn't really the question. The question is how do we prove to ourselves that we are confident enough to *be* ourselves and how do we show others that we are indeed human, warts and all?

Ask, don't tell

One of the biggest errors I see leaders commit is the amount of *talking* they do, compared with how much *listening*. Compulsive talking conveys that you believe what you have to say—and only you—is of paramount importance; active listening demonstrates that you value others' input. The higher you rise in your leadership journey, the more important it becomes to remember to ask questions and listen attentively to the answers.

Let's put it another way. The more senior your leadership position, the more knowledge you've probably obtained. How much of your time is spent telling others what you know versus asking people what *they* know? Do you find yourself constantly worrying whether those in your organization will see you as smart enough, capable enough, and accomplished enough to justify your senior role? Do you fret over the possibility that you might make a mistake? Instead of trying to portray yourself as the one with all the answers, make it your mission to learn as much as you can from others. The best way to do this is to be curious and ask lots of questions. Be a student, not a teacher.

Inviting Input

The best way to show that you aren't perfect is by inviting input from others. Show that you have a learning orientation by asking for people's perspectives on key decisions and then really listen to what they have to say. If people think you're asking their opinion just for appearances or they see you tuning out when they start to talk, you'll do more harm than good.

There are further benefits to soliciting the views of others. First, by getting them involved early, you create valuable buy-in. People are generally more willing to do new or different things when asked to offer their point of view, but resistant if a decision is simply forced upon them. Second, people around you may have great ideas percolating all the time, but they may be reluctant to come forward with those ideas unless they know you're willing to hear them. And finally, speaking of great ideas, you never know where they're going to come from, so open yourself up to the possibility that they might come from anyone at any time.

Let down your defensive walls

A very important part of being fallible is being, simply enough, *real*. Leaders who try to manufacture a veneer of perfection often come off as artificial instead. While such leaders may be seen as whip-smart, utterly focused, and professional to the bone, they may never truly gain the trust and partnership of others, because they inadvertently keep everyone at arm's length by revealing nothing of who they really are. A plastic leader is not an effective leader.

Show that you're a human being. Yes, be professional. Yes, be focused and ask the same of others. Yes, be calm in the face of crisis and show strength through the inevitable ups and downs. But don't mistake this for putting on a persona. Let people in. Show them a bit of the real you. It will make an enormous difference, not in the way they perceive you in a business context, but in the way they trust and invest in you.

Celebrate wins

What does this have to do with fallibility? Plenty. Celebrating wins lets your team know when they have satisfied expectations. The absence of such celebrations creates the perception that nothing they do is ever good enough— that no one can satisfy you no matter what they do or how much they achieve. This can lead to unintentional and highly damaging messages: "Nobody is as good as me," and "Nobody will ever meet my expectations."

Fallible leaders transmit the opposite message: "I have high expectations and will drive you hard, but when you perform, you will be rewarded."

Celebrating wins is easier when you make clear what "good" looks like. The value you get out of such acknowledgement is not just the positive reinforcement people get from being told that they've done a good job. It's also the fact of making clear for people where your performance bar is set, so they can strive to meet and surpass it.

Celebrations need not be elaborate affairs. A public pat on the back is sufficient; so is an e-mail blast. Your goal, as a fallible leader, is to recognize and acknowledge when a milestone has been achieved.

Find out what people have done and give specific recognition. A few years ago at RHR, our CEO started to send out "In Case You Haven't Heard" e-mails to everyone in the firm to acknowledge noteworthy efforts or achievements, including what the situation was, what the person did, and the outcome. The e-mail would not only point to what the consultant had done and why it was successful, but also how it aligned with the firm's strategy and benefited everyone in the organization as a whole. It may be just an e-mail, but it speaks volumes and sends a powerful leadership message.

Confront the fear of failure

Extraordinary leaders are driven not by fear of failure but by the desire to succeed. The latter outlook is a catalyst for innovation and risk-taking and the hallmark of a thriving, competitive corporate culture; the former is a recipe for stagnant growth, bureaucracy, lack of creativity, and political game-playing. Constant concern over failure also fosters corporate corruption and white-collar wrongdoing. If you're afraid of doing things because your efforts might fall short, then they probably will. More important, you'll keep everything close to the vest as a result of developing an instinctive paranoia about letting people know too much. This creates a false perception of infallibility and does little other than distancing you from your teams.

Instead, let people know that you believe the only way to succeed is to stick your neck out—to take risks, to make leaps, to jump across the occasional gorge. If you fall, you fall, and then you figure out the reasons for the fall, dust yourself off, and get back up again. People are surprisingly forgiving of failure if the effort behind that failure is well justified. As a leader, you'll gain much more respect and support from your people by taking defensible risks than you will by hunkering down against the possibility of disappointment.

Share your weaknesses

The essential failing of infallible leadership is that it causes people to hide their weaknesses or, more precisely, to try to create the perception that they have none. I don't know about you, but last I checked, there weren't too many perfect people walking around. When you try to come off as faultless, it only creates skepticism and wariness in your teams.

To leaders aiming for a perception of infallibility, weaknesses equal vulnerability, and vulnerability is bad. The opposite is true, of course. The more you share with people the challenges you face and the struggles you feel, the more they will perform to help you achieve what you've hopefully positioned as the *organization's* goals—not your own.

Revealing your weaknesses does not mean putting yourself in a weak position. I'm not telling you to be a doormat; I'm not telling you to act hard on yourself to win sympathy; I'm not telling you to be relentlessly self-deprecating at the expense of communicating successes. I'm just encouraging you to acknowledge what you're good at and what you aren't. On a more concrete level, make it very clear to people that, even if you're at the top position in the company, you're still committed to learning, growing, and improving. Give them a window into your own ongoing development. At the beginning of the year when you outline the company's objectives, reveal your own personal objectives too. Or, if you've done a 360-degree exercise, let people know what the results were. Give them a sense of the kinds of things you are working on in order to better serve them as their leader. "Let us go forward together," said Winston Churchill. People responded.

WHY IT MATTERS

In making themselves more real, leaders make themselves more relatable, more connectable, more believable, and more trustworthy. Leaders who regularly share with their teams, invite others' observations and views, ask questions, and, especially, admit when they are wrong, inevitably fare better in terms of the way they are perceived by others. Let's be clear on this point: People aren't looking for their leaders to be ineffectual or uncertain, but they do want to see in their leaders a willingness to take risks and to fail, and a constant orientation to adapt.

Leaders who strive to appear infallible, on the other hand, at best fabricate a false perception and, therefore, create distance between themselves and the people they are meant to lead, resulting in fragmented, often misaligned teams characterized by safe behaviors rather than bold risk-taking or innovation. By spending most of their time focusing on how to be flawless, such leaders miss much of the big stuff. They tend to ignore feedback. They have poor self-awareness. They operate with blinders on. Worse, their fear of showing any chink in their armor often pushes them toward fear-based behaviors—buck-passing, cover-ups, and finger-pointing. Leaders concerned with not making mistakes tend to hire people they think they can trust, talent notwithstanding. They want to know people will be in their corner should the need ever arise to sweep something under the rug. This is obviously not a recipe for success.

Fallible leaders, on the other hand, hire people they believe can do the job. They surround themselves with people who are ready to take on a challenging vision and look forward to pulling out all the stops to meet it. The result is forward-looking and forward-moving teams, united in purpose and allied in both their willingness to stumble and their ultimate resolve to persevere.

The Perils of Perfection: Part Two

As he continued to unspool the lines and sound bites, the crowd continued to eat it up. His remarks on the need for a more effective educational policy garnered huge applause. His statement about restoring the country's standing in the world community hit them at the very core. The reiteration of his commitment to getting the troops home sent them into a virtual frenzy.

It was at that point—at the height of the crescendo, the moment when everyone senses something momentous is about to be said and they're all on the edges of their seats hanging on the next phrase— that he chose to bring them back down. "I am reminded every day of my life," he said, "if not by events then by my wife, that I am not a perfect man."

Now they were with him again. Back in a place where they could really listen, be grounded alongside him, see him as the person they'd recognized him to be all along, someone with intelligence, reason, insight, and passion for his country.

"I will not be a perfect president."

They were a little stunned, maybe, but mostly they were grateful. Grateful and understanding. "But here's what I can promise you. I will always tell you what I think. I will always tell you where I stand. I will always be honest with you about the challenges we face as a nation. I will listen to you even when we disagree. And we're going to disagree sometimes. My wife and I disagree sometimes. We've been together fifteen years. This is a big, complicated country. We're going to disagree sometimes. But we can disagree without being disagreeable. We can focus on what we have in common. And do good work together."

Barack Obama, who before long would be president, stood and looked around at the 3,000 students and local residents surrounding him in the Ball State gymnasium. And as he scanned their expressions, a smile—big and happy and sincere—filled his face. They got it.

THE BOTTOM LINE

Don't try to be perfect. Influence others by showing that you *don't* have all the answers.

Endnotes

CHAPTER 1

1 Irwin, T. 2009. *Derailed: Five Lessons Learned from Catastrophic Failures of Leadership.* Nashville, TN: Thomas Nelson.

2 Sternberg, R. 1985. Implicit Theories of Intelligence, Creativity, and Wisdom. *Journal of Personality and Social Psychology*, 49(3), 607–627.

3 Baltes, P. B., Staudinger, U. M., Maercker, A., Smith, J. 1995. People nominated as wise: A comparative study of wisdom-related knowledge. *Psychology and Aging*, 10(2), 155–166.

4 Wetlaufer, S. 1999. Driving Change: An Interview with Ford Motor Company's Jacques Nasser. *Harvard Business Review*, 77(2).

5 Kilburg, R.R. 2006. *Executive wisdom: Coaching and the emergence of virtuous leaders.* Washington, DC: American Psychological Association.

CHAPTER 2

1 Young, M. J., Chen, N., & Morris, M. W. 2009. Belief in stable and fleeting luck and achievement motivation. *Personality and Individual Differences*, 47, 150–154.

2 Duckworth, A.L., Peterson, C., Matthews, M.D., & Kelly, D.R. 2007. Grit: Perseverance and passion for long-term goals. *Journal of Personality and Social Psychology*, 92(6), 1087–1101.

3 Shoda, Y., Mischel, W., & Peake, P. K. 1990. Predicting adolescent cognitive and self-regulatory competencies from preschool delay of gratification: Identifying diagnostic conditions. *Developmental Psychology*, 26(6), 978–986.

CHAPTER 3

1 American Psychiatric Association. 2000. *Diagnostic and Statistical Manual of Mental Disorders*, Fourth Edition, Text Revision. Washington, DC: American Psychiatric Association.

CHAPTER 4

1 Rousseau, D. M., Sitkin, S. B., Burt, R. S., & Camerer, C. 1998. Not so Different After All: A Cross-Discipline View of Trust. *Academy of Management Review*, 23, 393–404.

2 Hyland, K. Personal communication, October 8, 2009.

3 Google. 2004, August 13. Form S-1, Amendment 7.

CHAPTER 5

1 2007. Everything DiSC Research Report. Minneapolis, MN: Inscape Publishing.
2 Rath, T. 2007. *StrengthsFinder 2.0: A New & Upgraded Edition of the Online Test from Now, Discover Your Strengths.* Washington, DC: Gallup Press.

CHAPTER 6

1 Blatt, S. J. & Blass, R. 1990. Attachment and separateness: A dialectic model of the products and processes of psychological development. *The Psychoanalytic Study of the Child*, 45, 107–127.
2 Gardner, W. L. & Avolio, B. J. 1998. The charismatic relationship: A dramaturgical perspective. *Academy of Management Review*, 23, 32–58.
3 Weber, M. 1947. *The Theory of Social and Economic Organization*, ed Talcott Parsons. New York: Free Press. pg. 358.
4 Popper, M., Mayseless, O., & Castelnovo, O. 2000. Transformational leadership and attachment. *Leadership Quarterly*, 11, 267–289.
5 Towler, A. 2005. Charismatic leadership development: role of parental attachment style and parental psychological control. *Journal of Leadership & Organizational Studies*, 11(4), 15–25.
6 McKee, R. & Fryer, B. 2003. Storytelling that moves people: A conversation with screenwriting coach Robert McKee. *Harvard Business Review*, 81(6).

CHAPTER 7

1 Shapira-Ettinger, K. & Shapira, R.A. 2008. The Constructive Value of Overconfidence. *Review of Law & Economics,* 4(3), Article 4.
2 Dunning, D. 2005. *Self-Insight: Roadblocks and detours on the path to knowing thyself.* East Sussex, UK: Psychology Press.
3 Kruger, J. & Dunning, D. 1999. Unskilled and Unaware of It: How Difficulties in Recognizing One's Own Incompetence Lead to Inflated Self-Assessments. *Journal of Personality and Social Psychology* 77(6), 1121–34.

CHAPTER 8

1 Bandura, A., & Walters, R. H. 1959. *Adolescent aggression; a study of the influence of child-training practices and family interrelationships.* New York: Ronald Press.
2 Ibid.

CHAPTER 9

1 General Douglas MacArthur. Sylvanus Thayer Award Acceptance Address. Retrieved March 31, 2010 from http://www.americanrhetoric.com/speeches/douglasmacarthurthayeraward.html
2 Dawar, N. & Chandradekhar, R. 2009. Best Buy Inc.—Dual Brand in China. Ivey School of Business case study.
3 Duckworth, A. L., Peterson, C., Matthews, M. D., & Kelly, D. R. 2007. Grit: Perseverance and passion for long-term goals. *Journal of Personality and Social Psychology*, 92(6), 1087–1101.
4 Bloom, B. 1985. *Developing talent in young people.* New York: Ballantine Books.

CHAPTER 10

1 Winfrey, O. 2000. Oprah's cut with Martha Stewart. *O, The Oprah Magazine.*

Index